D1879777

WHERE INDIA CHINA AND BURMA MEET

WHERE INDIA CHINA AND BURMA MEET

BY

MAJOR SITARAM JOHRI

GYAN

© **Author**
All rights reserved. No part of this work may be reproduced, stored, adapted, or transmitted in any form or by any means, electronic, mechanical, photocopying, micro-filming, recording or otherwise, or translated in any language, without the prior written permission of the copyright owner and the publisher. The book is sold subject to the condition that it shall not, by way of trade or otherwise, be lent, resold, hired out, or otherwise circulated without the prior publisher's written consent in any form of binding or cover other than that in which it is published.

The views and opinions expressed in this book are author(s) own and the facts reported by them have been verified to the extent possible, and the publishers are not in any way liable for the same.

ISBN : 978-81-212-1698-2(HB)

First Published, 1933

Published, 2018

Published by

Gyan Publishing House
5, Ansari Road
Daryaganj, New Delhi-110002
Phone: 011-47034999, 9811692060
www.gyanbooks.com
E-mail: books@gyanbooks.com

Printed at: G. Print Process, Delhi.

DEDICATED
TO
MY MOTHER

ILLUSTRATIONS

CONTENTS

PREFACE

I visited Mansarovar in 1954 and met Swami Parmanand, F.R.G.S. of Almora at Thokar Mandi situated on the eastern bank of the sacred lake. During my short association I learnt much from the Swami. It was for the first time that I came to know about the *Inner Line Regulations*, as applicable to Garhwal and Kumaon, which restricted the entry of foreigners beyond the Inner Line and prohibited foreign missionaries' residence in the border areas. I understood that the Chinese protestations against foreigners and foreign missionaries had something to do with these restrictions. My curiosity to know something more about this barrier, specially pertaining to the North-East Frontier Agency, increased. With the assistance of Maj-Gen. Hiralal Atal—ex-Adjutant General of the Indian Army and now retired—I obtained the permission to visit the forbidden land.

During the period of my sojourn in the NEFA Divisions I visited Shillong twice. Both the times I travelled by road from North Lakhimpur to Gauhati (about 250 miles), and to reach Dibrugarh I passed through Nawgaon and Jorhat located in the heart of Assam. The journey offered me opportunities of meeting many Assamese intellectuals, and social workers, from whom I learnt more about NEFA than I could from the Agency officials, probably because the latter were inhibited by Official Conduct Rules. It soon became apparent that without visiting Majuli, an island of Brahmaputra on the northern bank, and other places of historical importance in Assam my trip to NEFA would be of very little value.

Therefore, I decided to see as much of Assam as I could. I studied old records in Gauhati libraries. Having done that I proceeded to Calcutta for further study.

I am grateful to Maj-Gen. Hiralal Atal without whose help I would never have been able to visit the North-East Frontier Divisions.

I thank all the Political Officers, Assistant Political Offcers and the Divisional staff who helped me to get a glimpse of the North-East territories. My thanks are also due to the Deputy Advisers at Shillong who issued me the necessary permits (in spite of the trying circumstances created by the entry of the Dalai Lama), to cross the Inner Line.

I am also obliged to Dr. P. C. Chaudhuri, M.A., PH.D., Assistant Director, Antiquarian Library, Gauhati, Dr. Mahesh Neog of Gauhati University, Shri P. D. Chaudhuri, M.A., B.L., Curator, Shri M. C. Das, M.A,, Assistant Curator, Assam State Museum, Gauhati, the Librarians of the Geological Survey of India and the Journal of Asiatic Society of Bengal, Calcutta and the staff of Asaf-ud-Daula Library, Lucknow. I pay my sincere thanks to these gentlemen.

SITA RAM JOHRI

Pithoragarh,
14.1.1962.

Abbreviations used

Journal of Asiatic Society of Bengal	JASB
Journal of Bihar and Orissa Royal Society	JBORS
Proceedings of Asiatic Society of Bengal	PASB
Memoirs of the Asiatic Society of Bengal	MASB
Journal of Royal Asiatic Society of Bengal	JRASB
North-East Frontier Agency	NEFA
The Naga Hill Tuensang Area	NHTA
Adviser to Tribal Affairs	ATA
Very Important Person	VIP
Political Officer	PO
Assistant Political Officer	APO
Lower Division Assistant	LDA
Village Level Worker	VLW
Junior Commissioned Officer	JCO
Other ranks or rank	OR
Asiatic Research	AR
All India Congress Committee	AICC
Press Trust of India	PTI
Inspector General	IG
High School	HS
Middle English School	MES
Lower Primary School	LPS
Cottage Industries Training and Production Centre	CITPC
Wet Rice Cultivation	WRC
Mile Stone	MS
Uttar Pradesh	UP
Central Provinces	CP
National Extension Block	NE BLOCK
National Cadet Corps.	NCC

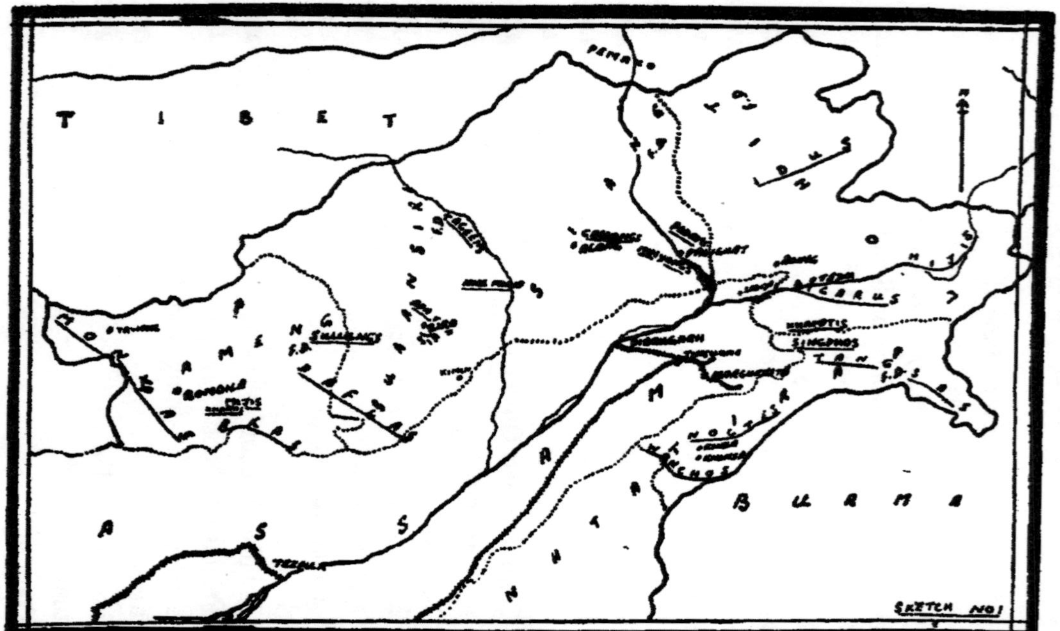

THE LAND WHERE INDIA, CHINA & BURMA MEET

CHAPTER I

INTRODUCTION

"I am alarmed when I see—not only in this country but in other great countries, too—how anxious people are to shape others according to their own image or likeness and to impose on them their particular way of living. We are welcome to our way of living but why impose it on others? This applies equally to national and international fields. In fact, there would be more peace in world, if people were to desist from imposing their way of living on other people and countries.

I am not at all sure which is the better way of living. In some respects I am quite certain their's is better. Therefore, it is grossly presumptuous on our part to approach them with an air of superiority, to tell them how to behave or what to do. There is no point in trying to make a second-rate copy of ourselves.

Now, who are these tribal folks? A way of describing them is that they are the people of the frontiers or those who live away from the interior of this country. Just as the hills breed a somewhat different type of people from those who inhabit the plains, so also the frontier breeds a different type of people from those who live away from frontier[1]."

Jawaharlal Nehru.

The North-East Frontier Agency is an obscure region to most people. The public generally associated the Agency with Naga ebullience and the Naga Hills, not realising that the Nagas, the inhabitants of Tirap form only one fifth of the population of NEFA, and that these Nagas have nothing to do with the so called 'Naga trouble' (some times violence is reported from the foothills of Margherita, but such exhibition of force has local significance only). The Press seems to have completely ignored NEFA. This neglect may have been due to restrictions imposed by Government upon visits of outsiders to this region, or perhaps the venture has not been considered worth the trouble. The Khampa unrest or revolt, the Dalai Lama's escape into India through the Kameng Frontier Division and the subsequent widely publicised happenings aroused the interest of the people. A furore was raised in the Lok Sabha (Indian Parliament) and the Government issued four 'White Papers' on the border violations by the Chinese forces and placed the Chinese version of the map which included NEFA as their territory before the House. Later, the Government of India published another document—'*Report of the Officials of the Government of India and the People's Republic of China on the Boundary Question*' for the benefit of the Indian Parliament. Interest breeds knowledge, and knowledge, if correctly obtained and assimilated, builds a right perspective against which problems regarding a subject whether political, social, cultural or pertaining to any other aspect of life are tackled and eventually solved. On account of the paucity of literature written by the sons of the soil in recent times, the problems of NEFA appear formidable.

The North-East Frontier Agency is constitutionally a part of Assam; it will be united, so is stated by Government of India, with the parent State when it reaches a sufficient stage of development. "Its present position as a centrally administered area is a temporary one[2]." Probably this has lessened the interest of Indian writers, excluding Government officials, in broaching the subject. One reads a number of articles here and there about NEFA in the Press, but invariably the articles do not embrace the entire area and if they do then most of the information imparted is indirect and only intermittent interest is displayed.

During the nineteenth century and in fact right up to 1947 many Europeans visited the Agency, always under Government patronage, and wrote about it. There were a few who along with their political mission wrote accounts of some of the tribal groups which are of anthropological interest. Nearly all of the authors have spoken disparagingly of the tribal people of NEFA. For Major Butler[3], the Khamptis were insubordinate, the Singphos were implacable, cruel and treacherous, the Abors were dirty fellows, the Mishmis were wild, the Nagas were very uncivilised and treacherous, the Akas were a ferocious band of dacoits and the Daflas were an uncivilised race of beings. Baker[4] considered the natives of Assam as 'Heathens' and the Westerners as civilised. What he thought of the tribal people can very well be guessed.

Every European adventurer before he came in contact with the tribal people of NEFA had fixed notions. The word 'tribe' reminded him of the Polynesians, the Maories and the Red Indians and he treated the tribals of the tract as a separate entity. Lt. Col. Waddel was the only officer who had conducted investigations in Nepal, Sikkim and Bhutan before he studied "such a variety of savage tribes" of NEFA and found the similarity of the latter with those of the Central Himalayan people.

Hatred begets hatred. The tribals were never reconciled to the British rule. In the beginning of the British regime there was a regular conflict between the rulers and the ruled. Raja Tagi, an Aka, in late 1820s wiped out a British post and the Khamptis attacked Sadiya and killed Lt. Col. White in 1839. The British had to expand the frontier constabulary to subdue such acts of violence.

From these references it is evident that the relations between the British and the people of NEFA were far from being cordial and the conditions in the foothills were completely devoid of peace. Under these circumstances. the British isolated the area. On March 7, 1873, the 'Inner Line Regulations' were enacted, and NEFA was cut off from Assam. But the Naga District, which provides access to Manipur State, was brought under the British Administration ; it was left out of the pale of these 'Inner Line Regulations'.

The British rulers could not subdue the tribal people of NEFA and they found the area unproductive. They for their own convenience and not for any humanitarian reasons brought about the isolation of the tribal areas of Assam. In doing this they had not the least consideration for India. The invasion and the occupation of Lhasa by the Chinese forces in 1910 provoked a renewal of the British interest in the northern hills. The Government of India established three outposts on the three known routes—the Lohit Valley, the Siang Valley and the Dirang Dzong track—, but did not lift the barrier—the Inner Line. Their real intention of slicing off the area from Assam was revealed to India when during the negotiations for the Independence of the country a proposal was brought forward for the formation of a 'Crown Colony' of the tribal areas. Of course when Independence came, it came for the whole country and NEFA was a part of it; and the question of the 'Crown Colony was shelved.

Thus NEFA was politically isolated, and thrown into the shadows of Indian History for more than one and a half centuries, yet there remained a wealth of records in Assam which give detailed and coherent information regarding the tribal people of this tract. These records were preserved in 'Buranjis', the historical accounts written in the Assamese and the Ahom script and handed down from father to son. During the 19th century some of the 'Buranjis' were translated into English. The British administrators also added quite a good deal of information and compiled records pertaining to the tribal people of NEFA which are even today considered valuable.

The inhabitants of NEFA were never an isolated people. They were in contact with the Buddhist culture in the north and east, and were a part and parcel of the Hindu culture of Assam in the south. Col. Dalton[6] traces the origin of the tribal colonisation of these hills to Aryan period. At any rate, it will be illogical to dub the inhabitants of NEFA as tribals, a term which conveys the idea of isolation, primitiveness and want of culture. They will be studied as the people of the region, of Assam and of India, and the problems of NEFA will be scrutinised in conjunction with the more important historical, geographical, economic, and cultural characteristics of the region and of Assam. NEFA is contiguous to Tibet, therefore, its problems cannot be fully appreciated unless a reference is also made to the current Sino-Indian Border Controversy.

India attained freedom on August 15, 1947, and inherited many intricate problems from the British. The Indo-Tibetan Border Controversy is one of them. The

British conduct in the Himalayas and the Himalayan States was guided solely by considerations of the security and integrity of India and to that end the British led Indian troops to Lhasa and assumed the role of guardianship over Sikkim and Bhutan. They explored Tibet, and these explorations served a dual purpose ; firstly, to develop a sound Sino-Indian policy and secondly, to keep up the spirit of adventure in British officers and diplomats. After Independence these objectives were forgotten and India kept herself strictly confined to the India of the Himalayas in the north, Pakistan in the east and west, and the Indian Ocean in the south. She did not fully appreciate and recognise the implications of keeping the frontier well-guarded. She was told that the British did not keep army detachments to guard the Himalayan border, but she forgot that Tibet was then, either by force or by diplomacy, a buffer State between India and China and there was no need to lock the Indian Army in the Himalayas which at that stage of scientific development were considered impassable. The British always considered Russia as a threat to India and as a safeguard against the Russian expansion they acted in collaboration with China, and concluded treaties and agreements with a deplorable lack of forethought. Free India followed the British footsteps ignoring the changed circumstances and political ideologies. She ignored history and believed in the credentials of her neighbour, China. The result is that India is faced with one of the most difficult problems in the history of her defence of her territory in these mountainous, inaccessible border regions. The tragedy is that the public lacks any real knowledge of the Himalayan region. And now that the defence of the frontier areas has come under the Foreign and Defence ministries, it is a special preserve for only a few high officials to discuss. It is too late to take the public into confidence and disclose all the facts, specially pertaining to the defence of 2,500 miles of Sino-Indian frontiers. The problem has assumed importance not only for India, but for the whole of Asia and the world. An attempt is made in this book to acquaint the public with the genesis of the conflict that has risen as a result of the Chinese incursions across the McMahon Line, and all that is involved in it. The problem is not new. It has been casting its shadow over India for more than three quarters of a century. Considering previous history and the Chinese proclivities of expansion as displayed from the beginning of the 18th century, it is safer to conclude that it will be years before the problem is solved and the signatures of the two Governments—India and China, are endorsed on any treaty or agreement. Or it may be that the two countries may not contract an agreement at all for decades to come. Therefore, the controversy is of long range interest and the author will be satisfied if the reader forms an intelligent perspective by which he may understand the implications inherent in the problem. The discussion of the Indo-Tibetan border dispute or of any problem pertaining to the two countries—India and Tibet—will, in general, be restricted to the North-East Frontier.

The author requests those who sympathise with the Chinese sentiments and International Communism to grant the same concessions to India that they are prepared to sanction to their so called Socialist State, China. If China is within her rights to liberate the people of the north—Tibet, Sinkiang and Inner Mongolia who on religiousical, cultural and religious grounds—though very doubtful, are claimed, to be akin to the Chinese, then India has a better claim to take upon herself the guardianship of areas in the Himalayan region vital to her own interest and which are inhabited by the Noctes, the Wanchoos, the Singphos and the Tangsas of Tirap, the Mishmis of Lohit, the Abors of Siang, the Daflas, the Hill Miris and the Apa Tanis of Subansiri, and the Monpas, the Akas, the Mijis and the Khawas of the Kameng Frontier Division, people who are ethnologically and otherwise also similar to their brethren of the Central and Western Himalayas and quite different from the people of Trans-Himalayan Tibet. It will be an act of treachery towards India on the part of those who may absolve China of expansionism and charge India with this evil design. If Peking can extend her frontiers up to more than 2,000 miles south in the Himalayan fastnesses then it is logical and natural for India to guard the barrier which has been a symbol of strength for her security and integrity since time immemorial.

1. Pt. Jawaharlal Nehru's Speeches—1949-53, Vol. II, pp. 41.

2. 10 Years' Progress in NEFA. A Brief Account of Administration and Development Activities in North-East Frontier Agency since Independence. Independence Day 1957.

3. Sketch of Assam (1847) by Major John Butler, pp. 38, 80, 81, 86, 206, 211.

4. The Planter's Life (1883) in Assam by Geo. M. Baker, p. 75.

5. JASB—1900 Vol. LXIX Pt. III, p. 5.

6. Descriptive Ethnology of Bengal by Col. E. T. Dalton, C.S.I. Introduction, p. vii.

CHAPTER II

ASSAM

Where nature is Prodigal and Earthquakes a Common Occurrence.

"The country of Kamrup is about 10,000 Li (nearly 1,700 miles) in circuit. The capital town is about 30 Li. The land lies low, but is rich and cultivated....On the east the country is bounded by a line of hills, so that there is no great city to the kingdom. The frontiers are contiguous to the barbarians of south-west China......After a two months journey we reach the south-west frontier of the province of Szechuen. But the air, the poisonous vapours, the fatal snakes, the destructive vegetation, and these causes of death prevail[1]."

Huin Tsiang (*643 A.D.*)

Assam is known to most of us as a country of jungles, wild animals and torrential rains. It was considered as a dark province of India. Whosoever entered Assam met with misfortune and for him Assam became a synonym for disaster. "It is from the misfortunes which have invariably befallen those who entered Assam, that the people of India have come to look upon the Assamese as sorcerers, and use the word "A'Sa'm in such formulas as dispel witchcraft[2]." Assam probably exceeds every other territory of comparable extent in the world in the number of her rivers, both small and large. These obstacles make social contact between the local people of different groups difficult. In the past, the Assamese suffered from a great want of intercourse with the rest of India and Assam made her own history in partial isolation from the main current of Indian History. Assam having its hilly tracts in the north, south and east, is a vast plain astride the Brahmaputra river, interspersed with shallow river valleys and channels at short intervals, where miles and miles of paddy fields, evergreen and ever-watered, greet the eye. The monotony of the landscape is broken by reserve forests where protected wild animals, a delight of tourists, roam unharmed by man. In Assam the sun, on clear days, is scorching and unpleasant, but generally it is hidden by threatening clouds all the year round. Some of the early historians and visitors have spoken highly of Assam. Tavernier wrote of Assam: "The kingdom of Assam as being one of the best countries of all Asia, for it produces all things necessary for human subsistence without any need of foreign supply[3]." Dr. M'Cosh's opinion of Assam was flattering. He said: "Its climate is cold, healthy and congenial to European constitution; its numerous crystal streams abound in gold dust and masses of solid metal; its mountains are pregnant with precious stones and silver: its atmosphere is perfumed with tea, growing wild and luxuriantly; and its soil is so well adapted to all kinds of agriculture purposes, that it might be converted into one continued garden of silk and cotton, of tea, of coffee, and sugar, over an extent of many hundred miles[4]." It is only once in the History of Assam when in 1665 rains failed to an extent sufficient to cause a complete failure of crops. But this beauty of landscape, fertility of soil and mildness of the cloudy weather is eclipsed by the geological failings of Assam. Here, in the east, the earth's crust is 'geosyncline', it dips downward towards the earth's axis resulting in the formation of depressions and abrupt elevations, The process is slow but continuous and the earth is constantly subjected to the pull. In the most strongly affected areas, during the monsoon season, torrential rains complete the picture of devastation ; rain water collects in the newly formed low-lying areas and changes them into marshy lands ; the trees are water-killed and forests of bare stumps of trees remain standing. At other places as the water soaks into the soil and further loosens it, landslides occur and river banks collapse. Debris so caused silts up the river beds and the rivers overflow their banks and cut wider channels. Thus rivers claim more and more of cultivable, inhabited or forested land and widen their courses to enormous width rendering bridge-building and road construction difficult and expensive. This destruction is repeated with every monsoon and the rivers remain untamed. Diversionary routes have to be constructed every year after the rains for the existing roads and tracks to keep them open for traffic. But even this does not complete the woe of the State. Assam also lies in the "Mediterranean Orogenic (Earthquake) belt[5]" stretching from Gibralter to Australia. The "Fault Line[6]" of this belt runs along the southern slopes of the northern hills and up to the north-east corner of the State where the Himalayan ranges change their direction abruptly from east-west to north-south forming a remarkable "hair-pin bend[7]" or a "deep knee-bend[8]" adding more strain to the earth's crust. Because of these geological faults Assam is literally known as the "home of earthquakes[9]" and "perhaps it is one of the most unstable regions of the world[10]." Although the recorded history of Assam speaks of earthquakes and their havoc since 1548, the most notorious ones are those of 1897 and of 1950. These were considered (up to 1959) to be two of the five strongest earthquakes recorded in the history of mankind. The loss of property caused by 1897 earthquake was incalculable, and the earthquake of 1950 was the worst in the annals of Assam. But as the people of Japan so those in Assam are still living and are reaping the fruits of nature's bounty.

NEFA is divided into five Divisions—Kameng (2,000 square miles), Subansiri (7,950 square miles), Siang (8,392 square miles), Lohit (5,800 square miles) and Tirap (2,657 square miles)—with a total population of about 300,000, the figures of 1961 census have not yet been published. These five Divisions are confined almost entirely to the hilly and mountainous terrain which encloses the Assam Valley of the Brahmaputra like a horseshoe. The Naga Hill and Tuensang Area is a separate unit. There is a move to take out Tirap from NEFA and merge it with this latter unit.

Territorially NEFA may broadly be divided into two tracts—the Northern Tract comprising Kameng, Subansiri, Siang and a major portion of the Lohit Frontier Division, and the Eastern Tract embracing the rest of Lohit and the Tirap Frontier Division. The Brahmaputra divides the two tracts in the north-east corner of Assam.

The Northern Tract foothills begin in the plains about 20 to 30 miles from the northern bank of the Brahmaputra river and rise to the main Himalayan range which roughly forms the Indo-Tibetan boundary—the McMahon Line*—along the international watershed. The tract has

* The McMahon Line, however, departs from well recognised geographical features at a few places. For example, the international boundary departs from the watershed near Tsari in order to include in Tibet the pilgrimage route of Tsari Nyingpa which is used every year by a large number of Tibetans. Similarly, the village of Migyitun was included in Tibet in view of the fact that the Tibetans attached considerable importance to this village. White Paper No. 2 p. 8.

the largest number of rivers of Assam which flow from north to south. These rivers—the Lohit, Dikrong, Dibong, Dihong or Siang, Subansiri, Kamla, Ranga or Painer, Kameng, Dirang Dzong Chhu and Tawang Chhu and their tributaries—are fed by torrential rains distributed almost throughout the entire year. Thus they remain flooded and their fast flowing currents and rapids have cut deep gorges through rocks which are geologically young. These gorges are difficult, if not impossible, to bridge. Construction of roads and tracks along river valleys is very expensive and the territory is devoid of good land communications. However, air-fields and landing strips and air services are being increased, though at exhorbitant expense.

The foothills, rising up from 6,000 to 8,000 ft. are covered, at least on the southern slopes, with dense subtropical evergreen forests below, and with semi evergreen temperate rain forests at higher altitudes. The middle or the Inner ranges from 8,000 to 14,000 ft. are forested with temperate or coniferous forests. Near the snow line the flora is Alpine.

The Northern Tract, like the rest of Assam, is a seismic area, and the earth's convulsions cause severe damage to life and property, specially in the Lohit Frontier Division where the earth has lost its cohesion and disintegrates at the slightest vibrations caused within or without it. A mere touch of a finger or a flight of an aeroplane may cause a huge landslide in the Lohit Hills, where landslips on some of the mountains appear of such magnitude that the fact of a village being occasionally swept away ought not to be wondered at. "On August 15, 1950, one of the most disastrous earthquakes in history caused widespread devastation throughout Upper Assam, particularly in the frontier tribal districts of the Mishmi and Abor Hills[11]." The epicentre of the 1950 earthquake was located in the Lohit Frontier Division near the Indo-Tibetan border. Mr. F. Kingdon Ward, who, in the company of Mrs. Ward, was touring the area and on August 15, 1950, was staying in Rima (a village in Tibet just across the McMahon Line in the Lohit Valley) recorded*: "........the crust on which we lay was really quite thin, and that it would immediately crack, break up, and let us fall through into the bowels of the earth. At the epicentre of such a convulsion, the word 'earthquake' conveys quite a false impression." The loss suffered by the Lohit Frontier Division was colossal and the Dibong Valley was the worst hit. This earthquake has changed the topography of the region and the Division stays in a highly disturbed state.

The Patkoi Range of about 6,500 ft. average height forms the Indo-Burma boundary of the Eastern Tract. The whole Tract is hilly and the hills geologically are the youngest in NEFA. Here the soil is soft and loamy, and the area is fairly stable and landslides rarely occur. Tirap and Tisa are the main rivers of the Tract and they join the Burhi Dihing river. Noa Dihing is another important river which waters the northern portion of the Tract. The Tract is tropical and experiences, at places, more than 200 inches of mean annual rainfall. The hills are covered with the thickest forests of NEFA, hence thousands of acres of land surface are never reached by the sun's rays. River valleys are very unhealthy and the inhabitants of the Tract strongly dislike to pass through

---

* A report written by Capt. Kingdon Ward which was made available at the Headquarters of the Assam Rifles in Lohitpur.

them. It is because of the insalubrious climate of the valleys that the tribal people live on the tops of the hills. The peculiarity about the Tract is that here the hills are detached from each other and seldom form a fairly long ridge. If one wishes to go from one village to another he has to cross a valley and negotiate steep gradients to reach his destination.

Because of the predatory propensities of the tribal people the fauna of NEFA is very poor. Forests are usually quiet, undisturbed by the chirpings of birds; tigers are rare; rhinoceros is protected; bison, deer and other quadrupeds are gradually decreasing in number. The elephant has so far resisted the onslaught of man and is found roaming in herds in the foothill forests.

1. A History of Assam by Gait, p. 23.
2. JASB 1872 Vol. XLI H. Blockman. p. 79.
3. The Calcutta Review Vol. XXI, 1853, p. 411.
4. JASB 1836, p. 194.
5. Geology of India by D. N. Wadia, p. 507.
6. Bulletin of the Geological Survey of India, Series By M. C. Poddar, p. 3.
7. Memoirs of the Geological Survey of India, Vol. 81 By M. S. Krishna p. 13.
8. D. N. Wadia, p. 8.
9. Poddar, p. 3.
10. Memoirs of Geological Survey of India, Vol. XXXV 1902 Pt. 2, p. 13.
11. Poddar, p. 1.

CHAPTER III

A Brief History of Assam

Ahoms' influence over the people of NEFA

"The complexity of the culture of any area can only be fully established when it has become possible to formulate a scheme of its history in harmony with those of neighbouring area of allied culture[1]."

W.H.R. Rivers

The people of NEFA are not like the other coloured aborigines who had continuously led a segregated life for centuries before they came in contact with the Western civilisation. They are not like the Red Indians of North America and the Australian tribals who, in the first contact with other civilisations, were decimated as Western settlers ruthlessly encroached on their tribal lands. The people of NEFA are surrounded by the Tibetans in the north, the Chinese and the Burmese in the east, the Assamese in the south and the Bhutanese in the west; they had social and economic contacts, according to the conveniences of communications available, with their neighbours. Their country is hilly and is surrounded by inaccessible mountains on all sides except towards the Assam Valley. Therefore, they had rare contacts with the Tibetans, the Chinese and the Burmese but were intimately connected with the Assamese. It will be futile to study these people in isolation from Assam or the Assamese. It is, therefore, imperative that, prior to understanding them, their history should be studied in conjunction with the history of Assam. The history of Assam is a broad subject and cannot here be written of in its wider aspect. In this chapter an attempt has been made to restrict it to the people of NEFA.

Pragjyotish of the ancient and Kamrup of the mediæval ages is the Assam of today. It may be differing in extent but the country is the same. Pragjyotish (or Kamrup) has been mentioned both in the Ramayana and the Mahabharata. "The Prabhu mountains are the eastern boundaries of Assam[2]", writes Lt. Col. Wilford. It was true in ancient times and it is true today. The Prabhu mountains according to Cshetra-Samasa are located in the north-east of Assam above the Mishmi Hills in the vicinity of Rima, about 187 miles from Sadiya. Gauhati for most of the time has been the capital of the State.

According to mythology, Daksha was once discourteous to his son-in-law, Mahadev or Shiva. Sati, the wife of Shiva, could not tolerate the insult shown to her husband and she died of shock. Shiva overcome by grief wandered all over the world carrying her dead body on his head. After some time her body started disintegrating and its different parts fell at different places. Her organ of generation fell on Nilachal, 3 miles west of Gauhati, where the temple of Kamakhya marks the site. Shiva continued the penance, and the other gods became apprehensive lest by this devotional penance, he should acquire universal powers. They accordingly despatched Kamdeo (Cupid) to make Shiva fall in love again. Kamdeo succeeded but he was reduced to ashes when Shiva opened his fiery third eye. However, Shiva later brought Kamdeo to life again. Since then the place where it happened has been known as Kamrup (the place where Kamdeo regained life). Coming to Assam, the word owes its origin to the Ahoms—Ahom and Assam are synonyms—who after the 13th century ruled the State. Assam means 'great' and the rulers named their kingdom as such.

Assam is the home of tribes who have been inhabiting the mountains, the hills, the jungles and the valleys of the State for such a long time, and with such an admixture of blood and races that, today, it is very difficult to differentiate one tribe from the other. However, the anthropologists, ethnologists, philologists and historians have agreed that the first people to migrate to Assam were of the Mon-Khemer or the Austric stock. The remnants of this stock are the Mundas of Chhotanagpur in Bihar, and the Khasis and the Garos of the Jaintia Hills south of the Assam Valley. Some historians trace the origin of the Bodo tribe, which is spread all over Assam to Mon-Khemer. The dissection of hair has indicated that the Nagas have traces of Negroid descent. This has confused the issue, because other tribes do not show any link with the Negroids. After the Austric people the Indo-Chinese, and the Tibeto-Burman (who may be called the Mongoloids) entered Assam and probably drove the Austric people to the southern hills where they, even today, reside. The Mongoloids spread to western hills, that is how the Newars of Nepal are connected with these waves of emigrants. The Mongoloids were followed by the Dravidians or by the Aryans or by both simultaneously. Those, who hold that the Aryans preceded the Dravidians, believe that the culture of the former was superior to the latter. The current trend is that the Dravidian's civilization, if it was not superior to that of the Aryan's, at least was developed to a level of which the Dravidians could rightly be proud and could hold their own before any contemporary civilization and culture. These advocates believe that the Dravidians entered Assam before the Aryans. The stories of Bana, Prahlad, Bhishmak and Shispal have given rise to the controversy. Even after the emigration of the Dravidians or the Aryans the people of Mongoloid stock continued to migrate into Assam up to the middle of the 19th century.

Although the ancient history of Assam is rich, yet very little is accurately known of that period. Whatever we know of Assam and NEFA of those days is from the Ramayana and the Mahabharata. Some of the legends are briefly narrated here.

Once Ugratara, the consort of Shiva, under the instructions of her husband proceeded to Kamrup to drive out all the inhabitants from the country. Whilst executing her mission she came to Vashisht and told the sage to leave Kamrup. Vashisht was so enraged that he pronounced a curse that all the inhabitants of Kamrup would turn mlechhas (non-Aryans) and would forget all the Kamrup 'Pithas'—the sacred shrines. Then Brahma felt the need of a sacred river flowing through Kamrup touching all the Tantra 'Pithas' so that anybody taking bath in the holy river would get the benefit of all the sacred shrines. According to the legend, the river sprang up as a sheet of water when a river-child was born from the womb of Amogha, the beautiful wife of Santanu, the sage who used to live on the bank of Lohit Sarovar. The child is said to be the son of Brahma and like him. The place where the child was placed after his birth became the source of the river and came to be known as the Brahma Kund (lake) and the river which began to flow afterwards as the Brahmaputra or the Lohit—the Red river.

Parasurama, the son of Jamdagni, under the direction

of his father had killed his mother with his pharsa or axe. Jamadagni granted seven boons to the son, but Parasurama's matricidal sin could not be washed away. Parasurama visited all the holy shrines, but he could not get rid of the gore and the axe remained glued to his hand. In this plight he visited Brahma Kund. He entered into the Kund for a holy bath. Lo! the battle-axe fell from his hand, and the blood stains disappeared.

In order to supply mankind with water of such admirable efficacy, Parasurama dug a channel with his pharsa for water to flow from the Brahma Kund to the Lohit Sarovar and then from Lohit Sarovar to the east. Then somewhere in East-North-East Assam on the eastern frontier of the State amidst the Prabhu mountains beyond Nara he rent a hill and made Lohit or Brahmaputra of pass through the gorge of Hemasringha and finally to flow through Kamrup covering all the Tantra 'Pithas'.

Brahma Kund is in the mountains of Tibet and in the north-west of which is Mt. Kailash; the river Tsangpo during its course through Tibet along the northern slopes of the Himalayas is the Lohit, the Red river, of the legend. There is no dispute about it. Sven Hedin[3], a famous explorer, reached the source of Brahmaputra in 1906-07. He places the source at an altitude of 15,958 ft. above the sea level and locates it about 60 miles to the south-west of Gurla, the highest mountain of the Tibetan plateau, immediately to the east of Mansarovar. But the learned pandits of Assam insist that the source of Brahmaputra lies in the range of mountains beyond Nara to the east-north-east-of Assam. Probably they refer to Lohit Sarovar where according to the legend quoted Parasurama brought the water of the Brahma Kund. Lohit Sarovar was evidently connected to Brahma Kund in former times by the river Tsangpo. In this case topographical upheavals caused by geological convulsions which are usually violent and very frequent in this region must have blocked the course of Tsangpo to Lohit Sarovar to the east and diverted it to its main stream, the Dihong, making the Tsangpo and Dihong as one and the same river.

Lohit Sarovar is lost in the Himalayas and from all accounts is inaccessible. From Lohit sarovar the Red River issues and forces its way through the famous chasm and the Pass of 'Prabhu Kuthar' cut at Himasringha, and rushes through the valley of Assam. Indian pilgrims visited this sacred place, 'Prabhu Kuthar' or the Lohit Sarovar, upto the middle of the last century[4]. Lt. Col. Wilford[5] informs us, according to Cshetra Samasa, that Prabhu Kuthar is about 125 British miles from Godagram, while Lt. Wilcox[6] considers the distance to be 150 miles. It is difficult to locate Godagram, but Col. Wilford further tells us that the Pass is about 120 miles from the present site of Brahma Kund, an imitation* of Lohit Sarovar or of Prabhu Kuthar. Col. Wilford writes :—

> "From the above pass to the Cunda, the journey is always performed in eight days, because the travellers must keep together, on account of the inhabitants, who are savages, great thieves and very cruel. There are fixed and regular stages, with several huts of the natives. The kings of Assam

* Among the old inhabitants of Tezpur in Lohit a story is prevalent that during the 18th century a sadhu established the present site of the Brahma Kund. The Kund is situated on the left bank of the river Lohit, 18 miles south of Tezu. Thousands of devotees visit the place for a holy dip on Sankrant Amawas, which generally coincides with the middle of January, every year.

> are some times obliged to chastise them, but in general they contrive to secure the friendship, and protection of their chief, by trifling presents. The country is covered with extensive forests, with a few spots cleared up, with little industry and skill."

From the nature of the terrain, the weather and the usual physical condition of the pilgrims, who are generally old, 'eight days' appears to be an understatement or the distance is less than 120 miles.

The British occupied Assam in 1826 and as a consequence conditions of insecurity prevailed in the Mishmi Hills. The number of pilgrims decreased. The ease with which the devotees could perform the pilgrimage to the present site of the Brahma Kund also discouraged the traffic. The final blow was given by the 'Inner Line Regulations' which segregated the area, and the pilgrimage to the real Prabhu Kuthar completely ceased; Prabhu Kuthar was forgotten. One hears a faint murmur of its existence near Walong, a journey of more than 10 days from Tezu, the Divisional Headquarters of the Lohit Frontier Division, but it is now lost to the noisy world.

The story suggests that only a century back Hindu pilgrims were trekking on the pilgrimage to Prabhu Kuthar up to which the domain of the Ahom Rajas extended.

During the Mahabharata period Bhishmak, the father of Rukmani ruled in Lohit. When Rukmani grew up Bhishmak arranged her marriage with king Shishpal, another chieftain of the adjacent territory extending to the banks of the Lohit river. A few days before the marriage Lord Krishna after receiving Rukmani's message arrived on the scene and kidnapped her. There was a fight between Krishna and Shishpal. Rukman, the brother of Rukmani, allied with the latter. Krishna crushed the opposition and captured Rukman. On his sister's entreaties Krishna released Rukman but as a token of victory he cut the latter's hair. Even today the Idus—the Chulikatas—observe that practice and claim their descent from Bhishmak. The Digarus trace their descent from Shishpal. The legend connects the Lohitians with the Aryan culture.

During the same period a similar drama was staged in the Darrang district. In this drama the chief actor was again Krishna, who visited Sonitpur, the present Tezpur, and forced the king Bana to marry his daughter to Aniruddha, Krishna's own son. The Akas of the Kameng Frontier Division trace their descent from this king Bana. Later Bana's grandson Bhaluk made his capital at Bhalukpung, at the foothills of Kameng, where the remains of old fortifications are still visible. The legend of Prahlad and his devotion to Vishnu is known to every Hindu child. Sonitpur was the place where this episode was supposed to have been enacted.

During the Mahabharata period Pragjyotish probably extended up to Eastern Nepal[7] and king Narkasur, a contemporary of Bana, ruled the kingdom. Narkasur, on account of Bana's non-Aryan influence, took to bad ways and started persecuting the Aryans. Krishna, to clear the kingdom of the evil influence, dethroned Narkasur and declared the latter's son, Bhagdatta, as the king of Pragjyotish. Bhagdatta took part in the epic war of the Pandavas and the Kauravas. He was an ally of the latter. There is a mention in Mahabharata of Bhagdatta's army having Kirata and Cina soldiers. "The Kiratas, with hair done in pointed top-knot, pleasant to look upon, shining like gold, able to move under water, terrible veritable tiger-men, so are they found[8]", says the Mahabharata. The epic emphasises the yellow colour of the Kiratas and the Cinas. The Kirata appears to be the generic term applied to the dwellers of the Himalayas, while Cina is likely to be the synonym of China and was probably applied to the allies or kinsmen of Kiratas who were of Mongoloid extraction. Abors of Siang display the nearest resemblance to the Cinas.

During the Christian Era Assam was a known king dom and had contacts with Gupta kings. According to Vincent Smith[9], in 428 A.D. a Raja named Yen-ai 'Moon-loved' (Chandra-priya) who was the lord of Ka-Pi-Li, a river in Assam, sent an embassy to the Chinese Court.

Assam by the beginning of the Christian Era had attained considerable power and a fair degree of civilization. Huin Tsiang, the Chinese monk, visited Assam in 643 on the invitation of the king of Kamrup. From the 7th to the 12th century Assamese history in connection with the tribal area is uneventful. Mohammadan invasions against Assam started by the end of the 12th century. Mohammad Bakhtyar Khilji's invasion in 1198 proved disastrous to the invader. Ghiyas-ud-din, a Governor of Bengal, reached upto Sadiya in 1227 but in the end was defeated and driven back to Gaur (Bengal). Ikhtiyar-ud-din Yuzbek or Tughrei Khan invaded Assam in 1278. He was killed and his army was completely routed. Thus Assam never came under the Muslim influence which, by this time, had infiltrated elsewhere in India.

The close of the 12th century or the beginning of the 13th witnessed changes which firmly established Assam on the historical map of India. The future rulers of Assam—the Ahoms—migrated to the State from Burma in 1324 and consolidated it. They remained in power till

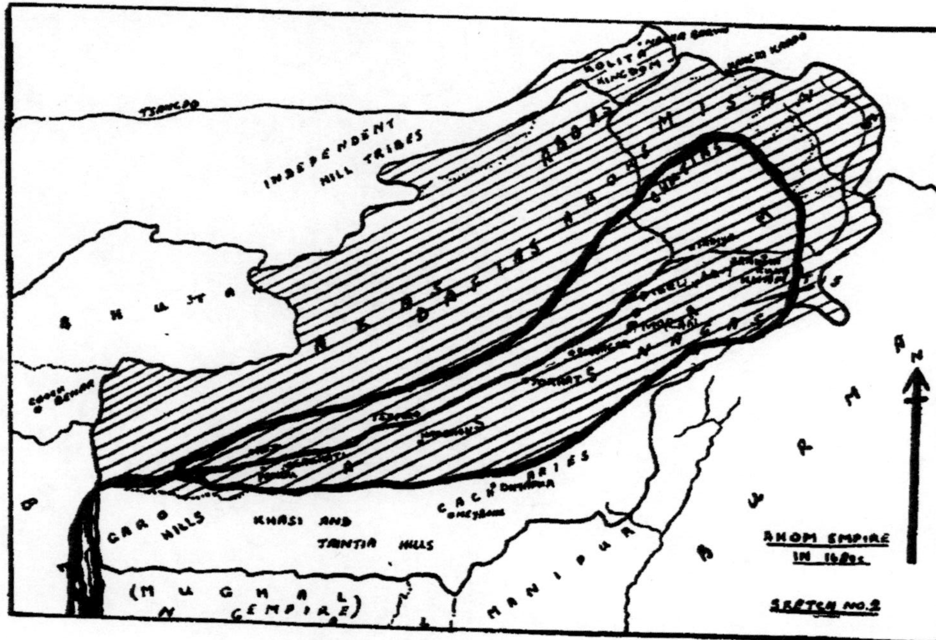

AHOM EMPIRE IN 1680'S

they were overthrown by the British in 1835. At the time of their migration Assam was not a unitary State controlled by a central power. It was divided into many small kingdoms and principalities. The Chutias, a tribe of Bodo origin, were ruling the Sadiya Tract, while the Cacharies, another tribe of similar origin, were dominating the territories west and south of the Chutia kingdom. The Nagas were supreme in Tirap and the Naga Hills. Gauhati and its surrounding territory was split up into many kingdoms out of which areas under the Kamta and the Bhuiyan Rajas were the notable States. Kamtapur was the capital of the former and was located in the west of Gauhati, while that of the latter shifted from place to place. The rulers of Kamtapur claimed their descent from the old kings of Kamrup, while that of Bhuiyan from Kanauj kings. In the southern hills Jaintia kings held sway, while Tripura and Manipur were known to have flourished at the time. In Bengal Muslims had gained a footing and their influence had penetrated up to Dacca.

Though Assam was divided into many small states, in emergency these states combined to ward off the common danger, specially from the West. That is how Assam escaped the domination and the cultural influence of Mohammadans.

The states were connected by roads and river transport was much in use. There was a regular traffic between China and India, through the Mishmi Hills because when Bhaskara Varma or Kumara, the king of Kamrup, invited Huin Tsiang to visit the State, he suggested that the latter "could take Assam on the way to China[10]."

The people of Assam were said to be short of stature

and dark-looking. They were simple and honest, but violent in disposition. They were persevering students and had a literature of their own. Their mainstay was agriculture and they also raised jack fruit and had cocoa plantations. They wore cotton and silken clothes and knew the use of wool. Their staple food was rice and fish supplemented by forest produce. Their towns had well maintained tanks or reservoirs.

Worship of the female or male principle of procreation—Saktaism—was the dominant religion of the people The temples of Tameshwari in the east and Kamakhya in the west were popular religious centres of Assam. The former was also known by the name of 'Kacha Khati' (eater of raw flesh) and was located in the Mishmi country. Human sacrifice was performed at the altar of the goddess. The temple priests were the Idu Mishmis. Besides these temples there were other innumerable temples of Shiva where animal sacrifice was performed. Temple women or prostitutes were a common feature of Assamese temple worship. Buddhism was tolerated but its adherents were very few in the State. Hajo, about fifteen miles from North Gauhati, was the Buddhist pilgrimage. It attracted pilgrims from Tibet, Bhutan and Tawang. These pilgrims combined trade with religion and attended an annual fair at Hajo. By the end of the 12th century Hajo had also attracted a few followers of Islam in its vicinity. These believers were the remnants of the defeated armies of the Muslim invaders who had elected to stay back and settled down in the country.

The social, economic and religious life of the Assamese influenced the dwellers of the eastern Himalayas. The Nagas had social contacts with the Cacharies, the Mishmis, and the Chutias, who performed human sacrifice. Some historians believe that the Abors visited Tameshwari for worship. In the west the Bhuiyans patronised the Akas and the Daflas, and the Monpas had trade relations with the ruling chiefs of Darrang and Kamrup districts. Nearly all the tribal groups contributed their share of soldiers to the local armies. The Nagas were known to have fought wars as the soldiers of their own army, while the other tribals fought under the banners of different chiefs.

In the north of Burma, contiguous to south China, the country is hilly. It is inhabited by the Shan race, a branch of Tais, who once expanded from this hilly cradle to Indo-China and India. The Khamptis, Phakials, Aitonias, Turung and Khamians are all Shan tribes who have, at different times, migrated to Assam after the spread of Buddhism in Burma. They professed and even today profess the same religion though their faith was influenced by Hinduism and the environments amidst which they lived. The Ahoms of Maulang (North Burma) were of the same stock, but they migrated to India before their conversion to Buddhism. Sukapha was the first Maulang king who established the Ahom rule in India.

Sukapha and Khunlung were two brothers. A conflict between the two brothers forced Sukapha, the younger of the two, to leave Maulang. He accompanied by 9.000 men and women of his clan entered India in 1225 and by 1228 succeeded in establishing his capital at Khamjan. After a series of changes he finally shifted the seat of his government to Chraideo in 1253.

For more than 150 years the Ahoms ruled the kingdom from Chraideo (at the foot of the Naga Hills) till Suhungmung (1497-1539) shifted his capital to the interior of the Naga country Tirap—on the banks of the Dihing river. After a lapse of a quarter of a century Sukhlungpha (1539-1552), the son of Suhungmung, made Gargaon his capital. The Ahoms built the Royal Palace and other buildings at Rangpur, a couple of miles from Sibsagar, and in the beginning of the 18th century made it as their capital. Till 1811 the town held this honour. Jorhat was the last Ahom capital and in 1835 witnessed the disappearance of the Ahom kingdom from Assam, after more than 600 years of rule.

The Ahoms liked the country of their adoption and tried hard to extend their rule to the whole of the Brahmaputra Valley. Slowly and gradually they dealt decisive blows to the Chutias, the Cacharies, the Bhuiyans and others, till they became the paramount power of Assam. By treaties and friendly alliances their suzerainty or sovereignty was recognised by the neighbouring tribes. Thus eventually the Ahom Empire embraced most of the territory known today as Assam.

At first the Ahoms tried to establish friendly relations with the Chutias. They contracted marriages with the Chutia women. Their overtures failed to achieve the desired result. The Chutias, in 1376, treacherously murdered the Ahom king Sutenpha (1364-1376) and thus invited the wrath of the Ahoms. Quarrel arose. There were armed conflicts between the two kingdoms. Finally during Suhungmung's (1497-1539) time, the Chutias were annihilated and their kingdom was annexed. A new officer, Sadiya Gohain, was appointed to administer the acquired territory. The remnants of the Chutia clan, in due course, were assimilated by the Mishmis of the Lohit Frontier Division.

The Cacharies stood longer than the Chutias against

the Ahoms. In 1490, king Suhenpha (1488-1493) dealt a severe blow to Cacharies from which they could not recover. During the period of the subsequent thirty years, their rule was confined to the Dhansiri Valley. The next crushing blow to this tribe, the second ruling race at the time, was delivered by the Ahom king, who, in 1527, forced the Cacharies to shift their capital to Dimapur. Suhungmung did not allow the Cacharies to live in peace. He attacked Dimapur and razed it to the ground. Pursued, they escaped to south and established their capital at Meybong in the Cachar Hills south of Lumding. By the end of the 18th century the Cacharies were a spent force.

Kamta Raj was a powerful kingdom. It was contiguous to Bengal in the south and Kamrup in the east. The Ahoms, once during the reign of Sukhanpha (1293-1332) and next during that of Sudanpha (1397-1407), attacked Kamtapur. On both the occasions the Kamta kings gave their daughters to the invaders in marriage to secure the friendship of the Ahoms. The Kamta king stood up well against the Muslim invaders of Bengal, but because of internal strife they became weak and eventually, in 1498, Hussain Shah overran the kingdom. Thus Kamta Raj also came to an end.

When he returned from Kamtapur Hussain Shah left his son Danyal to administer the newly conquered territory. Soon after his departure the rainy season approached. The Bhuiyans took advantage of the season and attacked Danyal. The defenders were easily overpowered and Kamtapur was annexed by the conquerors. Some of the troops of the vanquished army settled down in the Hajo territory. After about 40 years the Bhuiyan Raj was merged into the Koch kingdom.

A by-product of the Kamta Raj was the kingdom of Kochs which was established in the west in the vicinity of Barpeta in 1515. King Biswa Singh was the founder of the kingdom. Nar Singh, a descendant of Biswa Singh, on account of some internal strife, fled to Nepal and then to Kashmir. "It is said that Nar Singh subsequently became the ruler of Bhutan, and, though there is no confirmation of this statement, the occurrence is not altogether impossible[11]", writes Gates. Narnarayan, another successor in the line, is considered to be an outstanding figure among the Koch kings. He faced many Mohammadan invasions. Though he might not have warded them off successfully yet he did not suffer a crushing defeat at their hands either. He defeated the Ahoms and extended the Koch kingdom up to Namrup. Later he came to terms with the vanquished Ahoms and allowed them to re-establish their kingdom. Parekshit and his cousin Balinarayan, the subsequent claimants to the throne, quarrelled. The former sought help from the Mughals while the latter took shelter under the Ahoms. The result was that the Ahoms in the east and the Mughals in the west and south shared the Koch kingdom. The Koch Raj like that of Kamta Raj, by the 1640s, had disappeared from Assam. The Ahoms extended their rule to embrace Pandu.

In 1337 Mohammad Shah, the ruler of Bengal, sent an army of 100,000 horsemen well equipped to Assam, but the whole army perished in the country. After that not much was heard of Mohammadans invading Assam. During Suhungmung's reign Bengal rulers invaded Assam thrice, but were defeated. Gates[12] is of the opinion that the Ahoms used gun powder in the last of these wars. Previously to this there had been no mention of fire-arms being used in any of the actions. Tavernier[13], however, when narrating the results of Mir Jumla's expedition to Assam in 1663 writes: "The Assamese were the people that formerly invented guns and powder." According to him the invention first reached Pegu and then China.

For more than half a century peace prevailed in Assam. Then trouble was caused by the rivalries of Parekshit and Balinarayan, the two Koch princes. Balinarayan came to the Ahom Court where he was recognised as the vassal king of Darrang. This caused war between the Ahom king Pratap Singh (1603-1641) and the Muslim Governor of Bengal. The war proved a long drawn out affair. During this period Pratap Singh occupied Pandu and appointed a Baraphukan (Viceroy) to administer it. In one of the battles he completely routed the Mohammadan army and took the son of Sattrajit (a petty zamindar of Dacca) a prisoner and later sacrificed him to the goddess Kamakhya. However, Pratap Singh was defeated by the Mohammadans in 1637 and the boundary between Bengal and the Assam Valley was demarcated in 1638.

At Delhi the Mughal Emperor Aurangzeb came to the throne. He, after the Poona debacle against the Marhattas, appointed Mir Jumla as the Governor of Bengal and instructed him to conquer Assam. It is said that Aurangzeb deliberately ordered this move to teach Mir Jumla a lesson for his negligence shown at Poona. During Jaydhwaj's (1648-1653) reign Mir Jumla invaded Assam in 1662. He reached Gargaon and remained in its occupation for about nine months. Jaydhwaj fled to the Naga Hills. At an opportune moment he came down and pounced upon the Mohammadan army during the rainy season. Mir Jumla had already been afflicted with illness and his army was showing signs of exhaustion and was short of supplies. He agreed to a treaty with the Ahom king, then retired to Bengal and died soon after. The Emperor was correct if he had surmised that Mir Jumla would not survive the expedition.

The second victim of Aurangzeb's stratagem was Ram Singh, the son of Raja Man Singh, who had proved an irritation to the Emperor. On some pretext Ram Singh was ordered to overrun Assam. Sarai Ghat, near Gauhati, witnessed the resounding victory of the Ahoms and Ram Singh, in 1671, much harassed by the hostile weather of the country and the stalemate of the campaign left Assam disappointed. After a few years, Gauhati, through some intrigues among the Ahom high officials, fell to the Mohammadans. Gadadhar Singh (1681-1696), finally reoccupied it in 1682 and took possession of the entire territory as had been demarcated in 1638. Since then the territorial integrity of Assam was never threatened by the Muslim rulers of Bengal. Thus the Ahoms extended their kingdom to the entire Brahmaputra Valley, and the credit of this goes to Gadadhar Singh.

When the first Ahom king, Sukapha, migrated from Burma in 1324 to Assam, he encountered strong opposition from the Nagas of Tirap. He crushed all opposition and "caused Nagas to be killed and roasted, and compelled their relations to eat their flesh[14]." Having defeated the Tirapians he appointed his representative to administer the country. The terrain of the Naga Hills helped the people to keep the fire of revolt burning. Sudanpha's reign was marked by conflicts with the Nagas who were supported by king Nara of Burma. Eventually "a formal treaty was concluded in 1401 by which Patkoi was fixed as the boundary between the two country[15]"—Assam and Burma.

THE ROYAL PAI ACE AT GARGAON

SE LA

THE TWO LAKES EMBEDDED IN THE LAP OF THE PASS ARE BURIED UNDER SNOW

After the treaty peace prevailed in the Naga Hills till Susenpha's (1439-1488) accession when the Tangsu Nagas revolted. Intermittently this tribe gave trouble to the paramount power of Assam. Eventually by the end of the 15th century the Nagas were subdued by the Ahoms.

Suhungmung alias 'Swargnarain' or 'Dihingia Raja-1' ascended the throne in 1497. Because of the Nagas' persistent ebullient attitude he shifted his capital to the interior of the Naga country on the banks of the Dihing river. He appointed an officer to administer the provinces of Habung, Dihing and Balung. Dr. Wade writes: "Shookung abandoned the residence of his ancestors in the hills, and came to Dihing. From this station he despatched Taoomul, Deebank, Taoomung, Kamopaig with troops against Atoolia, a district of Nagas. On the approach of king's forces the inhabitants of the district were terrified into an entire submission to his command. They presented him with four virgins of rank and six elephants, as a pledge of their subjugation to his government[16]." Suhungmung seems to have forced all the Naga tribes contiguous to his kingdom to acknowledge the supremacy of the Ahom kings.. Whenever a tribe accepted the sovereignty of the Ahoms they offered the daughter of their chiefs to the conqueror as the token of submission. In addition they also payed tribute, prevalent at the time, to the king. Nagas now and then gave trouble to the central power, but their rebellious proclivities were held in check. They continued to owe allegiance to the Ahom kings.

The Sadiya Gohain[17] appointed by the Dihingia Raja-1 administered the Mishmi country and the Mishmis of the Lohit Valley were subjected to the Ahom law for punishment[18].

The Abors* were brought under taxation by the Ahoms and they were always considered as an ally of the latter and the subjects of the Assam king could pass through the Abor Hills without any formality. The Ahom influence extended up to the present Pemako (the promised land) district of Tibet. During the 15th century two sons of a Gohain (a minister in the Ahom Cabinet) migrated to this territory and established a Hindu kingdom thus extending the boundary of the Ahom kingdom beyond the Himalayan wall. " .....It appears that there was an Aryan settlement at a distance of fifteen days' march through hilly roads from the Ahom territory beyond the regions occupied by the Abors and the Miris. The people bore Hindu Vaishnavite names like Vasudeva, Harideva, Sakarsen etc. There was also a king in the land[19]." The name of the kingdom was Kolita Ramanand Dvija even gives the names of some of the Kolita villages as CEHEKHAMHAT and JINAIGRAM[20]. Neufville[21] also held this idea: "The country to the eastward of Bhot, and the northward of Sadiya, extending on the plain beyond the mountains, is said to be possessed by a powerful nation called Kolitas, or Kultas, who are described as having attained a high degree of advancement and civilization; equal to any of the nations of the East." According to the same author the kingdom maintained correspondence with the parent state of Ahoms. Wilcox[22] gives details of the route to Kolita and concludes: "From Sadiya to Kolita is a journey of forty-two days and six hours, in the middle of the way the route lies through hills, where the dense jungles make it very difficult to proceed." Rowlette[23] also confirms the

* Report on the Province of Assam by A. J. Moffal Mills—Moniram Diwan—Appx. JIXV.

feasibility of the existence of the kingdom. But Gates[24] ridicules the idea. He bases his observation on the visit of a French Missionary to Rima in the Lohit Valley and not in the upper reaches of Dihong, i.e. in the Pemako district. Secondly, when Gates wrote 'A History of Assam', the Englishman's opinion of Hinduism had undergone a change. Everything pertaining to the Hindus and Hindu civilization was fabulous and legendary. Bailey did make enquiries in right earnest and he was rghtly informed that the upper reaches of the rivers and streams in that area were populated by the Abors in the beginning of the last century and the Tibetans or the inhabitants of Tibet, Bhutan and other Buddhist regions in the Eastern Plateau had migrated to Mipi, a Mishmi village[25]. But then it was too late to claim the area of the Kolita Kingdom for India. Had the British made enquiries into this important historical fact earlier, India would not have lost such a valuable tract of land to Tibet. Logically the existence of the Kolita Kingdom seems sound. This area is warm, fertile and comparatively thickly populated. According to beliefs and legends prevalent among the Tibetans of the East the region was named as Pemako and was ordained to be inhabited by them. The Bhutanese, the Monpas and the Tibetans came to colonize this tract. In this region after every 12 years, the Monkey Fair, sacred to the Tibetans, is held around the Mountain Tsari and the pilgrims from all over Tibet attend it. Since Pemako is so attractive and important, no wonder that the sons of the Gohain were attracted to this region to found a separate and independent kingdom. Bailey's findings confirm that Indian nationals—the Abors—were inhabiting the area. The Assamese believe, and Neufville confirms, that the Kolita Kingdom was washed away by the great flood during the middle of the 18th century. Kolita might have been damaged but it was very unlikely that the entire kingdom was washed away by the flood. It was, most probably, wiped out by the Tibetans. It is to be noted that during the 18th century China launched the imperialist policy of territorial expansion and Ahoms at the time were a decaying power. From the Tibetan side territorial aggrandisement had started its pernicious activity while in the south the Ahoms, the paramount power of Assam, were helpless to despatch any succour to the detached Hindu kingdom of Kolita.

The Daflas paid tributes to the Ahom Kings. Once during the reign of Rudra Singh (1696-1714) the Daflas refused to pay the tribute and rebelled against the authority of the king. Rudra Singh despatched an Ahom official. Phukan, to crush the rebellion. "The Phukan suppressed the Daflas and promised them king's pardon, provided they would furnish 400 men from the western mountains and 200 Tageens (Eastern Daflas) for the invasion of Bengal[26]." The soldiers were recruited for the Bengal campaign which, on account of the death of the Ahom King, never, materialised.

There was a conflict in the east between Assam and Ava (Burma) but a formal treaty was concluded in 1401 by which Patkoi was fixed as the boundary between the two countries—Assam and Upper Burma. The relations between Tibet and Assam were cordial and Rudra Singh developed extensive trade with Tibet, hence no necessity arose for fixing the Indo-Tibetan frontier. In fact up to World War One, very few Asian countries could boast of having well-marked and internationally recognised geographical and political boundaries. The idea of defence had not developed so much as to warrant delimitation of national frontiers then. The countries were known and even now are known by the people inhabiting them. The people knew their frontiers and they decided the fate of the country. If they owed allegiance to any power then that *ipso facto* recognised the sovereignty or suzerainty, depending upon circumstances, of that power. During the Ahom rule, the Daflas and the Mishmis owed allegiance to the Rajas of Assam and the rulers of Kolita were a branch of the paramount power itself, therefore, the frontiers of Assam extended beyond the frontiers of present day NEFA. The people recognised the supremacy of the Assam Government and the government was fully justified in claiming the overlordship of the territory inhabited by them. The Patkoi Range in the east and a line touching the Lohit Sarovar, the source of the river Lohit, and the northern limits of the Kolita Kingdom and extending to the north of the Monpa country was the frontier of Assam, hence of India. The idea of a buffer state did not exist then, hence no state acted as a buffer to India either in the east or in the north.

The Ahoms were different from other rulers of Assam, in fact from the rulers of the rest of the country, in that they were keen historians and encouraged recording of facts of the State and employed writers for the purpose The history of Assam from 1228-1835 is a recorded history, though stored in Buranjis, the authenticity of which has been testified by Dr. Grierson, the linguist expert.

> "The Assamese are justly proud of their national literature. In no department have they been more successful than in a branch of study in which India is, as a rule, curiously, deficient. Remnants of historical works that treat of the time of Bhagdatta--

a contemporary of the Kuru Panchala war of the Mahabharata are still in existence. The claim of historical authenticity can be relied upon. These historical works or Buranjis as they are styled in Assam, are numerous and voluminous[27]."

The Ahom Kings were self-confident and proud. Though the rest of the country bowed down before the sword of Islam still the Ahoms refused to be subdued. They were good and stern administrators. Their Cabinet consisted of Burha Gohain (Prime Minister), Bar Gohain and Barpatra Gohain. The kingdom was divided into territories, each governed by a Barphukan. Below the Barphukan and Phukans there were many subordinate ranks and the lowest was the 'Bora'. Every rank was entitled to the free services of Paiks who were like territorial soldiers and were granted land for their subsistence. For all intents and purposes the Ahom Kingdom was a territorial camp which could be mobilised at any time to ward off any threat to Assam from any corner. The Ahoms took care to administer the tribal people. Raja Pratap Singh (1603-1639) appointed Kakaties to watch the movements of the tribals. The rulers punished offenders on the least suspicion and their punishments were barbaric. From 1670 to 1681 Assam Court remained unstable and as many as seven kings came to the throne. Six of them were murdered. At last Supanpha (1681-1696) alias Gadadhar Singh succeeded the throne. After his accession he dealt severe punishments to those whom he thought dangerous either to the State or to himself. Bhatdhar, ex-Barphukan and his son Madha were taken out of detention, slices from their bodies were then "cut off and made into curries like other edible meat. The father was made to eat the flesh of his son and vice versa.

Father was given the heart and liver of his son to eat and then beheaded[28]." By such actions, peace was restored in the country. The Ahoms rewarded the Nagas with 'Khats' and other concessions for the latter's good services to the State. "......, it is certain that several of the chiefs had received grants of khats or lands, and of bheels or fishing waters on the plains, and enjoyed assignment of Paiks like the ordinary Assamese nobility", writes Mackenzie[29]. The Ahoms did not make any distinction between the tribals and the plainsmen for social contacts. Suhungmung is said to have married the daughter of Khunbaw, a Banphera chief. The name of the bride was Karengpa and she bore a son named Tyachengmung to the king. Suhungmung also gave girls of good birth to the Nagas. Once he was obliged by a Khunbaw Naga to give him a princess in marriage. There is a story that one of the Supinpha's (1493-1497) wives happened to see a Naga chief, who had come to pay tribute, and praised his person in the king's hearing. The king was so enraged that he ordered the queen to accompany the Naga chief to his village. The queen was pregnant at the time of the exile. In due course she delivered a son, according to the people of Borduria, a well known Nocte village in Tirap, and died later. The name of the son was Senglung. Suhungmung, the next successor to the throne, on seeing the youth, was struck by the latter's high-bred appearance and after learning about the story of Senlung's mother, took the youth into favour. From the beginning of the Ahom rule the Burha Gohain and the Bar Gohain formed the Ahom Cabinet; Suhungmung created a new office of Barpatra Gohain in the Cabinet and nominated the youth for the office. After that the Ahom Cabinet consisted of three Ministers[30]. This is not an isolated instance of tribal youth occupying a high office. There are other instances also. Neog Gohain Barphukan[31] in 1631 was a Naga of the Banphera clan. The Nagas, the Daflas and the Miria joined the Ahom army. The last two were known for archery while the Nagas used to be employed in the offensive role. The Nagas did not only come down to the plains for service or for other material benefits. Very often they also gave shelter to the Ahom Kings when the latter sought one. Namrup at the foot of the Tirap hills was a well known refuge for fugitives.

Sudanpha was the 1st Ahom King who appointed Brahmans* in the court. Later Suhungmung, the 14th successor to the throne was said to have embraced Hinduism. Montgomery Martin[32] names the 14th successor as Chukum which does not differ much from Suhungmung. Other historians hold that Sutamala was the first Ahom King who accepted the Hindu religion. He patronised the Auniati Sattra (a Vaishnavite religious centre) though Samdeo, the image of the Ahom god, was still worshipped, and before a battle it was still a practice to call upon the Deodhais or the Ahom priests to tell omens by examining the legs of fowls. Some Hindu practices crept into the oath taking ceremony. "During the times of Ahoms,

---

* It is said that Sudanpha's father, Tao Khamti, had two wives. The elder of the two was jealous of the junior Rani. Once when the king was away the former framed false charges against the latter. It was so arranged that the charges were proved true, whereupon the junior Rani was sentenced to be beheaded. The Ministers, however, seeing that she was pregnant, did not kill her and set her adrift on a raft on the Brahmaputra. The raft floated to Habung village, where a Brahman gave shelter to the unfortunate woman. In due course the Rani gave birth to a son who eventually was declared the Ahom ruler. This ruler was Sudanpha.

it was necessary for the king on his accession to the throne to be washed in water brought from the place (Brahma-kund), and until this ceremony was completed he was not considered fit to take upon himself the reign of the government", writes Rowlette[33]. Another example is furnished by Gates[34] in regard to the reign of Sujinpha. His officers "were required to take a two-fold oath, one in the presence of the Brahmans before a Salagram of Lakshmi Narayan, a copy of the Bhagvat Gita and a Tulsi plant, and the other, according to the old Ahom method, by the shedding of blood before the great drum." Dr. Chatterji sums up the evolutionary process thus: "The Hinduism of the Ahoms, at first in culture and religion and then in language, commenced with great vigour in the 17th century, and by 1750 A.D. it was all over but complete[35]." The process was slow and gradual, therefore, it is not possible to allot a particular date and name of the king who specially called himself a Hindu. Had it been a case of conversion it could be done.

The Ahoms were a tribe and did not favour the caste system. It would not suit them. Further, Muslim culture did not influence the Assamese society and the women of the State remained free and did not observe parda. Widow marriages were in vogue and the Assamese women could contract series of matrimonial alliances.

At the same time faithful wives were adored in Assamese society. Jaimati, wife of Supanpha, is worshipped in every Assamese home for her heroic self-sacrifice to save the life of her husband. In spite of barbaric and inhuman tortures at the hands of her captors she did not disclose the whereabouts of her husband. For this she suffered death. Under such kings and circumstances the people of Assam lived and flourished.

"They (the Assamese) do not abstain from eating food cooked by Muslims and non-Muslims (alike) and partake of every kind of meat, whether of dead or of slaughtered animal, except human flesh......strength and heroism are apparent on the peoples of this country; they are able to undertake hard tasks; all of them are warlike and blood-thirsty, fearless in slaying and being slain...... The persons of their women are marked by beauty and delicacy of features, and loveliness of hands and feet...... Few of the men have two wives (only), most have four or five, and they mutually exchange their wives or buy and sell them......The common people bury their dead with some of the property of the deceased", writes Shahabuddin Bironi[36] who accompanied Mir Jumla's expedition. The same historian further comments: "The manners and customs of these people, (the Miris-Mishmis) agree entirely with those of Assamese, and their women surpass in beauty and grace the females of Assam." Shahabuddin's description is elaborate, informative and interesting, but it is tinged with a slight bias. He was a bit harsh on the Assamese. He did not spare the Assamese Muslims either from his adverse comments. This attitude might have been due to the atmosphere of depression which prevailed in the Muslim army on their retreat, or it might have been due to his preconceived ideas formed in the Mughal Court at Delhi. Assam was more secular than any other part of the country and the Hindus abstained from eating beef as is evident from the statement of an unnamed Dutch Sailor who also accompanied the same expedition. He writes about the Assamese as the people, "who worshipped a cow, and consequently never kill any of that kind[37]." However, it cannot be denied that the Assam rulers, with a few exception like Rudra Singh who sent his ambassadors to other courts in the country, neither favoured foreigners visiting the State nor permitted their own subjects to visit other countries. This self-imposed isolation did have a baneful effect. "The little intercourse the natives of Assam were formerly permitted to have with strangers, has rendered them bigoted to the forms and customs of their own country, and innovations which would even prove beneficial to them must be introduced, with some degree of caution. They are naturally of a distrustful and jealous disposition, and it will require time to get the better of their prejudices", reports Welsh[34].

The Ahom period is marked by the renaissance of literature and religion. This movement started in Western Assam. During the second quarter of the 14th century Hem Sarswati, Kavi Ratan Sarswati and Haribar Vipre wrote poetry in the Assamese language and helped the development of the indigenous literature. Shankar Dev gave a fillip to the movement by translating a number of Hindu scriptures into the Assamese language.

Swami Shankar Dev was born in 1449 in district Naogaon. He died at the ripe age of 118 years. He gave to Assam Vaishnavism which swept the State from East to West. Vaishnavism became the religion of the common man and claimed many adherents from the tribals of NEFA. During this period the Assamese Muslims also developed independent ideas of their religion. At Hajo a mosque was erected by one Ghiyasuddin Aulia who subsequently died and was buried near the mosque. Since then the Muslims regarded Hajo as 'Pao Mecca' or one fourth of Mecca.

So far Saktaism alone had dominated religious life in the State. By the introduction of Vaishnavism a rivalry developed which proved detrimental to the internal peace of Assam. Phuleshwari, one of the two wives of Siv Singh, the Ahom king, was a Sakta. She had no tolerance for the Vaishnavites and by her intolerant acts she enraged the followers of Moamari* Sattra and kindled the fire of revolt. Later one of the Ahom officials insulted the Moamari Mahant and one of the latter's disciples was unjustly convicted on a fictitious charge. This added fuel to the fire. The entire State was engulfed by the Moamari rebellion. The central power lost its authority and many principalities sprang up. The tribals of Darrang who were located far away from the Ahom capital took advantage of the situation and their neighbours the Daflas were the first to create trouble. As a result "an agreement was made whereby the Daflas were permitted to levy yearly from each family in the Duars, or sub-mountain tract along the foot of the hills, a pura of paddy and 323 cowries[10]." Pemberton describes the agreement as a "mutual compromise, between conscious weakness and barbarian cunning[10]." During the 19th century these claims were commutated for fixed annual payments—Rs. 1.740 for the Bhutias, Rs. 4.130 for the Daflas and Rs. 1,118 for the Miris.

The situation worsened and the intervention of outsiders—the British and the Burmans—was sought. Lord Cornwallis despatched two columns, one under Capt. Welsh and the other under Lt. Magregor, to Assam. The Moamari rebellion was suppressed, but the arrival of the Burmese troops in Assam created confusion. The Burmese started raiding the neighbouring states; they harassed the people and extended their aggression to

*Aniruddha, a disciple of Shankar Dev, established the Moamari Sattra which welcomed the tribals and the people of lower castes in its folds.

Cachar, which forced the British to fight the marauders. The Burmese were defeated and according to the treaty of Yandebo in 1826 Burma surrendered Assam to the British. After the treaty Purendra Singh, a claimant to the Ahom throne, was retained as the king of Upper Assam Purendra Singh had to pay Rs. 50,000 annually to the British, which he could not. As a result, in 1838, he was deposed and the new rulers annexed Upper Assam in the British territory. Thus the Ahom rule was wiped out in Assam. The British became the Paramount Power of the entire State.

After Rajeshwar Singh's (1751-1739) death Assam was subjected to the darkest perido in her history. Anarchy and chaos prevailed throughout the country. Moamaris were not the only insurgents to perpetrate bloodshed. They were joined by other recalcitrant elements of the country. Internecine strife among the courtiers and Ahom officials and rival claimants to the throne invited wave after wave of the Burmese army to come in and settle the internal issues. In 1816 we find that "some 8,000 Burmese troops and 8,000 auxiliaries crossed Patkoi into Assam, at the invitation of the Raja (Chandrakant)[41]", along the old route, via Bisa village. The route, then, was well maintained by the Burmese Government and provisions obtainable all along. Inside the country the Khamptis joined in with the Burmese. They took possession of Sadiya, ejected the then Sadiya Gohain, and took the Assamese inhabitants as slaves. Throughout the civil war they maintained and united with the Burmese interests. Singphos did not lag behind in the plunder. "Of late years they have taken advantage of the weakness of the Assamese Government, and have carried their ravages with fire and sword beyond the capital, Rangpur, laying waste the whole country, as far as Jorhat, and carrying off the wretched inhabitants into slavery; both banks of the river have been swept by their depredations, and the number of captives stated to have been carried off appears almost oncredible[42]", writes Neufville. The anarchy did not end with the arrival of the British. Raja Purendra Singh could not bring peace to the people. The consequence of this prolonged and continuous anarchy proved disastrous to the country. Lakhs of people left the Assam Valley and took refuge in the neighbouring states. Cities and villages were claimed by the encroaching forests and buildings were covered with thick layers of earth and clay. M'Cosh writes about the conditions in Assam thus: "....through-out (Assam) six-eights or seven-eights of its extent covered with a jungle of gigantic reeds, traversed only by the wild elephants or the buffaloes; where a human footstep is unknown, and the atmosphere even to the natives themselves is pregnant with febrile miasmata and death[43]."

It is not that every tribe adopted a hostile attitude in the insurrection. The Nagas[44] gave shelter to the Assamese who, to avoid the exactions and oppressions they were subjected to, took shelter in the Naga Hills. Many of the refugees stayed back and in due course were absorbed in the Naga community. From all accounts the Mishmis did not take any part in the trouble, and did not take slaves either. The Abors are said to have come down in large numbers, amounting to 20,000 to 30,000 to assist the Burha Gohain in repelling the Moamaris. The Apa Tanis though not very well known in the Assam plains also gave shelter to the Assamese refugees and treated them generously and did not place any obstacle for the latter's voluntary return to the plains[45]. A few of the refugees stayed back in the Apa Tani country and in due course were integrated into the society. Even the Akas[46] and the Daflas who were seldom well spoken of rendered aid to the Ahoms, but the Burmans appeared in overwhelming force and crushed the little man of Darrang. What followed the Burmese invasion is aptly described by Pemberton: "..... ......during the imbecile rule of its princes, and the anarchy which followed its conquest by the ruthless force of Ava (Burma), every bordering tribe would endeavour to extend its possession, by an appropriation of as large a portion of the lands at the foot of the mountains as it had power to retain[47]." Mackenzie[48] and Allen[49] have also expressed similar views. It might be true that these people (tribals) acted in the manner described but a power vacuum had been created in Assam tempting them to act as they did to safeguard their own interests, so they probably thought.

At the close of the Ahom rule the conditions in Assam were not peaceful. There was anarchy and no security of life or of property. Naturally self-preservation and self-interest predominated in the conduct of the inhabitants. Under such circumstances the reins of the administration in the State were passed on to the new rulers—the British—who shouldered the responsibility of bringing peace, prosperity and unity to the harassed people.

1. Psychology and Ethnology by W.H.R. Rivers, p. 163.
2. AR Vol. XIV Chapter VII, p. 373f.
3. Trans Himalaya by Sven Hedin, p. 97.
4. Description of Assam by W. Robinson, p. 247.

Descriptive Ethnology of Bengal by Col. E.T. Dalton, p. 14.
Topography of Assam 1833 by M'Cosh, p. 10.

5. AR Vol. XIV Chapter VII, p. 373f.
6. AR Vol. XVII, p. 354.
7. JASB 1897, p. 106.
8. JASB Vol. XVI Nos. 2, 1950, p. 165.
   Dr. Suniti Kumar Chatterji.
9. The Early History of India by Vincent A. Smith, p. 316.
10. The Real Tripitaka by Arthur Waley, p. 73.
11. Gates, A History of Assam, p. 48.
12. Gates, A History of Assam, p. 92.
13. The Calcutta Review Vol. XXI, 1853, p. 410.
14. Gates, p. 74.
15. JASB 1873, p. 235.
16. An Account of Assam by Dr. John Pete Wade 1800, p. 21.
17. Ibid.
18. Ibid.
19. The Mother Goddess Kamakhya by Beni Kant Kakoti, p. 60.
20. Vansi Gopal Chritara by Ramanand Dvija, Edited by Dr. M. Neog of Gauhati University.
21. AR 1828, p. 344.
22. AR Vol. XVII, p. 456.
23. JASB 1845 Vol. XIV Pt. II, p. 485.
24. Gates, p. 323.
25. No Passport to Tibet by Lt. Col. F. M. Bailey, p. 84.
26. Wade, p. 24.
27. Survey of India (Linguistic) by Dr. G. A. Grierson Pt. I, p. 396.
28. Atan Burgohain by Dr. S. K. Bhunyan, p. 220.
29. Mackenzie, North East Frontier (26.1.84), p. 91.
30. Gates, p. 323.

31. An old History of Assam, Edited by H. C. Goswami. p. 39.
32. Eastern India by Montgomery Martin, p. 603.
33. JASB 1845, p. 486.
34. Gates, p. 162.
35. JASB 1950, p. 175.
36. JBORS Professor Jadunath Sarkar, p. 179f.
37. Bengal Past and Present 1925 by an unnamed Dutch Sailor. The Title of the English Translation 'A Relation of an unfortunate Voyage to the Kingdom of Bengal'.
38. A Report of Assam by Major Welsh 1794.
39. Gates, p. 187.
40. Report on Bhutan by Capt. B. Pemberton, p. 10.
41. JASB 1879 by S. E. Peal, p. 71.
42. AR Vol. XVI, 1828, p. 338f.
43. Topography of Assam by M'Cosh 1837, p. 13.
44. JASB 1845 Capt. Bordie Vol. XIV Pt. II, p. 835.
45. Descriptive Account of Assam by William Robinson 1841, p. 363.
46. Gates, p. 232.
47. Pemberton, p. 10.
48. Mackenzie, p. 7.
49. Assam District Gazette Vol. V Darrang, p. 56.

MAP 3. The Ahom Empire at the end of the 17th Century.

CHAPTER IV

THE IMPERIALISTS' POLITICAL GAME

By the removal of the British power from India in 1947 we were, to some extent, thrown back to the days when the British first came. That is an interesting and good parallel to pursue in other ways too; but I shall not pursue it, because it may lead to controversial matters. When the British power established itself in India, it became evident that no other power in India could remain independent. Of course these powers could remain semi-independent or as protectorates or in some other subordinate capacity. Accordingly, the Princely States were gradually brought under the domain and suzerainty of the British power. Similarly, when the British left India, it was just as impossible for odd bits of Indian territory to remain independent as it had been during their regime. At that time Pakistan was, of course, out of the picture. For the rest, it was inevitable that the princes and others, whoever they might be and whether they wanted it or not, must acknowledge the suzerainty of the sovereign domain of the Republic of India[1].

Jawaharlal Nehru

Before their arrival in Assam the British, as the rulers of Bengal, had a good deal of experience in dealing with the Bhutan Government. In 1772 the Bhotias raided the villages of Cooch Bihar and devastated the countryside. The British took retaliatory measures. But on the receipt of a conciliatory letter from the Regent of Tibet, Teesho Lama, Governor General Warren Hasting's policy softened.

He tried to take advantage of the friendly feelings expressed in the letter and tried to develop trade relations with Tibet through Bhutan. He did not appear to have succeeded in the design. "In 1809", according to Lt. Rutherford[2], "the trade between Bhutan and Assam amounted to two lakhs of rupees per annum." But by the middle of the century it declined to extinction. The conditions for peaceful conduct of trade in border areas remained insecure and the Bhotias continued to encroach into the British territory and harass the ryots. Sometimes the British sent punitive expeditions to suppress the Bhotias and occupied duars, stations situated in the plains of the foothills that served as gates to the hillmen, and at other times the raiders were leniently treated and their territories restored. The Ahoms had made some arrangements with the Bhotias and bought the security of these duars under duress. This "purchase of a doubtful security on the part of Assam Raj, by a surrender of territorial rights which they had not the power to maintain[3]" was passed on to the new rulers who renewed and confirmed such arrangements. The Bhotias did not abide by the understanding or the agreement and continued their depredations against the ryots. Eventually the duars were annexed by the British in 1841 and a sum of Rs. 10,000 per year was allowed to be paid to the Bhutan Government, as a compensation. No written agreement was made regarding this arrangement. But the trouble did not cease and the Bhutan War was fought in 1864 and the border problems were finally settled. The duars remained in the British possession for which they undertook to pay the Bhutan Government, from the revenue of the duars, an annual sum beginning with Rs. 25,000 on fulfilment of the conditions of the treaty. Later the sum was raised to Rs. 50,000 per annum, then again (on the 8th January, 1910) to Rs. 100,000. Barring minor skirmishes since 1866 there was practically no trouble with Bhutan which eventually came under the British political influence in the beginning of this century.

Contiguous to Bhutan are the Aka Hills which needed the immediate attention of the new rulers. The Akas, like the Bhotias, were coming down to the plains for plundering the British subjects. Raja Tagi, their leader was arrested in 1829 and imprisoned at Gauhati. After three years' detention he was released. In 1842 he settled down in the British territory as a peaceful citizen. Now and then the Akas had clashes with the frontier patrols, but they were always subdued. Finally in 1888 they recognised the supremacy of the British and never gave any trouble to the Administration afterwards.

Like the Akas their neighbours the Daflas were also raiding the border villages but by the early fifties their raids were also stopped, and a few Dafla families came down to the plains for permanent residence in North Lakhimpur district in the vicinity of the Johing Tea Estate. Even today there are two Dafla villages, fifteen miles from North Lakhimpur town, the residents of which acted as a liaison agency between the Government and their compatriots to effect peace in the Dafla Hills.

The Abors were considered to be the most powerful and most respected of all the tribal groups of the Northern Tract. They claimed supremacy over the plains bordering their hills and a complete monopoly of all the fish and gold found in the streams flowing through their territory. The Ahoms in a way had recognised these claims.

In the plains there used to be numerous villages inhabited by gold washers and fishermen belonging to a tribe called 'Beehas', who in pursuit of their profession used to visit Dihong and its tributaries and payed a tribute to the Abors as an acknowledgement of the latter's superiority. In 1847 the Abors carried off a gold washer for whose restoration a small party of troops under Capt. Vetch was despatched to the Abor Hills. After that the relations between the British and the Abors became strained. The former, as a conciliatory measure granted many concessions such as giving the latter salt, opium, tobacco etc. free of cost from specific shops, but these overtures proved of no avail. The Abors remained resentful and unpredicted till in 1911 they killed Mr. William, the Political Officer of Sadiya, and Dr. Grierson, the Linguist, because of some misunderstanding. In 1912 an expedition consisting of 3,000 troops and 3,500 to 4,000 Naga coolies under General Hamilton Bower, C.B. was despatched to the Abor Hills[4]. The Abors yielded to the inevitable and recognised the supremacy of the rulers so much so that by 1913/14 they were reported "to of bringing their disputes in increasing numbers for settlement by the Political Officers at Pasighat[5]."

The Khamptis are recent arrivals in Assam. In fact Col. Dalton informs us that "in 1850 a large colony of fresh settlers from Bor Khampti—between three and four hundred individuals—under a chief, a scion of one of their best families, migrated to Assam in a body[6]." The Khamptis cooperated with the British in restoring peace in the area in 1824 and after the occupation of Assam Capt. Neufville recognised the office of Khampti Sadiya Gohain. Some administrators believe that the Khamptis cooperated with the Singpho rising in 1830 while others expressed doubts. At any rate, the British did not have implicit faith in the Khamptis, and after some time tension mounted between the two. The Khamptis showed signs of insubordination and the rulers deprived them of their gun licenses and deposed the Sadiya Gohain. Recommendations were made to the Governor, both in 1835 and 1837 to shift the Khamptis away from Sadiya. This annoyed the Khamptis. On January 28, 1839 the Khamptis made a surprise attack on the British garrison at Sadiya. Both sides suffered casualties and Lt. Col. White was killed in the skirmish. However, the Khamptis were pardoned in 1843 and were allowed to settle down in Sonepura (a village on Assam-NEFA boundary in Lohit) and eventually at the present site.

The Singphos are also a newcomer to Assam. During the Burmese invasion and occupation of Assam from 1821-1825 the Assamese were taken slaves in thousands. The Singphos by that time had not been emotionally attached to the country. They cooperated with the invader in the massacre and deprivation of freedom of their own countrymen. "Capt. Neufville, received from Singphos alone upwards of 7,000 Assamese captive slaves, and perhaps there are 100,000 Assamese and Manipuris still in slavery throughout the dominions of Ava[7]", writes M'Cosh. These slaves were economic units for the Singphos, who on account of this free labour, gave up working with their hands in their fields and resented the release of these serfs. They revolted in 1830 in vain. The British armed might and diplomacy brought them round and afterwards they never gave trouble to the Administration. Time healed their wounds.

The Nagas also practised slavery. "......an extensive and infamous trade is carried on in slaves, who are stolen indiscriminately by all in that quarter, and sold to the Bengali merchants who go up for cotton. Muneepories were sold for Rs. 3[8]", writes E. A. Grange. Here the system of harassing the plainsmen was different and carried on slyly. It did not involve mass violence or insurrection on the part of the Nagas.

During these turbulent days the Lt. Governor of Bengal administered Assam from Calcutta. Reorganisation of the State was considered absolutely essential. In this reorganisation the frontier areas, with their trade and the new opportunities they offered, played an important part. Areas which had the least prospects of trade were neglected to be tackled at an opportune moment. There were three trade routes, along the Dirang Dzong Valley, the Dihong Valley and the Lohit Valley, which were given first priority for reconnaissance and development.

The first passed through Tawang which was administered by a Raja. Because the Raja recognised the British authority in India and in 1844, undertook to act "upon any orders[9]" from the latter, it was not thought necessary to pay more than cursory attention to the Indo-Tibetan track. The track was and is fit for animal transport. It crosses a terrain in Tibet which ordinarily places the defenders in an advantageous position over the invaders from the Plateau. Moreover a regular and constant traffic passed along the route and Tibetan information could easily be had from local sources. Therefore, its reconnaissance and development was postponed to an indefinite date.

The second ran along the Dihong Valley across the Abor country. The Abors were an almost independent race and were dreaded by the Tibetans. They had offensive and defensive alliance[10] with the Tibetans, and their trade activities were confined to the frontier areas only. But for some unknown reason they drew a "veil of mystery over their intercourse[11] with the Tibetans." The British started wooing them but with little success. Capt. Neufville[12] observed that sufficient confidence had not been inspired among the Abors so as to encourage them to visit the British Administrative Headquarters at Sadiya. Later, Mackenzie advised the Government not to annex the Abor Hills. "To annex Abor Hills would only bring us into contact with tribes still wilder and less known, nor should we find a resting place for the foot of annexation till we planted it on the plateau of High Asia, perhaps not even then[13]."

Coming to the Lohit Valley inhabited by the Mishmi tribe the same story was repeated. The Mishmis who had always owed allegiance to the Assam Government and were under the exclusive control of the Ahoms reacted differently. The Mishmis of the interior, according to Col. Dalton, "were always hostile to the British Officers[15]." Angus Hamilton candidly writes: "In spite of all that was then done and continued to be done to win over the Babijiyas (Mishmis) as the years passed, this people continued to maintain an attitude of defiance and detestation of our wishes and of ourselves[16]."

Therefore, conditions in the Dihong and Lohit Valleys were not peaceful. Despite this the British administrators and adventurers continued to try to penetrate through the Abor and the Mishmi Hills.

Apart from the above areas conditions elsewhere were also not such so as to be termed as peaceful. Reference has already been made to the Akas' and Tagi's hostilities towards the British which lasted till the close of the century. In the eastern hills bordering Burma, the Nagas who had never seen a fixed boundary dividing them from the plains[17] and who used to pay tribute to the Ahoms and in return were granted the Naga Khats (land grants), the benefits of which are even today enjoyed by the chiefs of Namsang and Borduria, regularly carried on a considerable trade in cotton and other hill produce in exchange of rice, thus contributing to a mutual good understanding between themselves and the Assamese. The trade and Khat concessions were a restraining influence. Abolishing of duties by the British in early 1841 on salt which the Nagas manufactured from brine springs at the foot of their hills was also a great stimulous to their intercourse with the plainsmen. These measures should have created conditions favourable for smooth administration, but all such hopes were belied. "The Nagas who live to the south of Sibsagar and on the western slopes of the central range are not open to our influence, and have to be dealt with as Abors and Mishmis, and other tribes", reported the "Pioneer" of March 24, 1780. The position for the rulers was so unrewarding that Baker recommended the extermination of Nagas.[18] Expeditionary columns used to be despatched to the Naga Hills and the Nagas continued to remain alert and suspicious of the British incursions. On February 2. 1875, Lt. Holcombe and 80 of his men were murdered and Capt. Badgeley and 50 men were injured by the Nagas of Banphera village.

On the above exposition the conclusion is obvious The attitude of the tribals of NEFA was not friendly towards the British. Muffat admits that "except the clans immediately in the hills on each side of the Brahmaputra, none can be said to be in friendly communication with us[19]."

To obviate such feelings the British resorted to two remedial courses—introducing Christianity where possible and raising units of the Frontier Constabulary. The Naga land was considered a virgin soil for Christianity "Among a people so thoroughly primitive, and so independent of religious profession, we might reasonably expect missionary zeal would be most successful[20]", wrote Butler. Missionaries were encouraged to open Government aided schools[21] in the Naga Hills—Mr. Brown and Mr. Clark opened such schools—and Christianity did succeed in some parts. Side by side with this peaceful acculturation the strength of Frontier Constabulary was increased. During the Ahom rule only 9 companies of sepoys were used to keep the bordering tribes under control, but under the new regime each company was raised to battalion strength. Even then the relation between the tribals and the British did not ease. Moniram Diwan, an Indian patriot who was sentenced to death on the suspicion that he took part in the so called Sepoy Mutiny of 1857, though at the time of the outbreak of the uprising he was at Calcutta, attributed the constant state of war between the British and Hill tribes and mutual loss of life and money to an objectionable treatment meted out to the latter by the former[22].

Trade as carried on between Assam and Tibet and China along the three well known high ways, and elsewhere also in the State, was also important for the reorganisation of Assam. Considerable traffic passed between India and Bhutan. Ralf Fitch[23] in 1583 had observed that there were merchants who came from China, and probably from Moscow to sell musk, blankets, agates, silk etc. to Assam. Even in 1837 M'Cosh[24] noted that the commerce between China and Ava and Assam was of much consequence, and was every day increasing Blockman[25] confirms that "the traffic between Bengal and Tibet in the old days, and even up to the reign of Akbar, seemed to have been considerable." The traffic consisted chiefly in gold, copper, lead, musk, yak tails, honey, borax, falcons, and hill ponies. But by 1840s Indo-Tibetan trade completely ceased. No attempts were made for its revival. The Indo-Tibetan trade did not influence the reforming of Assam.

The Abors, the Mishmis and the Nagas carried on trade with the plains. The Abors had "capital roads[26]" leading into their country and they brought brass pipes, beads, copper pans, silver ornaments, salt and yaks (obtained from China in exchange for medicinal herbs indigenous to their hills) to the plains for sale. The Mishmis, the inveterate traders, also regularly attended the Sadiya bazars specially during the winter. The Nagas, the Daflas, and the Akas etc. also carried on trade with the plains according to the local resources available, and attended weekly bazars in the foothills. In due course the supply of raw materials depleted and trade practically ceased. Mr. P. T. Carnegy, Assistant Commissioner of Sibsagar wrote: "........It appears for the present they (the tribals) have killed the goose which laid the golden eggs, for the two latest parties who were here complained that their trees had ceased to yield rubber, to which their Katogi added that it was no wonder, for they had been chopping them all over from the roots to the upper branches[27]." This state gave rise to competition and hard bargaining. At times there were heated arguments over a deal between the tribals and the plainsmen creating new problems of law and order for the rulers.

Tea is an indigenous plant in Assam, and it for noticed growing wild in the frontier jungles. The common belief among the Assamese is that Moniram Diwan discovered the plant. Others dispute it. Anyhow, the

Government took notice of the plant and encouraged the tea industry. By 1852 the Assam Company, the oldest in the province, had 15 tea gardens in Sibsagar, with a cultivation varying from 15 to 500 acres in each. Besides these there were other plantations also managed and owned by private individuals. The number of plantations was on the increase requiring more and more labour. The labour either had to be recruited from outside and imported into the Province or it had to be secured from tribal volunteers. First the encroachments of tea gardens into the tribal areas and secondly the coming in contact of the tribal people with the plainsmen created complicated problems for administration. Where compensation could be paid for bringing lands belonging to the tribals under cultivation, settlements were effected, for instance the Borduria Raja was given 200 bighas of land free of revenue while the Namsang Raja was granted an amount of Rs. 450 per year on account of the Hakanjuri tea garden. At other places resentment among the people persisted. "The unrestricted intercourse that formerly existed between British subjects in Assam and the wild tribes living across the frontier frequently led to quarrels and, sometimes, to serious disturbances. This was specially the case in connection with the traffic in rubber brought down by the hillmen, for which there was a great competition. The opening out of tea gardens beyond the borderline also at times involved the Government in troublesome disputes with the frontier tribes in their vicinity[28]."

Therefore, in spite of the best efforts of the British conditions could not be ushered in to enable the tribal trade to flourish. What was the remedy? It appears that the isolation of the tribal people was considered as the best remedy. The Inner Line Regulations were enacted on March 8, 1873, but the policy of declaring NEFA as a secluded area had been advocated long before the enactment. Peal[29] had condemned this policy in 1872, and there were comments in the Press. On March 27, 1870, the "Pioneer" had printed: "Baffled at length by the inveterate savagery of the people and the difficulties of their hills, the Government fell back on a policy of absolute non-interference and defence; and the Imperial Dalhousie emphatically pronounced the game not worth the candle. We had nothing to gain, he said, by annexing a wild people and their barren hills. So we relegated them to a kind of political 'Coventry'. In the year 1851 our troops withdrew......The first attempts to open up the Naga territory were made rather in the interest of Manipur than of India, and was due to the fact that Raja Gumbhir Singh was desirous of strengthening his hands against Burma by intimate trade relations with Assam, and it was thought well to encourage him in his policy."

This clearly removes any doubt about the motive behind the 'Inner Line Regulations' of 1873. The rulers did not consider it worth a while to bring in peace in an area which was barren and devoid of any future trade prospects. They for their own convenience and not for any altruistic motives or for the good of the people affected the isolation of the tribal area from Assam. Thus a rift was created between the tribal and the Assamese. This policy of isolation or so called non-interference left the tribals on their own. Butler writes: "At this juncture, we find our local officers frankly declaring that our relations with the Nagas could not possibly be on a worse footing than they were then, and that the non-interference policy, which sounds excellent in theory, had utterly failed in practice[30].'

During and before the 19th century the United States' and United Kingdom's policy towards the aborigines of North America or Australia was to disregard their rights. The twentieth century brought a change. After the settlers' gains were consolidated, administrators started viewing the tribals with a 'Patron's eye'. J. P. Mills belongs to that class of administrators. He has written an elaborate report describing the evil effects of modern civilization vis-a-vis the Nagas. There were others who were alarmed by the encroachment of civilizing influence in the tribal areas in the name of Science.

> "Unfortunately for science, however, no steps are being taken to record the rare vestiges of pre-historic society which still survives here; but which are now being rapidly swept away by our advancing civilization."
>
> "........, this unique mass of material which is thus available for solving such important problems lying at the very basis of civilization and culture is being allowed to disappear unrecorded."
>
> "Surely it is a duty which Government owes to science and to posterity that it, as the agent which is removing pre-historic customs, should take steps to record this fast vanishing knowledge, before it is irretrievably lost to the world for ever[31]."

Similar views were expressed by a few other administrators also. In response to these views the Government deputed many investigators to write Monographs on the tribals who came under the normal jurisdiction of Government of India. The tribals of NEFA were the last to be touched. Haimendorf was the first Anthropologist to live in Subansiri for a year. His books –'The Himalayan Barbary' and 'The Naked Nagas' are still considered authoritative works on the Apa Tanis, the Hill Miris, the Daflas and the Konyak Nagas*. The work is still continued. Divisional Research Officers are being employed to write accounts of various tribes though under different garb. A few of such tribal accounts have been published in 1960, one from each Division.

However, isolation excluded NEFA from the political map of India and segregated the tribal population from Assam. The first relapse was made up in the beginning of the present century when the invasion and occupation of Lhasa in 1910 by the Chinese brought new British interest in the northern hills of NEFA. The Government of India established three outposts on the three known routes—the Lohit, the Siang and the Dirang Dzong tracks—without meeting any opposition from the locals, and cartographers included the NEFA area in the political map of India. Though belatedly, but the mistake the rightly rectified. The second relapse, the isolation of the people, stays.

Having erected the artificial barrier of the Inner Line, Assam, in 1874, was organised into six districts—Goalpara, Kamrup, Darrang, Nowgong, Lakhimpur, and Sibsagar—and was raised to the status of a Province to be headed by a Lt. Governor. The District Commissioners or Magistrates of border areas were entrusted with the task of dealing with the tribals contiguous to their border. For the security and maintenance of integrity of NEFA and of Assam, Indo-Tibetan relations occupied the second place in the scheme of things.

* Konyaks are the inhabitants of Tuensang Area which in those days was included in NEFA. At present this area is included in NEFA.

The political history of Nepal, Sikkim and Bhutan is a bit confusing in its early stages. During the Hindu and the Buddhist period the Hill States were within the Indian sphere of influence, but the advent of Islam into the country closed all doors leading to the plains in the south, and the Nepalese, the Sikkimese and the Bhutanese looked towards the north for spiritual and cultural guidance and sometimes for protection also. By the time the British completed the occupation of India these States had virtually accepted the Chinese Protectorate. The British reversed this phase of Himalayan History and regained the confidence of the hillmen. As Islam diverted the Nepalese, the Sikkimese and the Bhutanese to the north the British attracted them to their mother country. If the reclamation of lost nationals is imperialism then certainly there is some imbecility in the understanding of those who consider the occupation of Tibet by the Chinese as an act of liberation.

As in Assam so in NEFA, Islam did not influence the history, and NEFA politically and otherwise remained attached to Assam. Later its border history became the history of Sino-British relations which revolved round Tibet.

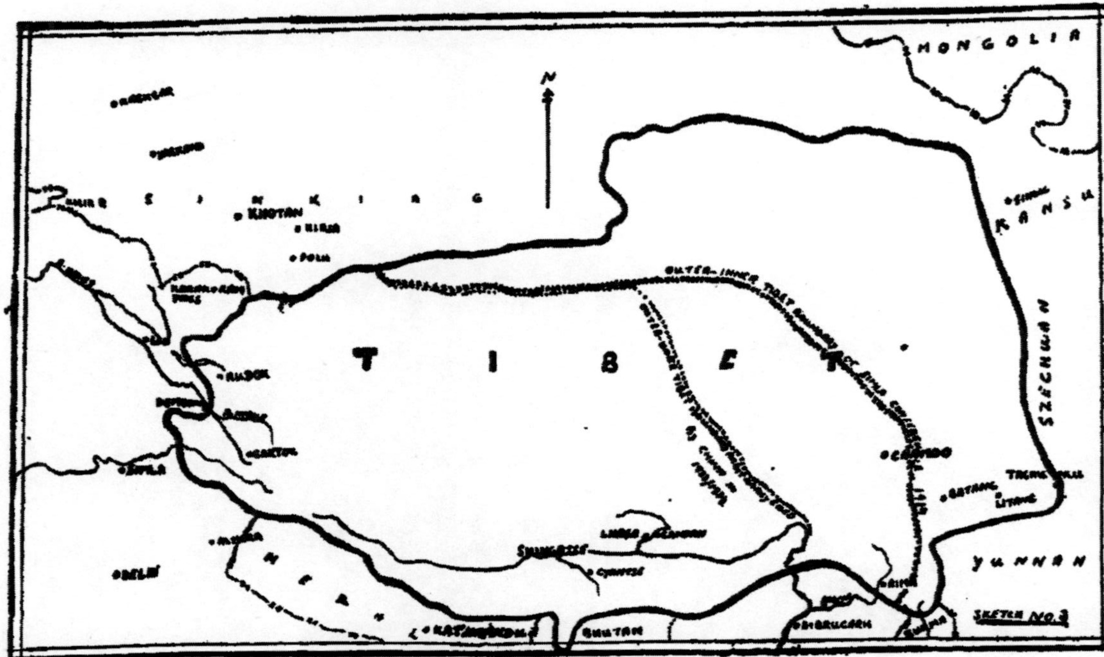

THE LAND OF LAMAS : TIBET

The Chinese occupation of Tibet has drawn iron curtain over Tibet and it is rather difficult to outline its boundaries with any precision. According to Gordon East and Spate[32], the division of the Tibetan Plateau can be traced from the later part of the Manchu period, Sikang and Chinghai being the Provinces of Inner Tibet. One has to fall back to the 19th century for a correct definition of the Tibetan boundary. CSoma de Koros defines the Tibetan boundary thus: Tibet is bounded in the north by the countries of the Turks and the Mongols whom the Tibetans call Hor, and Sok-po (Hor-Sok). On the east by China (Gyanak in Tib). On the south by India (Gyagar in Tib). On the west by India, Cashmir, Afghanistan, Tazik-Tul and Turkistan.[33] Ralph Linton[34] also confirms that the new provinces of Sikang and Chinghai have been chipped off Tibet's more densely populated fringes in the east and south-east.

Tibet before 1950 was territorially divided into three Divisions—Tibet proper or U-Tang around Lhasa, Kham-Tul or Eastern part of Tibet, and Nga-Ri, or North-Western part—. Lhasa, Shingatse, Tse-Thang and Chamdo being its main cities.

Tibet was always a familiar name in the Vedic Era. It might have been referred to as 'Swarg Lok' because Mahadev is supposed to have resided on Mt. Kailash on the northern bank of Mansarovar and Raksh Tal, which are believed to be the water reservoir of all the big and sacred rivers of North India. Or it might have been referred to as a portion of Uttra Khund in our religious scriptures. During the Mahabharata period Karna, the son of Surya from Kunti, was supposed to have come from

Tibet to participate in the epic war. Some scholars hold that Tibet was unified by King Rupati or by a descendant of the Lachchhavi branch of the Sakya family. Chinese historians believe that the name of Tibet in about 2225 B.C. was San Wei. Later the Chinese chronicles refer the Plateau as the land of the Kyan tribes. Herodotus in the fifth century B.C. refers the people of the Tibetan Highland as cannibals. Probably he misinterpreted the funeral practice of cutting the dead into pieces, as cannibalism. Neither the Sanskrit nor the Chinese literature records ever mention cannibalism as a prevalent creed in the Highland. Beyond these references very little is known about Tibet till the 6th century A.D.

Shi-Pu-Ye also referred as Pu-Gye was the first Tibetan king of the pre-historic era. Another king who is known to every Tibetan was Lha-Tho-Tho-Ri-Nyen-Shey. King Son-Tsan Gam-Po a descendant of the latter was born late in the 6th century and came to the throne in 620 A.D., thus establishing the rule of the To Fang Dynasty of Tibet which lasted up to 842 A.D.

Gam-Po's reign was marked by the outstanding services of Tho-Mi Sam-Bho-Ta and Gar-Don-Tsan, who great statesmen of that period. The former together with 16 companions was sent to India to study and work out an alphabet for the Tibetan language. On his return Sam-Bho-Ta gave an alphabet of 4 vowels and 30 consonants to his country, while Gar-Don-Tsan played an important part in arranging Gam-Po's marriage in 640 to the Chinese Emperor's daughter, Princess Wen-Chen. The Princess was a Buddhist. Though the Emperor married his daughter to the Tibetan king because of the latter's military prowess, still the Emperor Tai Tsung boasted: "Without drawing a sword, by the power of virtue, China receives tribute from countries so far away that grass does not grow in them[35]." Son-Tsam-Gam-Po also married Bhrikuti Devi, a Nepalese Princess, who was also an ardent Buddhist. The Princess brought several 'murties' or idols of Buddha to Tibet which were installed in various temples of Lhasa. She also helped in spreading the religion in Tibet. Thus Buddhism entered the Plateau both from India and China during the 7th century. For the next two centuries the royalty patronised Buddhism, while the nobility continued to favour Bon-Po, the pre-Buddhist religion of the country, which was not very different from Chinese Taoism. Eventually, in 1842, Monarchy was abolished by the Tibetan nobles, but the conflict between Buddhism and Bon-Po continued.

The conflict between the king and nobles was violent and resulted in a civil war. Out of this chaos and the synthesis of Buddhism and Bon-Po, the two rival religions, Lamaism grew and developed. By the beginning of the 13th century three Lama Sects—(*i*) Ka-dam-Pa, (*ii*) Sa-Kya-Pa, (*iii*) Ka-Gyur-Pa (and later the fourth a Ge-Lu-Pa) were established and the country was actually divided into principalities administered by local sects.

In India Islam was making inroads thus raising a barrier against the continued social contacts of Tibetans with their southern neighbours. Finding the southern doors closed Tibet was naturally attracted more and more towards China. In 1240 the Yuan Dynasty came in power in China and Kublai Khan the conqueror of China was converted to Buddhism in 1245 by Phas-Pa of the Sa-Kya-Pa Sect, thus establishing a religious bond between Tibet and China. The Khan concluded a temporal alliance with Tibet and proclaimed Buddhism as the national religion of his empire. In 1247 a Sa-Kya pandit was invited to the

Imperial Court. The pandit paid tribute to the Emperor. The Sa-Kya-Pa Sect remained popular in Tibet till the fall of Yuan Dynasty which came in 1359.

The new rulers of China were from the Ming Dynasty (1368-1644), and Tibet continued to keep her religious ties with China. Nearly all the Lama Sects sent their representatives to the Chinese Court to pay annual tributes. The crowd of Monks visiting the Imperial capital used to create many civic problems for the inhabitants. In 1509 the Ming Emperor had to pass a decree according to which the tribute was to be paid after every three years and not annually as before. This measure eased the transport difficulties.

The Ming Emperors never exercised political control over Tibet and the attendance of the Lamas in the Chinese Court could be interpreted as more of gaining a royal favour than seeking any advice or recognising the supremacy of the Chinese Emperors. Such opportunities were not available to the Lamas in India because by then the Hindu ruling classes had discarded Buddhism in favour of Hinduism which was more militant than the former, and secondly the Mohammadan kings naturally would not favour the preaching of this pacifist philosophy of Lamaism among their subjects. The result was that the Northern Asia alone experienced the full impact of Buddhism. The Mings were overthrown by the Manchus who ruled the country from 1644 to 1911. The seasonal exodus of the Lamas to the Chinese capital had a baneful effect on Tibet. The more the religious relations between Tibet and China developed the more the presents, as a tribute, were offered to the Chinese Emperors and the more the Imperial Court assumed that tribute from Tibet was a right. Pemberton's dictum that "a gift long granted as a favour in the eyes of an Asiatic is soon considered as a right[36]" proved true and Tibet had to suffer the consequences of the tribute which she continued to pay to China for a long time.

During the declining years of the Kublai Khan's Yuan dynasty in the 14th century an important event occurred. Tson-Kha-Pa, the founder of Ge-Lu-Pa Sect was born in 1357. He founded, in 1409, Gan-Dan Monastery, a little more than a day's journey south-east of Lhasa. From this monastery later originated the Ge-Lu-Pa Sect—to which the Dalai Lama belongs—which had to wait until 1642 for fortune to turn in its favour. From the fifteenth to the seventeenth century the Sect was presided over by five Dalai Lamas So-Nam Gyan-Tsho was the third Dalai Lama, and he laid the foundation of the secular power of the Ge-Lu-Pa Sect and established the Dalai Lama series. He visited Mongolia in 1578 and 1587. The Mongolian king awarded him the title of Vajradhara Dalai Lama. The fifth Dalai Lama was born in 1617, and in 1641 with the help of the Mongolian prince dethroned the Tibetan king Tsan-Pa and thus became the secular head of the State. During the fifth Dalai Lama's rule, belief in the reincarnation of the Pancham Lama was also established. This was a very unwise step on the part of those who recognised his rank, and since then there has always been rivalry between the two leading Lamas of Tibet. The Dalai Lama claims superiority over the Pancham Lama and the latter over the former. It may be by coincidence or by manipulation that China always supported the Pancham Lama, even today he is said to be co-operating with the Chinese in Tibet while the Dalai Lama in India is pondering his future action under the shade of the cedars at Macleodganj, Dharamsala.

The sixth Dalai Lama from Tawang—an independent state then and located south of the Himalayan watershed—was installed in 1683. Soon after he was dethroned by the Chinese Emperor. It is said that the Lama*, a youth, indulged in wine and women and was useless. How far this is true one cannot say because the dethronement was very much resented by the Ge-Lu-Pa Sect. The ruler of Ili (north of Mongolia) was approached by the Sect and asked to intervene. He welcomed the opportunity and in 1716 captured Lhasa. The Chinese Emperor K'ang Hsi† despatched a Chinese force and drove out the intruder. The Emperor in 1720 put a boy Lama from Eastern Tibet (under Chinese influence) on the throne in the Potala Palace and proclaimed him the seventh Dalai Lama. *This was the beginning of the Chinese interference in Tibetan affairs.* To stop further intrigues and trouble the Emperor Chiang Lung, in 1726, appointed a Chinese Amban (Minister) in the Lhasa Court. According to the new arrangement Tibet was not allowed to negotiate directly with any foreign power. On China's part she undertook to

---

*An anonymous poet of the time stated to have described the Lama thus:— "A king I sit in Potala
A god on earth am I
But in the town, a prince of Rogues, and boisterous revelry."

'Tibet Past and Present by Sir Charles Bell—1924. P. 39.'

†The earliest attempt to map the whole of Tibet was made by the order of this king. He deputed a couple of Lamas to draw a map of the Chinese Empire in the south. They included whatever territories they heard of in the map drawn by crude methods. A copy of this map was sent to France. The European atlases based on it their information about this part of the world up to the middle of the nineteenth century. This is map that China is using now to advance her claims over the Himalayan regions.

protect Tibet against any foreign invasion. The new relationship has been termed as 'Chaplain-Patron' partnership. By this time Buddhism had claimed the whole of Mongolia and the Chinese chauvinists argue that China could not be secure without Mongolia; and to keep a hold on Mongolia Tibet's annexation was justified on the ground of the security of China. And who knows that China, tomorrow, may profess that for the security of Tibet the liberation of the Himalayan States is a necessity and the story of annexation may end up on the shores of Bay of Bengal. In 1950 China proclaimed that the liberation of Tibet was a "sacred duty[37]" and tomorrow she may over-burden herself with the responsibility of liberating India!

The history of the 13th century and after is the history of recent times, the period when British Imperialism was expanding and making inroads into Asia. The British on their part were always apprehensive of Russian Imperialism. In their anxiety they wooed China as an ally with them against the increasing influence of Russia over Tibet. Pemberton reports: "........ the agent of Russia have found their way to that celebrated capital of Central Asia, and with that view they have been sent may be safely inferred from their proceedings in a still more conspicuous field further West[38]." Thus Tibet was a pawn in the political game and she suffered. To this covetous game the Gorkhas were a new comer. King Prithi Narayan, a Gorkha chief, who traced his descent from the Rajas of Chitor, defeated the Malla Dynasty of Nepal and established his Capital at Khatmandu in 1769. He launched a campaign of annexation and extending his kingdom up to the Kangra Valley in the west and, in 1687, invaded Sikkim in the east. Sikkim ultimately beat off the attack. In the meantime a brother of the Pancham Lama persuaded the Gorkhas to invade Tibet, which they did. They came in contact with the Chinese in the adventure, and in 1792 they had to retire and accept Chinese terms. Twenty-four years later, in 1816, they faced the British and were defeated by General Octerloney. The Gorkhas ceded most of their territory in the west and in the Tarai (submountain region) to India, but a major portion of the latter was restored to them after the Sepoy Mutiny in 1857 for the unstinted support they rendered to the British. In 1856 the Nepalese army marched into Lhasa for the second time and defeated the Tibetan army. A treaty was concluded according to which Nepal was granted extra-territorial rights in Tibet and an annual tribute of Rs. 10,000. *China Failed to Aid Tibet.* This is the first of three instances when Tibet was let down by China, her so-called Patron, and the latter lost the claim which is now being so eminently trumpeted by the pro-Chinese elements. They attributed the failure of China to the declining influence of the Manchus from the middle of the 19th century. This defeat of Tibet could have been exploited by the British but in their anxiety to appease China they remained passive onlookers. The result was that Tibet bracketed the British with the Chinese and being suspicious of both she did not welcome their visitors into the country. Mr. Huc[39] during his journey from Lhasa to Batang in the 1850s noticed that the Tibetans refused oola (work levy) to the Chinese, while Bailey in 1912 was refused the same by the Monpas of Tawang. Bailey[40], probably, was taken as a Chinese ally.

However by the seventies of the last century realisation of Chinese designs dawned on the rulers of India. They moved to make the Indian frontier contiguous to

Tibet secure. They arranged the 1876 Treaty with the Chinese according to which they obtained the right to send an officer to Tibet on scientific explorations. The Tibetans resented the concession and prevailed on China to annul it. China withdrew the concession but at the cost of losing Burma under the 1886 Treaty. The Tibetans were jubilant over this superficial slight shown to the British. In the meantime, slowly and gradually Sikkim had come under the British influence and was made a Protectorate by 1869. The Tibetans judging wrongly the strength of British arms invaded the small Hill State and faced defeat. The 1890 Treaty was signed according to which Government of India's protectorate over Sikkim was confirmed and the Tibeto-Sikkimese boundary marked. *This was the second time that China failed Tibet and did not protect the latter's interests.* The treaty was followed by a set of regulations in 1893 governing trade, communication and pasturage between Tibet and Sikkim giving leverage to the former to encourage agitation in Sikkim. To stop this nuisance the famous Younghusband Expedition marched into Lhasa in 1904, the year when Russia was pre-occupied in the Russo-Japanese War and China was a helpless onlooker. Beyond expectation Lhasa put up a stiff resistance but was crushed on the arrival of reinforcements from Bengal. The Dalai Lama fled to Mongolia, and the Lhasa Convention of 1904 was signed between Great Britain and Tibet. Later the high dignitaries of England and China confirmed the Convention. Besides other minor points of the Convention the two main ones were that the British established the precedence of negotiating *Directly with Tibet,* and, second, Tibet agreed neither to permit any foreign power to interfere in her affairs nor to send her representative outside. *This was the third time that China failed to come to the aid of Tibet.* This was a potent point and it emboldened Nepal and Bhutan to cut free from Chinese domination. Since 1904 these countries have maintained their independence and have developed friendly relations with Government of India.

China realising the seriousness of the situation contrived with Britain to hold the Peking Convention of 1906. The Convention recognised the suzerainty of China over Tibet. The word 'Suzerainty' appeared for the first time in the political relations of Tibet vis-a-vis China. By virtue of "suzerainty" China became the protecting power of Tibet. China paid an indemnity of two and a half million rupees to Britain and later signed the Tibetan Trade Regulations of 1908 which allowed England to maintain armed guards in Tibet and granted extra-territorial rights for the three trade agencies of Yatung, Gyantse and Gartok. The Trade Regulations also authorised telegraph-postal service and a string of Dak-Bunglows from the Indo-Tibetan frontier to Gyantse. In 1907 *Russia recognised the Peking Convention, and hence the 'Suzerainty' of China over Tibet.*

The Peking Convention removed the disability of China which had been imposed under Article 9 of the Lhasa Convention which classed her as a foreign power. Now she was not a foreign but a protecting power. By recognising the suzerainty of China the British lost whatever they had gained in the Lhasa Convention of 1904. They, in fact, lost Tibet and "delivered her into the power of China[41]", and China was not slow to take advantage of the opportunity. In 1910 she invaded Tibet and occupied Lhasa. The 13th Dalai Lama who had returned from Mongolia in 1908 fled to Sikkim. The Chinese who in the course of their occupation of Tibet during the 18th and

19th centuries had informed the Khampti chief that he was a subject of the Imperial Government of China, this time, ordered the Mishmis to cut them a road to India. Lt. Col. Shakespear writes: "In fact it would seem that China had been desirous of extending her rule right up to our borders, and that this was possibly a fixed principle of her statesmen in the past. It may so happen that under a new and stable Government and a rapidly modernising China this idea will come to the front again[42]." Times have proved the truth. The Chinese invasion shocked the British. They realised the folly of leaving NEFA as an administrative vacuum and appointed Political Officers and Assistant Political Officers to administer the tribal areas.

In 1911, due to her internal disturbances, China became weak and lost her grip over Tibet. In 1912 the Dalai Lama returned to Lhasa and regained his political and spiritual powers. The Chinese Minister and the Chinese army personnel were packed off to China via Calcutta and *Tibet declared her Independence*. But China never gave up her claim of 'suzerainty' over Tibet. The political tension persisted and finally, on April 27, 1914, a Convention was initialled at Simla by the three plenipotentiaries of China, India and Tibet. The Convention divided Tibet into two zones, Outer Tibet and Inner Tibet. The former was nearer India including Lhasa and Chamdo; while the latter was the part touching China. The British kept their extra-territorial concessions in the Outer Tibet but the 'suzerainty' of China over the whole of Tibet was again recognised. China undertook not to convert Tibet into a Chinese province, and the British also gave such an undertaking for Outer Tibet. The Convention fixed the hitherto undefined Indo-Tibetan frontier along the great Himalayan range known as the McMahon Line. In drawing this frontier Tibet ceded Tawang and Dirang Dzong Valleys to the Government of India as a token of appreciation for arranging the Simla Convention. Unfortunately, in keeping with her tradition of not committing herself to any agreement, the Chinese Government repudiated its representative's actions and refused to sign the Convention. Subsequently, however, China never challenged the validity of the Convention in her correspondence with the Government of India. The McMahon Line was never under dispute. China did raise an objection over the eastern boundary dividing Inner and Outer Tibet. She wanted the Inner-Outer Tibet boundary to be fixed 100 miles west of the 1914 boundary to include Chamdo, while Great Britain and the Tibetan authorities maintained that it should be pushed further east by 300 miles.

Tibet was again a sufferer. Previously, when she stood against the British, China chastised her by denying her the promised protection. Even when she declared her independence she could not free herself from the yellow menace which has been infringing on her integrity since 1726. No wonder "Lhasa believes that to be politically attached to China is more a liability than an asset[43]."

Immediately after the Simla Convention World War I started. British attention was diverted towards its prosecution, and China was pre-occupied with her internal revolution. The Convention was forgotten and China never ratified it.

In 1917 the Tibetan pushed the Chinese back as far as Gyam-Da, but had to retire under Chinese pressure in 1930, and the Chinese arbitrarily fixed the Inner-Outer

Tibetan boundary about 100 miles to the east of Lhasa, thus bringing Chamdo, 370 miles east of Lhasa, into Inner Tibet.

In 1924 a controversy arose between the Dalai Lama and the Pancham Lama. The latter took refuge with the Chinese in Chinghai and died there in 1937.

In 1934 the Chinese Government despatched a mission which opened an office at Lhasa. The British reacted and they installed their own representative in the Tibetan capital thus putting China on equal footing with Great Britain. As the latter was a foreign power in Tibet so the former also became. The British thus regained whatever they had lost in the 1906 Convention. In 1940 a Chinese representative attended the present Dalai Lama's installation ceremony. This was an ordinary courtesy attendance, but later the Chinese interpreted it as a sign of the willingness of the Tibetans to continue the 'Chaplain-Patron' relationship with them. In spite of these assertions and manoeuvres Tibet continued to maintain her independent status. The British considered Outer Tibet as a buffer state between India and China, and it never occurred to them to enlist Tibet as a member of the League Of Nations, or at least to make an attempt in that direction. Probably they thought the overture risky. This passive attitude was reflected by Western acquiescence in being always favourably inclined towards China and tacitly recognising her suzerainty over the Plateau, and never effecting any modification of this attitude or annulling it as warranted by political and ideological changes occurring in Europe and Asia. In the meantime the Second World War started. China, under force of circumstances was drawn into the Allies' camp. Historic imitation is a strong point in Chinese polity and whenever she was unified under a strong government she always attempted to extend her territorial limits, never forgetting to reiterate her old claims irrespective of whether they were genuine or fictitious. Whether the rulers of China were the Nationalists or the Communists their outlook towards weaker Asian nations was the same Whether it be Burma, Indo-China, Bhutan, Sikkim, Nepal, Ladakh or Tibet, they never forgot to lay claims on their erstwhile protectorates. Not only this but they also gave an indication that they were aspiring to seize even those territories where not a single Chinese national had put a foot from the beginning of civilisation. In 1945 the Kuomintang Government issued maps according to which China's frontier with India runs along the edge of the Assam plains, skirting the tea-gardens, and incorporating villages in the Abor Hills which have long been administered by the Government of Assam. At that time General Chiang Kai-shek was a great friend of the Allies, specially of the United States of America, therefore it was thought that the matter would amicably be settled to the satisfaction of the parties concerned. It was a delicate problem and needed time and opportunity for its solution. Unfortunately time and opportunity never arrived. The British with the termination of the War departed from India leaving the problem as a legacy of their rule over the country. General Chiang fled to Formosa leaving China to be ruled by the Communists.

At the close of British rule, peace and prosperity prevailed in Assam. There was security of life and property. The province became one of the chief exporters of tea to the Western market. Politically and culturally also Assam did not lag behind. But instead of uniting Assam the British had divided it into reserved or excluded and semi-reserved or semi-excluded areas thus leaving a serious problem for Government of India to tackle.

1. Pt. Nehru's Speeches 1949-53 p. 247
2. Report on the State of Bootan by The Hon'ble Ashley Eden—1864 p. 127
3. Pemberton p. 12
4. In Abor Jungles by Angus Hamilton p. 74
5. Assam Administration Report 1913-14 p. ii
6. Ethnology by Dalton p. 7
7. JASB 1936 p. 99
8. JASB No. 79. 1838-47 by E. A. Grange p. 452
9. White Paper No. III by Government of India p. 94
10. The Mishmi Hills by Cooper p. 129
11. Ethnology by Dalton p. 28
12. AR Vol. XVI 1828 p. 336
13. NEF by Mackenzie p. 55
14. Descriptive Account of Assam by William Robinson p. 369
    Angus Hamilton p. 192
    JASB 1837 p. 336
    Butler p. 120
15. Ethnology by Dalton p. 6
16. Angus Hamilton p. 201
17. JASB 1872 S. E. Peal p. 19
18. Tea Planter's Life by Geo. M. Baker p. 72
19. Muffat Mills Appx. M cxxvii
20. Butler p. 150
21. Mackenzie p. 92
22. Muffat Mills Report Appx. P ixv/ixvi
23. Bhutan by Ashley p. 128
24. Topography of Assam by M'Cosh p. 67
25. JASB 1875 No. 1 p. 383
26. Cooper p. 247
27. Mackenzie p. 400
28. Gates p. 334
29. PASB p. 78
30. JASB 1875 p. 313

31. JASB 1900 Vol. LXIX Pt. III by Lt. Col. L. A. Waddle, I.M.S. p. 2
32. The Changing Map of Asia p. 375
33. JASB 1832 Vol. I by CSoma de Koros p. 122
34. Most of the World Edited by Ralph Linton p. 53
35. The Peagent of Chinese History by Elizabeth Seegar p. 182
36. Pemberton p. 168
37. K. M. Panikar—In Two Chinas p. 105
38. Pemberton p. 96
39. Tibet, Tartary and Mongolia by Henry T. Prinsep (1851) p. 129
40. No Passport to Tibet by F. M. Bailey p. 236
41. Out of This World Tibet by Lowell Thomas Jr.
42. Shakespear p. 239
43. Tibet and Tibetans by Shen & Liu p. 62

CHAPTER V

India Attains Freedom

"At this solemn moment when the people of India, through suffering and sacrifice, have secured freedom, I........ a member of the Constituent Assembly, do dedicate myself in all humility to the service of India and her people to the end that this ancient land attain her rightful place in the world and make her full and willing contribution to the promotion of world peace and the welfare of mankind[1]".

Pledge.

It is said that history is to society what navigation is to the marine or airman. Therefore, to understand any problem and its implication, it is essential to know how it has grown. The fact of India's Independence is a reality but what factors lie behind the national freedom are of historical importance; a clear conception of these factors may also lead to conclusions of far reaching significance.

The history of Independence, for the purpose of this chapter, begins with the history of British rule in India. The British entered North India from Bengal. They faced opposition from the Hindus. They did not like the obstructionists and endeavoured to halt the ingress of Hinduism among the tribal people of Assam and Bengal. "The old tribal beliefs are gradually being abandoned; and the way in which Hindu priests established their influence over non-Aryan chiefs and gradually drew them within their folds is repeatedly exemplified in the pages of Assam history[2]", writes Gates. Author after author can be quoted as holding this opinion. To neutralise the evolutionary influence of Hinduism, Christianity was introduced among the so-called non-Aryans in the 1840s under the patronage of Government. The temper of the country did not welcome the move and the Christians, who were mostly from the lower castes, were treated as outcastes by the general public. The assimilation of non-Aryans into the Hindu told continued. Various suggestions were made by vested interests to make Christianity a success. "Considering as a measure of policy, a Christian population, holding a decent rank in the motley throng of tribes and castes, would tend to consolidate the strength of the State, and add to the probable duration of the empire. A colonization of the nature alluded to, far from being likely to terminate in the separation of the colony, would rather serve to perpetuate the Union by the addition of a tribe whose interests and doctrines much attach them to their European superiors[3]", wrote Hamilton in 1820. The same writer further expresses his view: "......, and until some such improvement is effected the temporal causes that oppose the conversion of the Hindus will continue to operate." Attempts to depopularise Hinduism were set afloat. As a result Christianity succeeded in some areas and in others the absorption of the people into Hinduism completely ceased. Side by side with this political expediency motivated the rulers to support Mohammadans in India. The uprising of 1857 provided a temporary set back, but the core of the policy remained the same. As late as 1791 Muslims were in an insignificant minority in East Bengal. Dr. Wiss writes: "When English magistrates first came in contact with the people of Bengal, they arrived at the conclusion that the Mohammadans only comprised one per cent of the population and their estimate, formed on insufficient ground, was generally assumed to be approximately correct[4]." This points to the conclusion that the pre-independence predominance of the Musalman element in East Bengal was mainly due to the change of the religion of the people. This conversion on such a large scale—by the beginning of this century the Mohammadans were in majority in East Bengal—was brought about during the British regime—a period of about 150 years only—and not, as is the general belief, during the Muslim rule which lasted for more than four hundred years in these parts. Assam for some reason escaped. It remained a Hindu majority province.

In 1905 Lord Curzon divided Bengal in two and united East Bengal with Assam making the unit a Muslim majority territory. Fortunately by then the Bengali Muslims had not so estranged themselves from their Hindu countrymen as to oppose a movement launched by the revolutionaries of the province to unite the two Bengals. The movement succeeded and in 1911 the order of partition was reversed by Royal Command. Regarding the partition, Spate writes:

> "By and large it seems impossible to avoid the conclusion that on every logical and rational criterion the partition of Bengal was a profound mistake. But in view of the general irrationality of human affairs, to say that does not mean that there was any alternative to partition, still less that what is done should be undone[5]."

It was the first attempt to convert a frontier province into a Muslim majority State and it failed.

Simultaneously with the partition of Bengal, Muslim migration to Assam commenced. The Census Report of 1931 speaks about it in no uncertain terms:

"Probably the most important event in the province during the last twenty five years—an event, moreover, which seems likely to alter permanently the whole future of Assam and to destroy more surely than did the Burmese invaders of 1820 the whole structure of Assamese culture and civilisation—has been the invasion of vast hordes of land-hungry Bengali immigrants, mostly Muslims, from the districts of Eastern Bengal and in particular from Mymensingh.

Without fuss, without tumult, without undue trouble to the district revenue staffs, a population which must amount to over half a million has transplanted itself from Bengal to the Assam Valley during the last twenty five years.

It is sad but by no means improbable that in another thirty years Sibsagar district will be the only part of Assam in which an Assamese will find himself at home[6]."

In the 1911 census the Muslim population of the Assam Valley was only 355,320. But this number had grown to 1,305,902 by 1941 according to the Census Report which was the last taken by the British.

Following the same imperial policy of 'divide and rule' the British supporting the Mohammadans, in 1905, created 'Muslim League', a political-cum-communal organisation. Muslim League's apparent aim was to oppose the Congress Party and to delay the Independence of the country. The climax of the struggle was reached during the Cabinet Mission negotiations in 1946 when Assam was grouped with Bengal to placate the League. After the intervention of Sri Gopi Nath Bardoloi, the Chief Minister of Assam, who had prevailed over Mahatma Gandhi and through the Mahatma over AICC, the Cabinet Mission Plan was rejected. As a natural sequence the League also rejected the Plan. According to Dr. Abul Kalam Azad, the then Congress President, a few of the minor mistakes of Pandit Nehru and Sardar Patel and the stubborn attitude of Mr. Jinha led to the partition of the country. It is a well known fact that the British Conservative Party had always preferred the Division of India. The idea of 'Pakistan' by then had taken deep root in the minds of the Muslim League Leaders. The Hindus were apprehensive that Pakistan, if such a nation came into existence, would, in collaboration with their co-religionists of the South West Asian countries, dominate India. Any plan other than partition was not to the liking of Mr. Winston Churchill and his Party. Lord Wavell, the then Viceroy of India, firmly believed that communal accord was prerequisite to independence, while the circumstances demanded independence first and everything else afterward. Wavell failed to bring about a compromise between the two political parties and resigned on the issue. He was replaced by Lord Mountbatten, a 'Conservative by birth and by his whole make-up'. Lord Mountbatten naturally advocated partition. "It must be placed on record that the man in India who first fell for Lord Mountbatten's ideas was Sardar Patel", writes Dr. Azad. He continues, "Lord Mountbatten was extremely intelligent and could read the minds of all the Indian colleagues. The moment he found Patel amenable to his idea, he put out all the charm and power of his personality to win over the Sardar[7]." Within a month of Lord Mountbatten's arrival Pt. Jawaharlal Nehru also started showing signs of cracking under the nervous strain created by the hostile and stubborn attitude of the League. Pt. Nehru at last became willing "to cut off the head in order to get rid of the headache[8]." Dr. Azad further remarks: "I have often wondered how Jawaharlal was won over by Lord Mountbatten. Jawaharlal is a man of principle, but he is also impulsive and amenable to personal influence. The arguments of Sardar Patel must have had same effect, but could not have been decisive. Jawaharlal was also greatly impressed by Lord Mountbatten, but perhaps even greater was the influence of Lady Mountbatten. She is not only extremely intelligent, but had a most attractive and friendly temperament. She admired her husband greatly and in many cases tried to interpret his thought to those who would not at first agree with him[9]." Whatever might have been the circumstances that led to the truncation of India, it is a fact that the people in general—the Hindus, the Muslims, the Parsees and the Christians—were not prepared for partition. Even Mahatma Gandhi did not favour partition of the country. Lord Pathick Lawrence writes:

> He (Mahatma Gandhi) was firmly convinced that the partition of India was contrary to God's will and that, as such, to resist it was a holy duty. Against such a conviction, sustained by his inner voice, merely political argument about the political consequences of a refusal to compromise, or about the desirability of choosing the lesser evil, counted for nothing. It was man's business to act in accordance with God's will as he understood it. If he did that the fruit of action did not rest with him. They rested with God[10]."

The vivisection of the country was contrary to the modern conception of historical facts. Burma, under the strain of the Karen revolt refused partition; while in China when the Communists were fighting the Kuomintang forces and the position of the latter was very precarious, General Chiang Kai-shek was strongly pressed to accept partition. He did not agree. "The Nationalists and Chinese nationalism in general had all along insisted that there must be only one Government, and that it must include all China, certainly all of China, in which the Chinese predominated and preferably all that had been embraced in the empire when it had been ruled by Manchus. There were even some who dreamed of occupying all the lands, that had at any time accepted Chinese suzerainty, including much of Indo-China and Burma[11]", records an American Report. The Communists are not different from the Kuomintang, and the current policy of China confirms this. The Imperialist Policy of Great Britain was short sighted and India was a victim of this pernicious design—the partition of the country. The destiny of India rested in the hands of a few and they gave up in the end. "Our national organisation had taken a decision in favour of partition but the entire people grieved over it[12]." Obviously a part could not be as strong as the whole and India became weak. To add to the misfortune of India and Pakistan the Kashmir issue sprang up interlocking the armies of both as belligerents Weakness turned into invalidity.

To make matters still worse Congress did not share the administration of the country with non-Congress nationals. Pt. Jawaharlal Nehru did include some non-Congressmen in the Union Cabinet, but, after a few years, they were on one pretext or the other either expelled or made to resign from the Cabinet. Outside the Cabinet, non-Congressmen received similar treament; while Congress members and sympathisers were given preferential treatment in public and other voluntary services on the plea that the latter had undergone sacrifices for the national cause. This created disappointment and frustration in the public mind. Congress forgot that the birth and the presence of the Indian National Army during the Second World War, and disaffection among the Defence Forces and policemen were other equally important factors that hastened Independence. It may be argued that this disaffection was a by-product of the national awakening brought about by Mahatma Gandhi. This is correct but the credit of the awakening goes to Mahatma and Mahatma alone and not to any political party. However, the fact remains that the British, who always considered the Defence Services and the police as the two main pillars of the Indian Empire, lost confidence in the guardians of security and law and order. Discretion is the better part of valour. They decided to quit India in time and with grace. Therefore, it is safe to say that violence and non-violence both played their respective roles in the struggle. In fact violence was more effective, because defections in the army and police were a signal for future violence on a vast scale. The British fully realised that any delay in handing over the reins of the country would be inviting the wrath of the Indian people and in that mood everything was possible. The army could revolt and a civil war could start, or the country might go Red and injure the Imperial Interests. At the same time they were quite sure that their interests were safe in the hands of the Congress leaders who came from the higher strata of society and as such would oppose sudden and revolutionary changes in the political or administrative set up of the country, so with what grace they could muster they made a hasty retreat. The unconditional withdrawal of the British encouraged the Congress to attach undue emphasis to the efficacy of non-violence and its ancillary pacifist ideals.

Non-violence gave birth to co-existence, Panchsheel and non-alignment. Non-alignment or positive neutrality, as some would like to call it, was adopted as our Foreign Policy. The policy succeeded in the international field and India's neutral influence was recognised when General Thimaya was appointed as Chairman of the Neutral Nations Commission in Korea and Sri Rajeshwar Dayal as the UN Secretary-General's personal representative in Congo. How far the policy has succeeded in dealing with China has yet to be seen. In the teeth of the Chinese challenge India is sticking to her policy of non-violence and non-alignment. In spite of deliberate provocation she has decided to act calmly and to settle the dispute through negotiations, however prolonged the negotiations may be. Professor Toynbee praised India for her non-violent approach to the controversy and said: "...... You, the people of India, are finding it difficult at this moment in your relation with China. But you have incurred a rather formidable obligation both to Gandhiji and history—I mean the obligation to go on setting an Indian example of non-violence to the rest of the world.

If India were ever to fail to live up to this Indian ideal which is the finest, and therefore the most exacting, legacy in your Indian heritage it would be a poor outlook for mankind as a whole. So a great spiritual responsibility rests on India. Your action, whichever way it goes, may do much towards giving the spirit of man a decisive turn for better or for worse—and that means a turn towards self-preservation or towards self-destruction seeing that we are now living in the atomic age[13]."

Internally India is facing a crisis. It is a historical fact that whenever a strong and benevolent ruler was at the helm of affairs India was united and whenever hypocrisy and weakness guided administration, fissiparous tendencies raised their heads and India disintegrated. The country is now passing through the latter phase. Apart from the yellow threat in the north and its effect on the Himalayan States the five autonomous districts of Assam are demanding separation from the parent State. In their demand they have included NEFA also. On what grounds they have done this is only known to the spokesmen of All-Party Hill Leaders Conference. On one side the Government of India is wedded to non-violence and on the other it rewards violence. That is a contradiction. The birth of Nagaland has proved that violence pays. This feeling was at the root of the recent trouble in Assam and it may create serious repercussions elsewhere. Its impact is creating ferment among the Tirapians. They have become restive and are expressing their dislike for the present Administration of NEFA. The infection may and probably will creep into the other Divisions. Leaving alone the problem of the proposed integration of NEFA with Assam, the disintegration of Assam itself is a political certainty unless, of course, the Government of India starts acting on the basis of practical considerations. The security and integrity of India demands a united and strong Assam as a frontier State; every impediment to a united and strong Assam must be removed. The Inner Line mentality is the greatest of these impediments.

Partition made India weak and the Kashmir dispute locked the bulk of her army in the far north-west. She preferred to sacrifice the defence and consolidation of her northern frontier areas in order to safeguard her integrity in Kashmir and to hasten the economic development of the whole country. China was quick to discern that. India's Foreign Policy prevented her from rendering military aid even to Tibet, her neighbour, which had acted as a buffer State and as a safeguard to India's security and integrity in the north. China was emboldened and marched her troops into Tibet unhindered, in spite of Tibet's assertion of independence, and occupied Lhasa. It is said that China was apprehensive of India's intervention but she was officially assured of India's neutrality. Nepal was another 'Independent Country within Independent India' which could have despatched military aid to Tibet, but could she do that on her own? Under the circumstances India watched the Rape of Tibet passively. If India could not intervene in this debacle effectively, at least she was capable of sending a nominal force, as a protest, to hinder the occupation. But she did not do even that. What were the reasons for her passive attitude? The rulers of India may advance other reasons, best known to themselves, but a few have been detailed in the following paragraphs, after a thorough study of the literature now available on the subject.

First, India firmly believed that the Indo-Tibetan policy she had inherited from the British was wrong and it was China's internal affair to deal with Tibet in the manner she liked (condemning the British Imperialism and blessing the Chinese expansionism)! This view is confirmed by Shri K. M. Panikar, "a friend of China[14]" and India's Ambassador to that country at the time of the Rape of Tibet.

> '"The only area where our interests overlapped was in Tibet, and knowing the importance that every Chinese Government, including the Kuomintang, had attached to exclusive Chinese authority over that area, I had, even before I started for Peking, come to the conclusion that the British

policy (which we were supposed to have inherited) of looking upon Tibet as an area in which we had special political interests could not be maintained. The Prime Minister had also in general agreed with this view[15]."

The upholders of such views, probably, drew a parallel between the Sino-Indian relations and those of the Naga Hills with NEFA. They forgot that these Naga territories were never known as independent entities and to equate them with Tibet was erroneous. Probably Tibet was herself responsible for the origination of the view that she was an internal problem of China. Historically, off and on, she had been flirting with China and had been playing the Chinese tune in the political field. Even during the late forties of this century she did not change her tactics.

Second, in 1946-47, Kuomintang Government despatched as may as four protests to the Government of India in connection with a small territory in NEFA, while a fifth one was handed over in November 1949 which "merely stated that China had not signed the Simla Convention[16]." The Tibetan Government followed suit. The Indian Mission in Lhasa forwarded to the Government of India a telegram, dated the 16th October 1947 from the Tibetan Bureau. "The telegram asked for the return of alleged Tibetan territories on boundaries of India and Tibet 'such as Sayul and Walong and in direction of Pemako, Lonag, Lopa, Mon, Bhutan, Sikkim, Darjeeling and others on this side of river Ganges and Lowo, Ladakh, etc. upto boundary of Yarkhim[17]." No wonder that India welcomed a change of the Chinese Government when the Communists took over.

Thus the second reason is linked with the first because India expected a better deal from the Communist Government. The Government of India hoped that Tibet would be allowed to "maintain the autonomy it has had for at least forty years[18]" and that China would respect the people's (Tibetan's) opinion. Tibet would become autonomous without firing a shot: It was purely wishful thinking on India's part if she thought that like Outer Mongolia, Outer Tibet would also form an autonomous State. India forgot that Russia had had to interfere in Outer Mongolia from 1921-28 on behalf of the Mongolian 'freedom fighters' to compel China to accede to Mongolia's autonomy. In 1921 Chinese power grew weak in Outer Mongolia and in a series of revolts (with Soviet's active support) the Mongolians secured their present status as a Republic. Probably by now the Chinese regard Tibet as an autonomous State under Greater China, but Tibet and India know better than this. The People's Republic of Mongolia is entitled to be a member of the United Nations, while Tibet cannot dream of that privilege. She is a Chinese 'servile' colony—Chinese are encouraged to migrate to Tibet, and the target of this migration is said to be about 10 millions* while the population of Tibet is estimated to be not more than 3 millions.

Ethnologically Tibetans are different from the Chinese and belong to Central Asian stock. China professes to let the Tibetans develop according to their own desires. This is false. The Chinese will absorb the Tibetans who will soon lose their identity. The favourite Chinese slogan since 1911 has always been: "A Republic of five races meaning, the Hans (original Chinese who arrived in early

* According to reports current in the Border Districts of India the number of Chinese who have already migrated into Tibet is about 7 millions.

times from Central Asia), Manchus, Mongols, Mohammadans and Tibetans. In recent years a sixth group, the Miaos, has been added. The actual number of ethnic groups to be found in China is, of course, much greater[19]" writes R. Linton.

The hopes of the Government of India that the Chinese would respect the wishes and opinions of the Tibetan people were rudely destroyed. India was very unwise in having faith in such a democratic idea in respect to China. She failed to recognise the force of science as used to compel people to change their opinions. She failed to understand that the opinion of the people could be moulded; she also failed to learn much from the Russian Revolution and now she is blaming China because after the same manner, China did not and does not respect the opinion of the people. Those, whose opinions she did not respect, have either been removed from this world or have migrated to India for eventual extinction.

The third reason for India's inaction was a serious one for which India paid heavily. It has the inexperience of India's national leaders nurtured by Satyagraha and passive resistance. The present day leaders are those who made sacrifices for the national cause in a gentlemanly way. They had not passed through that blood-bath which is inevitable in a revolution and they could not understand the implications of the political game in which Tibet was the football. In fact they could not make up their minds about the role to be played by India in Tibet. After independence India replaced the British representative at the Lhasa Court. Chen & Liu writes: "Thus India came to be represented in what has been described by its own (India's) leaders as 'undefined capacity'[20]." She could have received political advice from countries who were used to such games but her Foreign Policy debarred her from that too. Whatever advice was available was from people of her own way of thinking. Under these circumstances India's passive action was inevitable.

If India were convinced that for her security, Outer Tibet's autonomy was essential, she could have done something about it. It was certain that India could not go to war against China. It is also true that the British had recognised the suzerainty of China over Tibet in the 1906 Convention and India could not repudiate the previous treaties. Some quarters have suggested that India had two years, 1947 to 1949, at her disposal to recognise the independent identity of Tibet and thus could have neutralised the suzerainty of China over the latter. Such critics fail to appreciate that by 1947 Tibet had joined the Kuomintang camp. How was it possible then for India to take advantage of this short period of two years to persuade Tibet, an unwilling party, to declare herself independent ? The only possible course for the Government of India to pursue was to postpone the signing of the 1954 Treaty till the settlement of the Sino-Indian Frontier and to delay the withdrawl of the extra-territorial privileges from Tibet. This would have given India sufficient time to study the real intentions of the Chinese Communists; if required, she could also in this time arouse an international conscience against the atrocities committed by the Chinese in their programme for the annihilation of Buddhism and extermination of the Tibetans themselves. Probably India acted in the manner that she did thinking that she could keep the cold war away from her northern frontiers, but, on the contrary the cold war has penetrated the Himalayan wall. By letting down erring Tibet India has let herself down very badly. History will hold the top Indian Administrators and their advisers responsible for this political betrayal.

Foreign Policy is usually the legacy of the whole nation and it is, generally, not easily changed. If it has to be changed then changes should be effected after ascertaining the public opinion. The British took more than a century and a half to understand the intentions of the Chinese and then another thirty years to secure extraterritorial concessions in Tibet, but India knew the Chinese Government's designs before the Chinese Communists came to power and she took hardly six months to come to the decision to withdraw her (India's) privileges from Tibet, and to execute that decision. The public hardly knew the implications of this inexplicably hasty action. There was a faint murmur in the Indian Parliament, but it was drowned by the towering personality of the Prime Minister. Shri Panikar's observation may throw more light on the subject :

> "To add to my troubles, by the middle of the month, rumours of a Chinese invasion of Tibet began to circulate. The Chinese reply was equally strong. It practically accused India of having been influenced by the imperialists, and claimed that China had not taken any military action but was determined to liberate Tibet by peaceful means. Our rejoinder though couched in equally strong words, recognising Chinese sovereignty over Tibet and disclaiming all desire to intervene in its affairs, but emphasised once again our desire that the issue between Tibetans and the Chinese should be decided peacefully and not by the use of force. Both parties had made their point of view clear and were content to let it rest there.

I had expected a virulent campaign against India in the Press. But for some reason the Chinese, apart from publishing the correspondence, soft pedalled the whole affair. The controversy was seldom mentioned in the Press. But on our side matters were not so easy. The Indian Press, egged on by the sensational reports of the American correspondents and the blood-curdling stories issued from Hong Kong Taipeh agents, kept on talking about Chinese aggression. Even Sardar Patel, the Deputy Prime Minister, felt called upon to make an unfriendly speech. In the meantime Equador which was then a member of the Security Council, threatened to bring up the Tibetan question before the United Nations. Knowing the temper of the Indian public and the attitude of some of the officials I was nervous that the government might take some hasty step. My own prestige with the government was at low ebb and I was being attacked for having misled the Prime Minister about Chinese intervention in Korea. But the Prime Minister was not so easily moved. He kept calm and allowed the public feeling to die down[21]."

When Shri Panikar left China he wrote: "The Tibetan issue was simple. ...... The main issue of our representation at Lhasa was then satisfactorily settled and I was happy to feel that there was no outstanding issue between us and the Chinese at the time of my departure[22]." What about the Tibeto-Indian border issue?

After the occupation, China summoned a Tibetan Commission to sign the famous seventeen point agreement. The Agreement of the Central People's Government and the local Government of Tibet on measures for the peaceful liberation of Tibet was initialled on May 23, 1951 by the authorised representatives of the two countries. The 3rd paragraph of the preamble of the same is reproduced as under :

> In order that the influences of aggressive imperial forces in Tibet might be successfully eliminated, the unification of the territory and sovereignty of the People's Republic of China accomplished, and national defence safeguarded; in order that the Tibetan nationality and people might be free and return to the big family of the People's Republic of China to enjoy the same rights of national equalities as all the other nationalities in the country and develop their political, economic, cultural and educational work, the Central People's Government, when it ordered the People's Liberation Army to march into Tibet, notified the local government of Tibet to send delegates to the central authorities to conduct talks for the conclusion of the agreement on measures for the peaceful liberation of Tibet.

Thus the 'peaceful liberation' of Tibet was accomplished with bayonets! According to the Dalai Lama the Agreement was signed under duress. The highlights of the Agreement were : (i) China guaranteed the autonomy of Tibet with no change in the Dalai Lama's status, (ii) the Pancham Lama's position was to be restored, (iii) Military and Administrative Committees were to be set up and, (iv) Tibet's external affairs were to be handled by the Chinese.

Immediately after signing the Agreement a three pronged movement of the Chinese armies—from Chamdo in the east, Nga-Ri in the west and Chinghai in the north—

was launched in July 1951 and Tibet was admitted into Greater China's familly. Later a strong military base was built upon the Asian High Plateau to threaten India. The Dalai Lama's status was neutralised to such an extent that he made a bid to leave the country, but his attempt either failed or he gave up the idea. That is what happened to the 'autonomy of Tibet'. A new interpretation of the word 'autonomy' was coined by China, all previous undertakings were thrown to the wind and Tibet was changed into a Chinese province. The Pancham Lama entered Tibet with pomp and show behind the bayonets of the Communist China. The third and the fourth provisions of the 1951 Treaty were reinforced and strengthened with authoritarian ruthlessness. These are the provisions which established the Chinese Military and Administrative Committees.

During these hectic days China continued to print maps showing more and more Indian territory as her own. There was agitation in the inner administrative and army circles in India to force the Union Government to take cognisance of the Chinese attitude and to settle border problems once for all. The Government of India began to press the Communist Government to amend their maps according to the existing treaties and agreements, but China on the plea of gathering information and lack of time kept postponing the issue. On one side, she increased her military might in Tibet and encroached on the Indian territory, and on the other side she signed the Trade Agreement of 1954 which recognised Indian traders' right to carry on normal trade in Tibet and advocated a 'status quo' on the border. The Government of India, to avoid suspicion in good faith, never handed over the defence of the border to the Army. In NEFA the Assam Rifles, a kind of frontier constabulary, continued to guard the border as a checking authority. Slowly and gradually it dawned on Government of India, and this Pt. Nehru had to admit in the Lok Sabha that China had committed an all round 'Breach of Faith'. The Dalai Lama fled from Tibet and entered India for political asylum. He was followed by thousands of Tibetan refugees. The stream of refugees continues; up to December, 1960, more than 45,000 Tibetans had entered India, Nepal, Sikkim and Bhutan.

Since the signing of the 1954 Trade Agreement there have been border violations by the Chinese army in NEFA. In October 1957 a small party of Chinese troops entered Dichu Valley and came as far down as Walong in the Lohit Frontier Division. Again another Chinese army detachment consisting of one officer and approximately 50 men camped inside the Indian border after crossing into the same Division on September 27/28, 1958. This detachment later moved towards Tazung Dam which lies in Burma. In the Subansiri Division the Chinese incursion, bordering on aggression took place on August 26, 1959. On that day a strong Chinese detachment opened fire on the Indian outpost at Longju killing one soldier and wounding several more. The Indian detachment was forced to vacate the post and the Chinese occupied it. The post was in occupation of the Chinese up to November, 1960. According to the "Times of India" of December 10, 1960, "Mr. Nehru today confirmed in the Lok Sabha that the Chinese had vacated Longju on account of an epidemic and had retired to a distance of about three miles to the north." Further Pt. Nehru told the House that India, in view of the Sino-Indian understanding, would not seek to reoccupy Longju. In Kameng

Frontier Division Chinese troops have intruded twice, once in 1959 and next on June 3, 1960. In the latter case they penetrated four miles into Indian territory in spite of the fact that both countries had expressed their intention not to patrol a strip 12 miles on either side of the Indo-Tibetan border. The Ladakh tragedy* was the climax. This caused furore in the Lok Sabha and the Union Government handed over the Indo-Tibetan border defence to the Indian Army. Thus for the first time the Indian Army obtained a say in matters concerning NEFA.

As far as Tibet is concerned China's attitude is firm and final. "The Tibet Region is an inalienable part of China's territory. The quelling of the rebellion in the Tibet region by the Chinese Government and following that, the conducting by it of democratic reforms which the Tibetan people have longed for, are entirely China's internal affairs, in which no foreign country has any right to interfere under whatever pretext or in whatever form. In Tibet, just as in other national minority areas in China, regional autonomy shall be implemented as stipulated in the Constitution of the People's Republic of China. *In this matter which is purely China's internal affairs, the Chinese Government has no obligation to give assurances to any foreign country, nor can it tolerate others under the pretext of a so-called different interpretation of autonomy, to obstruct the Chinese Government's exercise of its State sovereignty in the Tibet region to make semi-independent*

*In Ladakh the Chinese had constructed the Tibeto-Sinkiang road through India's territory. In October, 1959, the Indian border police patrol suffered heavy casualties. This wanton destruction of 10 lives (9 were declared killed and the 10th—Constable Makhan Lal—missing) was condemned by the world democracies.

or even to turn it into a sphere of influence of a foreign country or buffer zones[23]."

(Italics are mine)

As regards the settlement of the Indo-Tibetan border controversy again the stand taken by both Governments is firm and there is very little likelihood of any compromise being reached between them in the near future.

> "The Chinese Government is of the opinion that no matter what views the two sides may hold about any specific matter concerning the boundary, there should no longer be any difference of opinion about the most basic fact known to the whole world, that is the entire boundary between the two countries has indeed never been delimited, and is therefore yet to be settled through negotiations. Recognition of this simple fact should not create any difficulties for either side, because it would neither impair the present interest of either side, nor in any way prevent both sides from making their own claims at the boundary negotiations. Once agreement is reached on this point, it could be said that the way has been opened to the settlement of the boundary question[24]."

A sinister suggestion! If accepted the existence of India as a political unit is as good as extinguished. Pt. Nehru rightly rejected the proposal. "In the latest note from the Government of the People's Republic of China, emphasis has been laid on entire boundary never having been delimited. *That is a statement which appears to us to be wholly incorrect, and we cannot accept it.* On that basis there can be no negotiations[25]." (Italics are mine). However, the negotiations continued. The two Prime Ministers—the Prime Minister of India and the Premier of the State Council of the People's Republic of China—decided that officials of the two Governments should examine the factual material in the possession of the two Governments in support of their stands. The two official teams so designated met at Peking, Delhi and Rangoon and studied documentary materials in accordance with the decision of the two Governments. The proceedings of these meetings have been compiled into a book known as '*Report of the Officials* of the *Government of India* and the *People's Republic of China* on the *Boundary Question*'. On page 244 of this Report India's stand with respect to NEFA is briefly stated as:

> "The Indian side brought forward positive evidence to show that Indian political authority had always been exercised over the stretch of territory between the foothills and the main Himalayan range. The British Indian Government, which inherited this political authority from the Ahom rulers, exercised administrative control over these tribes in the same manner as over other Indian tribes—those in the North West Frontier areas of undivided India as well as those in the tribal areas in the heart of India. The Indian side showed how subventions were paid, and homage and tributes realised, through the Political Officers responsible for these tracts, in acknowledgement of the controlling authority of the Indian Government. Numerous undertakings were given by the Bhutias, Akas, Abors, Daflas, Miris, Mishmis and other tribes from 1844 onwards explicitly confirming their acceptance of the sovereign authority of the Government of India and promising good behaviour. To protect the distinctive features of tribal life, the Govern-

> ment of India restricted entry into these areas, and no one could cross the *Inner Line* without permission from the Government. A special form of administration was also developed for these areas......."

As expected the Chinese side declared that India's stand is untenable. "From the above analysis of the various categories of evidence provided by the Indian side, it is not difficult to see clearly that the area in the eastern sector disputed by the Indian side has never been Indian territory and the 'inner line' defined by the Indian Government throughout the years is in substance precisely the international boundary between China and India. It was not until 1914 that the so-called McMahon Line was illegally marked out through a secret exchange of letters, thereby showing this area within Indian territory. However, even up to the thirtees and forties of the 20th century the Indian side still failed to exercise authority in this vast area". (CR p. 147-148).

China persisted in her claim over the entire territory of NEFA less Tirap. Thus each side completely disagreed with the other and the negotiations have virtually ceased. Although the Indian leaders think, and rightly too, that India's case has been proved to the hilt, still there is no likelihood that China would vacate the areas of Indian territories occupied by her armies unilaterally. In spite of China's expression of good will towards India and vice versa the chances of an agreement or a treaty are very dim indeed.

Part II—Nefa Administration

What was happening to NEFA during this period? The British established, in 1912, Assam Rifles checkposts in the Lohit and Siang Valleys under the Governor of Assam and the jawans started patrolling these valleys up to the Tibeto-Indian border. The administrative void in Subansiri and Tawang was left for the Union Government to fill. After the recommendations of Mr. Haimendorf and Lt. Col. Baites the Subansiri Divisional Headquarters was established at Zero in 1949, and Tawang was brought under regular administration in February 1951.

The NEFA area was divided in two—the Western Section and the Eastern—each under the charge of a Political Officer. In 1911 these sections were named as Balipara and Sadiya respectively. In 1942, Tirap Frontier Tract was carved out of the latter, and in 1946 the former was divided into Se-La Sub-Agency and Subansiri Area. In 1948, the remaining portion of the Sadiya Frontier Tract was divided into two divisions, namely the Abor Hills and the Mishmi Hills. Formerly the Deputy Commissioner, Naga Hills administered the Naga Hills, but in 1951 it was formed into a separate district, and in 1953 named as the Tuensang Frontier District. Finally in 1954, the Divisions were given names of Kameng, Subansiri, Siang, Lohit, Tirap and Tuensang. In 1956 the last was amalgamated with the Naga Hills District and the area came to be known as the Naga Hills and Tuensang Area. The present Naga Hill trouble is entirely confined to NHTA. NEFA has nothing to do with it. It is through lack of publicity that the general public confuses NEFA and NHTA. These are separate territories with separate administrative machineries, though both come under the Assam Governor.

The North-East Frontier Agency is an independent administrative unit under the Foreign Ministry with the Governor of Assam acting as the agent of the President of India. The Governor is assisted by an Adviser and a full fledged Secretariat. The Adviser is assisted by many special Advisers, Assistant Advisers and Deputy Advisers. Of all these the Adviser for Tribal Affairs is very important. His official status is not clearly defined. Dr. Verrier Elwyn himself writes: "As Adviser for Tribal Affairs, I am not technically a government servant and this has made it possible for me to study the work of NEFA Administration with some objectivity[26]." The ATA receives his honorarium and is provided the full facilities of a super official when he visits the NEFA Divisions. He is supposed to assist the Adviser to the Governor at the same time, says he, he studies the administration with some objectivity! He has his Divisional Research Officers, one in each Division. These officers are supposed to be under the Divisional Political Officers but in actual practice they are directly controlled by the ATA; and they carry on their researches among the tribal people. In 1958/59 they were kept busy in writing accounts of various tribes. These monographs were published in 1960.

There are five Divisions and each Division is under the control of a Political Officer. The PO is assisted by the heads of various departments at Headquarters. The PO, the APO, the Area Superintendent, the Upper Division Assistant and the Lower Division Assistant belong to the Administrative Cadre, and each rank carries authority and prestige, the envy of the non-administrative specialists.

In 1954 a new Adviser took charge of the Agency. Side by side with this appointment Single Line Administration was also introduced in NEFA. This system is a replica of the army administration where "Administration is ordinarily discussed as the art of 'getting things done'[27]" and the Administrative planner plans for a thing assuming that it can be done. "His function is to assess the requirements of success, and the degree of administrative risk involved[28]." Therefore, the meaning and the task of administrative planning is to channel the entire administrative machinery towards achieving a specific and well defined aim. If extraneous considerations demand cognisance then these, instead of guiding the course of action should, rather must, accelerate and facilitate it to achieve the desired aim. Ordinarily, 'the achievement of an aim at any cost' is not a routine procedure in civil life. Indeed it cannot be, because the society is busy in multifarious activities channelled to achieve a number of aims, and if this principle—'to achieve an aim at any cost'—is applied then its (society's) entire structure will have to extend itself beyond its resources; it would not be able to stand the strain for long and it would collapse. This is what happens in an authoritarian state.

Therefore, the principle of 'getting things done' or 'to achieve an aim at any cost' is, in practice, only adhered to in an emergency and emergencies are not a daily occurrence. The Army's chief aim is to liquidate the enemy and all other objectives are subordinate to it. A soldier may me confronted with the enemy once or twice during his life or he may never have to face this situation. Even so every soldier is trained for years with this one aim in view—the annihilation of the enemy—until he is thoroughly disciplined, and has developed a sense of duty in the performance of which he might have to sacrifice his personal interests, and to kill or be killed in the process of achieving the aim becomes natural with him. There are various factors, most of them interconnected, which go to develop respect and *espirit de corps*, the former of which in many instances leads to the latter. *Espirit de corps* animates many to perform deeds of valour. Military Law is another important factor that goes a long way in inculcating the sense of security and assurance of fair play among soldiers. This agency is greatly dreaded by the recalcitrant elements.

In NEFA, as long as it was a social problem, no emergency existed so as to warrant the Single Line Administration. If there was one then certainly neither the administrative machinery nor the tribal people could stand its strain for six years—from 1954 to 1960—, unless a rot had set in in the machinery right from the beginning. In Single Line Administration it is imperative that every worker be as disciplined as an army soldier. Do the facilities exist for inculcating the army type discipline among the members of the NEFA staff? The NEFA government servants are like the other government servants in the rest of the country and they do not receive any sustained training for a long period to cultivate the required standard of discipline. They are recruited from all over the country and from every class and community to join the unfamiliar Agency and that too on temporary basis—80% of the APOs II were serving on temporary contracts in 1959, and quite a good percentage of them had served for more than four years. How one can expect that such government servants will develop self-respect or *espirit de corps* or loyal desire to serve under the NEFA Administration? In the army there are innumerable tiers between a soldier and the Chief of Army Staff strengthening discipline and discouraging any one from injuring the interests of his subordinates lest he invites trouble for himself. Injustice, in the normal course, is unknown in the army and Military Law and its procedure is such that nobody comes out of a Court Martial room grumbling or complaining. In NEFA on the other hand there are a very few tiers between a government servant and the Political Officer which are authorised to exercise disciplinary powers with the result that the future of the former hangs on the whims of the solitary PO. No doubt the army procedure is applied in investigating a charge and in holding a court as well, but it is very seldom that the victim gets a square deal. It is evident, therefore, that the prerequisites for Single Line Administration were not present and in any case there was no real need for such a system to be introduced in NEFA. If efficiency was the criterion in view then the attempt was a half-hearted measure.

Then it is proclaimed that the Single Line Administration avoids delay in execution of plans and inculcates co-operation. How far the development plans were executed will be shown later and regarding co-operation one has to meet the NEFA Specialists. The engineers arranged their exit from the NEFA Administration and the CPWD took them under its protection. The Forest Department comes entirely under the Assam State. Medical specialists are the only professionals who come under the control of the NEFA Administration. Now an ordinary clerk—Lower Division Assistant—can aspire to be a PO, but this is denied to the medical specialist; the LDA of today may be the future boss of the doctor tomorrow. This has created disaffection among the doctors and it is not unusual for a doctor to try to get himself transferred to the administrative branch and say good bye to his profession. In Kameng there were instances where an engineer and a doctor had opted for the said branch. The former was serving as an Area Superintendent and the latter as APO II. In the army the necessity of suppressing the official status of specialists and raising that of the fighting soldier would not arise, because, each specialist has his own corps and rank by virtue of which he has equal rights, privileges and opportunities for promotion along with his compatriots of the fighting arms.

In NEFA whether the Single Line Administration is beneficial to the locals is a doubtful point, but certainly the system does have its benefits. It provides good opportunities for praising the work of one's colleagues in literature sponsored or patronised by the NEFA Administration. Such praises are reminiscent of the British days. For instance Major John Butler went out of his way to praise the Governor of Assam in his book 'Sketch of Assam'[29]. The praise inserted by a junior for his superior must have created a good impression on the Governor. This tendency is prevalent in the NEFA Administration also, and it is accentuated by the Inner Line Regulations, because there is no chance of confirming or criticising the official version or of getting any adverse comments published in the Press for the general information of the public. The sole judges of the Administration are a limited number of high officials who naturally cannot afford to let any information leak out regarding the drawbacks of their Administration. Therefore, in the eyes of the public everything in NEFA and its Administration appears to be wonderfully good. The VIPs who visit a Division even for a few hours are so pleased that they praise the administrative officers on the spot to such heights that officials outside of the

Agency have started doubting the genuineness of such routine utterances. On the other hand the slightest disrespect shown by a junior towards his superior, or by a junior's family towards that of the senior, is likely to ruin the career of the junior. If there are instances of quick promotion there are instances of victimisation as well, though the former are known to the big bosses but the latter pass off unnoticed.

The Single Line Administration is also likely to give undue importance to NEFA officials. A PO is like a king in the Division and he is very unwise if he does not act in that manner. High officials when visiting the Divisions may be adored like national leaders and their photographs published in NEFA literature. Briefly the NEFA official class is so drugged with adulation that it would never advocate the 'open door' policy in the territory lest their privileges might be curtailed. The NEFA, therefore, must remain an inaccessible Shangrila for the public.

The Tribal Policy of the British in NEFA ran parallel to that which they adopted in Burma. Burma was divided into 'partially excluded' and 'excluded areas'. According to Mr. J. L. Christian "'excluded areas' are those whose inhabitants differ from the other peoples of Burma in kind of civilisation, and where an almost complete reversal or abandonment of tribal customs would be necessary before they could be incorporated into the political life of the remainder of Burma[30]." In spite of wide social contacts indicated by the previous history of the people of NEFA, the region for all practical purposes was kept and treated as an 'excluded area'.

Whether in British times, it was for ease of administration or for keeping the people divorced from the political current flowing in the country or for satisfying the desire of a few officials to keep the tribal folks happy by leaving them on their own, the fact is that the people were forgotten and there was neither any regular administration nor any definite policy for administering the area. We have to fall back on the administrative areas of tribal people of Assam to read the British mind. Haimendorf has outlined the British policy of administering the Nagas and it is not wrong to assume that had the British stayed in India they would have pursued the same in NEFA also.

> "Government's policy has been to avoid any sudden disruption of Naga culture, respect tribal custom where it does not prejudice the maintenance of law and order, and tamper as little as possible with the old village organisation. The ousting of the products of village crafts by foreign imports is discouraged, and government interpreters are indeed forbidden to wear Western clothes. With their land closed to traders, money lenders and land-hungry settlers from the plains, the Nagas have been saved from the exploitation which has caused the ruin of so many aboriginal tribes in other parts of India. Respect for the old order has, however, not meant a policy of *Laissez Faire*. The Naga has been given security, cheap and effective justice within the spirit of the tribal law, hospitals and dispensaries, a good many schools and improved communications. Not, it is true, motor roads which would not benefit the tribesman, but good bridle-paths with bridges crossing all major streams[31]."

Government of India's policy of administering the tribal people is the policy of Pt. Jawaharlal Nehru, the Prime Minister and is enunciated by Dr. Elwyn, "a missionary of Mr. Nehru's gospel[32]", in his 'A Philosophy for NEFA'. It has been framed from the Prime Minister's various utterances and applied for the benefit of the tribal people. The present policy of the Government of India is not very much at variance with the policy outlined by Mr. Haimendorf above.

1. Jawaharlal Nehru's Speeches, Vol. I, 1946-49 p. 26
2. Gates Introduction p. ii
3. Hamilton Hindustan Vol. I p. xxiv
4. JASB 1894 Vol. LXIII Pt. III p. 28f
5. India and Pakistan by O. H. K. Spate p. 552
6. Census Report 1931 p. 50f
7. India Wins Freedom: An Autobiographical Narrative by Dr. Abul Kalam Azad p. 183
8. Mahatma's Correspondence with the Government 1944-47: Forword by Sri Pyarelal p. xxix
9. Azad p. 183
10. Mahatma Gandhi by H. S. L. Polak, H. N. Brailsford, Lord Pathic Lawrence: Chapter xxiii p. 313
11. The American Record in the Far East 1945-51 by Kenneth Scot Latourette
12. Azad p. 207
13. The "Pioneer" February 25, 1960
14. In Two Chinas by K. M. Panikar p. 129
15. In Two Chinas by K. M. Panikar p. 102
16. White Paper III p. 96
17. White Paper II p. 39
18. Nehru's Speeches 1950
19. Most of the World Edited by Ralph Linton p. 797
20. Tibet and Tibetans by Shen & Liu p. 52

21. K. M. Panikar p. 112
22. K. M. Panikar p. 175
23. White Paper I p. 73
24. White Paper III p. 80
25. White Paper III p. 83
26. Dr. Verrier Elwyn Preface to Second Edition
27. Administrative Behaviour by Herbert A. Morison p. 1
28. Lindsell's Military Organisation and Administration, 27th Edition
29. Sketch of Assam by John Butler p. 13
30. Modern Burma by John LeRoy Christian p. 106
31. The Naked Nagas by Christoph Von Haimendorf p. 561
32. Dr. Elwyn Preface to Second Edition

CHAPTER VI

The Nefa Divisions and the People

"When we talk about tribal people, I wonder whether we all have the same idea in mind. So far as I am concerned, we are all tribals, whether we live in Delhi or Madras or Bombay or Calcutta or in the hills or in the plains. To call some people primitive and to think of ourselves as highly civilised is basically wrong.......... There are differences between people living in the hills and the people living in the plains. Geography and climate account for differences of food and clothing and living conditions. That is inevitable .... But I am sure that to think of the tribals and non-tribals as people qualitatively different is wrong ....[1]."

Jawaharlal Nehru

"In the foothills between the plains of India and the mountain ranges of Tibet lived a number of primitive and savage tribes. Quarrelsome, treacherous and riddled with suspicion, they were continually at war with one another. They regarded strangers as welcome only as possible victims of extortion by pacific or violent means, or as allies from whom they might obtain weapons with which they could massacre their neighbours more efficiently than with their simple implements of death[2]."

F. M. Bailey

It is established beyond doubt that the tribal people of NEFA, historically, had social contacts with the Assamese, and their segregation was effected by the Inner Line Regulations of 1873. At the same time it does not mean, and it is impossible to conceive that under such geographical and climatic conditions as exist in the Northern and Eastern Tracts of NEFA, the culture of tribal groups developed uniformly. Their cultural differences were marked by natural barriers; the greater the barrier dividing two groups the more the cultural differences between them. The Lohit, that is the Brahmaputra, the greatest barrier, divides the Northern Tract from the Eastern Tract and also the culture of the Mishmis from that of the Nagas. Then in the Naga Hills, river valleys and thick virgin forests divide the Naga society itself into innumerable clans proportionate to the number of natural obstacles, each clan developing in isolation from the other. Similarly in the Northern Tract, the rivers Subansiri and Kameng isolate the Dafla Hills from the Abor Hills on one side and from the Monpa country on the other and are thus responsible for a Dafla culture which is different from Abors in the east and of the Monpas in the west. Therefore, it is natural that the Agency area is inhabited by a large number of groups differing in social habits and culture and probably in their racial heritage as well. In this chapter the main tribal groups will be described.

The political Divisions of NEFA more or less coincides with the group divisions of the people. There may be an overlapping of tribes (in areas contiguous to the inter-Divisional boundaries) but it is not so serious that it warrants repetition in the chapter very often. As the tribal groups differ among themselves so do the NEFA Divisions, each having its own characteristics.

Tirap Frontier Division

In 1954 the Tirap Frontier Division was given its present name, after the river that flows through it. It is surrounded by Lohit Frontier Division in the north, Burma in the east, NHTA in the south and Assam in the west. Its main approaches are from Sapekhati, Namrup, Naharkatia and Margherita railway stations. In fact, at the present moment, it is the most easily accessible region of NEFA. Khonsa (4,500 ft.) its Divisional Headquarters is connected with Margherita on one side and Naharkatia on the other by a motorable road recently constructed by the Administration with the help of the locals.

The Margherita-Khonsa road is jeepable and after about four miles run it enters the Tirap hills. It touches the northern fringes of the local coal mine and zig zags its way to the tribal region where with a keen eye one notices villages perched on the tops of isolated hills and screened by luxuriant foliage from the observer's view. The country is covered with large trees, beautiful ferns and evergreen creepers. The atmosphere is damp but the area is conspicuously devoid of springs and rivulets. Thus the country has very few bridges. When a bridge has to be built the engineers find an acute scarcity of stones and suitable sites for abutments. From Margherita to Khonsa, a distance of about 70 miles, the road crosses only one nullah and that too near the Divisional Headquarters. After passing through Khonsa, situated on an open piece of land, the road passes through Borduria, Boga Pani, Jungli Camp, and Jaipur. If one wishes to see the thickest forests of India then he should break journey at Jungli Camp and should trek to Namsang via Deomali Camp, the Conservator of Forest's Headquarters. The visitor may not find game to his liking but he will be interested in seeing herds of elephants and may step over a female python hatching her eggs under the perpetual shades of the giant trees.

Changlang and Nuisa are the sub-Divisional Headquarters of Tirap. The former is about 34 miles from Margherita on the main road, while the latter is situated in the south-west corner of the Division and is also connected with Khonsa by a 45 mile road constructed during 1958-59.

The Khonsa-Nuisa road passes through the Nocte villages of Lebnan, Toopi, Lonju, Kapoo and Baira, and then the Tisa valley, a veritable hell, infested with all sorts of flies, mosquitoes, lizards and reptiles. From Tisa to Nuisa, a distance of 22 miles, there is only one water source at Sinua Camp, and that also dries up in the summer months. Probably the denudation of forests is responsible for such a water scarcity.

Apart from the two roads described, every administrative Headquarters is connected by porter tracks constructed and maintained by CPWD. In the Naga Hills foot slogging is most uncomfortable. Gradients are steep; mud, slush and reptiles are on the ground, insects are in the atmosphere, the tree trunks are thorny and there is no spring water to drink. These things are enough to try the strongest nerves. This is why marching stages here are fixed for intervals of 8 to 10 miles only.

In the north-east corner of the Division is the Pangsu Pass, which has played an important role in the history of Assam. It was this Pass through which the Ahoms, the Khamptis and the Singphos entered India and influenced the Assamese culture. It was through this Pass that the Burmese Army, in waves, invaded Assam and coloured the Assam Valley with the blood of thousands of Assamese men, women and children. Then again during the Second World War the Indian Army marched through the Pass to roll up the Japanese forces from north to south.

Though the area is covered with tropical forests, it does not appear as sinister as that of Deomali. Here a shikari usually can get a shot at a panther or a deer. On account of the slight altitude of the area the climate is also not particularly uncomfortable. This is the only Division of the Agency where the Nagas* form a major portion of the population. Besides them there are other minorities like the Singphos and the Tangsas who inhabit the area bordering Burma.

The Nagas of Tirap are divided into two endogamous groups—the Noctes (12,000) and the Wanchoos (20,000)—united in culture and descent. In 1226 they were the first to oppose the invasion of Ahoms and they paid heavily for it. They were the next-door neighbours of the Ahoms whose punishments were barbaric and who felt happy to see the heads of their enemies piled up before them. The ruled learnt what the rulers taught. "Widespread burning, scalping, and killing became the order of Indian warfare, but in this the Indians only did as the white man did[3]", writes Baldwin while describing the characteristics of Indians of the USA. Therefore, we cannot blame the Nagas for their head-hunting propensities if we take the harshness of the Ahom times into account.

During the Ahom period the Nagas used to be enrolled in the Assam army and they owned allegiance to the Ahom kings. In the British Era Capt. Bordie[4], in 1842 and 1844, was the first to visit the Nagas of Tirap. There were other administrators also who visited the tract. Out of them Peal[5] was quite notable. The Nagas' prolonged isolation, forced on them by Patkoi in the east and a belt of about 20 miles of thick forests in the west has deve-

* Naga is derived from Nok which means a man in one of the local dialects. Gates p. 300.

loped a recklessness of life and indifference to physical comforts in them. They appear to be free of wordly worries; their cheerful and gay attitude is reflected in their dances for which they decorate themselves elaborately. "Like most savages, the Naga seems to aim to make himself look as hideous as possible, and their dances at times of festivity have solely that object[6]", observes Peal. Others would call such decoration a manifestation of love of colours and hence of art. Constant living in the company of nature and the forest has made them fearless and shrewd hunters. Once I watched them laying a ring round a small herd of deers. While working on the Khonsa-Nuisa road in the Tisa valley a group of Wanchoos spotted the herd. The news went round the surrounding villages and by 11 A.M. the entire male population of the area assembled with their shining 'daos' and rusted guns to encircle the patch of forest where the animals had been spotted. By 2 P.M. they started closing the circle. The sight was so frightening that even a tiger would not dare to break the ring and like a lamb would surrender for the slaughter. I was told that the hunters would not break off for the night untill they had killed their prey. Having done that they would, according to the Naga custom, share the flesh of the animals among the participants of the hunt. The Nagas would not miss the chance to kill an elephant even. It is only Government restrictions that are preserving the massive animal in the Tirap forests today. The Hoolook, a monkey of Assam that walks on his hind legs like a human being is the only quadruped that escapes their notice, because of sentimental reasons.

The Nagas live a community life. If one house is destroyed by fire then the whole village works for repairs. Of course during such emergencies the Government grants

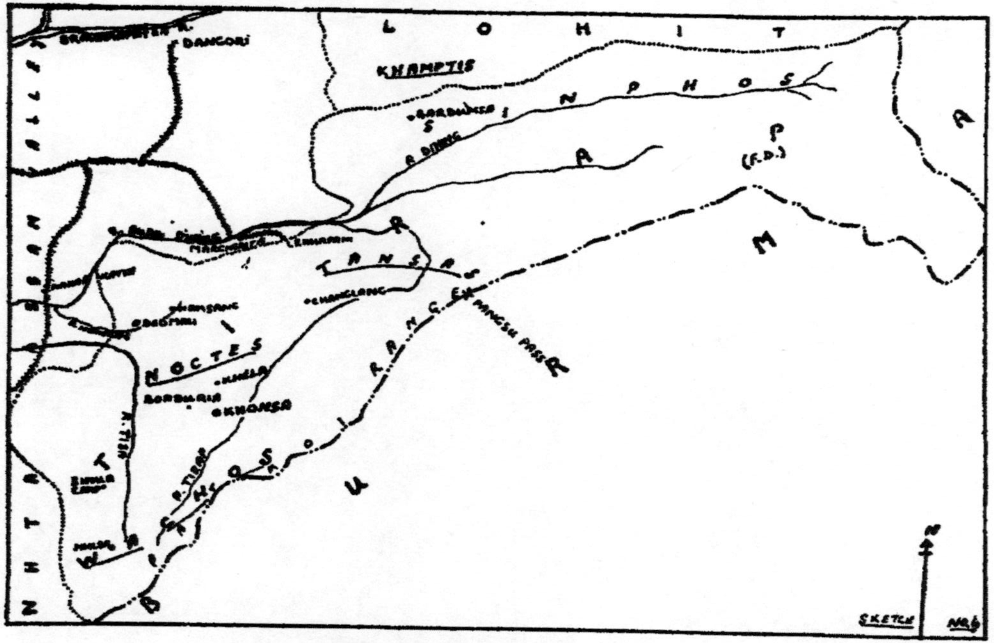

TIRAP FRONTIER DIVISION

SINGPHO GIRLS OF BORDUMSA
In their working dress

A NOCTE COUPLE FROM THINSA

IDU MISHMIS WITH THEIR FAMOUS LEATHER BELT SLUNG ACROSS THEIR BODY LIKE 'YAJNOPAVIT'

a substantial sum for the construction of the new house. Naga villages are big, each having more than 300 houses. They are congested and there have been instances when the blaze of a single burning house engulfed the entire village. The size of a house varies with rank; a chief's house is seldom less than 300 ft. in length. Boys and girls before puberty sleep in the parental house. When matured they go to sleep in the respective village dormitories called 'Morangs'. The Nagas, like most of the tribal groups, are vertically divided into various clans and marriages cannot be contracted within the clan. Therefore, there are as many 'Morangs' as there are clans in a village, and each youth knows where to sleep for the night. For instance a young man knows where his sister sleeps and he will not go there. At night the boys go to the giris' dormitories and may stay there up to cock crow in the morning. It is wrong to believe that a boy can sleep with a different girl every night and that the girls make free love with many boys. The boy knows his girl and vice versa. If a girl becomes pregnant then marriage between the couple is considered auspicious for future happiness. Some laxity is permissible in the society before marriage. After marriage fidelity is the general rule. VD and other diseases resulting from laxity of sex are unknown among the Tirapians. Monogamy is popular but there are cases where chiefs have more than one wife. After marriages couples build their own houses and land for their subsistance is allotted by the village chief. If the bridegroom happens to be the eldest son then he may continue to stay with his parents, otherwise he has to make his own arrangement for his living.

The life of a Naga is very busy. The Naga women wake up first in the morning and prepare the meal for the family. Having eaten their morning meal they immediately proceed to the fields carrying cooked rice and 'lao pani' (rice beer) for the midday meal. They work in fields while their menfolks perform hard jobs, for instance cutting trees in the forest and hunting for food. After finishing the outdoor work the family returns home in the evening and again the women cook the last meal. Thus the Nagas have three meals a day.

Each Naga clan is ruled by its council, and no important measure concerning the welfare of the clan is undertaken without the consent of the elders. But the Naga chief wield considerable powers in deciding matters of life and death and the punishment of offences committed by any of his clan. A village has a minor chief; a few villages organise into a unit and come under a great chief. Thus the chiefs of Borduria, Namsang and Ninu are great chiefs and some times are addressed as Rajas. The Government appoints gamburas as the village leaders. They are not very popular among the people.

The Noctes come in contact with the plains more frequently than the Wanchoos, therefore, they are changing faster. They are Vaishnavites and the Goswami of Baraghar Sattra, near Nazira, is their religious teacher. He pays them a regular annual visit. They do not drink milk and profess not to eat beef. They have started lending their milch-cows to government dairies and official on hire.

Among the Wanchoos the women of good birth (chiefs' families) are allowed to wear their hair long while others have to shave their heads. The former do not work outside in the fields and spend their leisure in embroidery work. Probably these customs are a legacy of slavery among the Wanchoos. It is surmised that only slave women worked in fields, and they were not allowed to wear long hair because of the danger of a hair falling into the food served by them to their masters.

Although the mainstay of the Nagas is agriculture, yet they are poor agriculturists. They practise shifting cultivation and practically all of their available land is used up, especially in the Wanchoo area, where the situation has become alarming. The Naga Hills in the Tirap Frontier Division experience scarcity of food during the rainy season.

Tangsas, though few in number, are a promising community of Tirap. They migrated to India from Burma a few centuries ago and even today they maintain contacts with their relatives across the border. They are intelligent and enterprising. Agriculture is their mainstay and they practise, where possible, wet rice cultivation. They also grow edible fruits and have started taking contracts and opening general merchandise shops. Many of their girls are studying in schools and colleges in the plains and have married into Assamese families. Their staple food is rice supplemented by pork, beef and fowl. The use of opium is prevalent among the Tangsas, and those who live near the Patkoi Range cultivate the drug. They also grow tobacco for local consumption. They are industrious and their women are good weavers. Gams, the government appointed village officials, act as the village chiefs. Among the Tangsas monogamy is in vogue and divorces are unknown.

Like the Tangsas the Singphos (2,500) are new commers to this country. They are the Kachins of Burma. They migrated to India in the later half of the eighteenth century and settled down in the area presently occupied by them in the vicinity of Bardumsa in the north-east corner of the Division. Capt. Neufville[7] in 1826 was the first officer to visit them. He found them warlike and aggressive. The Singphos were considered the Afghans or the Pathans of Burma in the 1880s, but by the end of the 19th century they started showing signs of deterioration. Now their degeneration is complete, and they are a decadent race. Their mainstay is agriculture and they produce sufficient rice to sustain themselves. Like the Tangsas they bury or cremate their dead according to the status of the deceased. Their Gams look after the administration of their villages. "The Shan is the written character used by the Singphos .... they write on leaves and a peculiar kind of paper[8]." From this we know that the Singphos had their own script, but now they have forgotten it. They are Buddhists and practise polygamy and abhor infanticide. Inheritance laws are peculiar in the Singpho society in that only the eldest and the youngest sons inherit and the intermediate sons get nothing. The eldest inherits the estate and the family title, while the youngest receives the movable property and goes off to found a new settlement.

Lohit Frontier Division

Located in the north-east of India is the Lohit Frontier Division. Two mighty rivers, the Brahmaputra and Dihong, water it. Three fourths of Lohit is mountainous and is sparsely populated. Geologically it is the most sensitive region of Assam. Lt. E. A. Rowlette visited it in 1845 and wrote: "........ and the landslips on some of the mountains appear of such magnitude that the fact of a village being occasionally swept away may not be wondered at and I was told that the village of Macrus was so destroyed last year, and that many of its inhabitants together

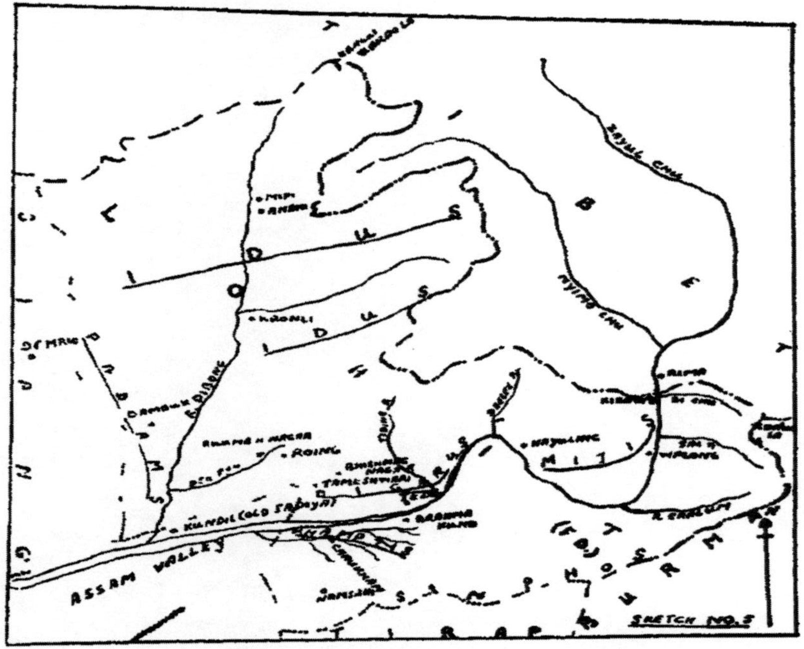

LOHIT FRONTIER DIVISION

with the chief of the village were involved in the destruction[9]." In recent times, in 1948, Minuatang, a village in the Lohit Valley, was buried under a huge landslide; Mr. Campbell, the APO and more than 1,000 people lost their lives. Then, the colossal loss suffered by the Division in the 1950 earthquake is not forgotten by the Lohitians. One year and a half after the debacle, on February 17, 1952, the abutment of the Tiding Bridge then under construction collapsed killing three men and injuring 9. The latest tragedy is that of the Airipani landslide in the Dibong valley claiming an Assistant Engineer and his party; in all 52 men were buried under the debris in May 1958. The new track leading to the Indo-Tibetan border out-post bypasses the site. Because of its geological failings, Lohit is a highly disturbed area and the earth here is constantly shaking requiring special material* which can absorb such constant and ceaseless shocks for road construction. It is said that in the United States of America such material is available but its cost is prohibitive for India.

The Division is terrritorially divided into two administrative units—the Lohit Valley and the Dibong Valley—with Headquarters at Tezu and Roing, each being connected with Kundil (Old Sadiya) by motorable roads. People of different races have migrated into the Division from Tibet, China, and Burma along the river valleys from the north, and through the Pangsu Pass from the south-east. In this Division one finds the remains of an ancient civilisation, in ruined city sites, stone defence works, tanks etc., now entirely buried in the densest forests imaginable. It is this Division through which a national highway leading into China passes. The British wanted

*USA used such material in rebuilding Sanfrancisco, a seismic town.

to explore this direct route to China, and in this quest many British adventurers undertook the journey to Rima. The national highway leading to Rima more or less runs along the Lohit river. It is motorable up to Lohitpur, beyond which one has to march. After passing through Denning and Hayuling the highway reaches Walong beyond which going up to Kibithoo, the frontier outpost, is very difficult. On the border the Lohit river is crossed by a rope-way which tests the nerves of the user.

Apart from this national highway another porter track running along and parallel to the Dibong Valley leads to Anani, an outpost near the Indo-Tibetan border. There is a lateral track also which joins the Lohit and Dibong valleys in the north. There are many small tributaries of the two main rivers—the Lohit and the Dibong—along which local village tracks run.

This historic Division is populated by the Mishmis, the Khamptis, the Singphos and the Padams.

The Mishmis in appearance are 'almost like Aryans' from whom they trace their descent and they take pride in expressing pro-Indian sentiments. Lt. Wilcox[10] in 1827 and Wm. Griffith[11] in 1837 visited the Mishmis and described the people as friendly and inoffensive. As late as 1907 Noel Williamson[12] when dealing with the China route along the Lohit writes: "........, the whole route lying through a country occupied by a quiet, peaceable people, who at present look to us as the paramount power, and from whom we may expect nothing but obedience; a people amongst whom no trace of Tibetan influence is found." Unfortunately the Mishmis, like any other people of Assam of those days, were averse to any foreigner visiting their hills. Lt. Rowlette in 1845 recorded that the Tibetans of Rima "were prohibited by their own government from visiting the plains of Assam[13]", and probably these instructions were passed on to the Mishmis who under such compulsion could not permit foreigners to enter South-Eastern Tibet through their country. Because of this attitude, whether natural or imposed, they sometimes violently opposed the intrusion of foreigners and jealously guarded their seclusion. Father Kirk once travelled to Rima and returned to Assam safely. Again in 1854 in the company of another missionary, Bouri by name, he trekked to Tibet through the same country i.e. the Mishmi country. This time both the missionaries were murdered near Rima. This cold blooded murder gave the Mishmis a bad name. All of their good attributes were forgotten and their shortcomings were magnified. Even the Ten-Year Brochure[14] lukewarmly upholds the foreigners' opinion : "These fascinating but wayward people created a bad impression on the early travellers who were never tired of speaking of their dirty appearance and rude manners but who curiously enough overlooked their physical charm. The Digaru and and Miji women posses great physical beauty ;..........". Dr. V. Elwyn had read adverse remarks pertaining to the Mishmis before he visited their hills. He wrote : "I had read this and when I first went into this wild country it was frankly with some apprehension. Within a few days I discovered the curious fact that these old botanists, administrators and traders seem to have had something wrong with their eyesight. Not one of them had even bothered to say that the Mishmis were beautiful[15]." So the present official trend is not to contradict the writings of the previous adventurers but to divert the attention of readers to the beauty of the Mishmis and their women, a fact which had been recognised by Shahabuddin[16], Cooper[17] and others as well. Col. Dalton, a friend of

Tribal people, writes about M. Kirk's episode: "......but unfortunately in his journey across the mountains he gave dire offence to an independent Mishmi chief, called Kaisa, refused to submit to his extortionate demands and making a circuit to avoid passing through his territory. The incensed savage armed, followed the party to Sammeu, and in utter disregard of the authority at Rima attacked and murdered the two priests, carried off all their property as plunder, and their servant Singpho as a slave[18]." Later the servant was allowed to return to his village. Dr. Elwyn[19] refers to another murder of a Hindu Sadhu, Parmanand Acharaya, but the purpose of the mendicant's visit to the country is not mentioned. Kintup, a British agent, and all other explorers entered Tibet in those days disguised as Sadhus and Acharaya probably was one of them. It is not uncommon for secret agents to have to pay the penalty of death for the mission they are employed on, and Acharaya was not an exception to the rule.

There are three territorial divisions of the Mishmi tribe—the Chulikatas or the Idus (20,000) of the Dibong Valley, the Digarus or the Taraons (11,000) of the foothills of Tezu, and the Mijus (14,000) of the east and remote north of the Division—each differing from the other in minute details. The Mijus and the Digarus let their hair grow long, and twist it into a knot, secured on the top of the head by a wooden pin, while the Idus cut their hair around their heads in a peculiar fashion. On account of eating and smoking opium the Mijus and the Digarus are not so physically strong as the Idus who are more warlike and virile.

The Mishmis are a quiet, industrious and inoffensive people. They are good weavers and keen traders. They bring aconite, teeta and musk to the plains for sale. The

A PADAM COUPLE FROM MEBO

APA TANI VILLAGES

'mithune', a hill bison peculiar to NEFA, is their wealth and with it they buy as many wives as they can afford. Like the Daflas, the son inherits his father's wives, barring his own mother. Their weapons consist of bows and arrows, a dao or heavy chopper blade, a spear and a knife. The Mishmis are good hunters.

In some respects Hinduism has influenced the Mishmis. They have a separate house for woman's period of confinement; after delivery, in case of a boy, the mother stays in it for ten days and, in case of a girl, for eight days. The poor burn their dead or throw the dead bodies into a river. The eldest son takes the title of gam, or chief, and holds a yearly feast in honour of his deceased father. The Mishmis believe in a god of destruction, the equivalent of Siva or Mahadev of the Hindus.

The Mishmis rarely commit crimes. However, if need arises, an assembly of gams collected from distant villages acts as a court. Since the advent of the Administration, serious cases are dealt with by the POs. In the past the crime of adultery, provided it was committed without the consent of the husband, was punished by death.

The Mishmis who form a majority of the Divisional population lead an isolated life in the hills, where their villages often consist of one house only. The provision of adequate medical care and implementation of village water supply schemes and so forth is naturally difficult under these circumstances. Probably similar difficulties in undertaking social work among the Mishmis prompted Capt. Dalton[20] to try to induce them to congregate in selected villages on the banks of the Brahmaputra, but without success. With the same idea in mind the present Administration has started an experimental pilot project of a model Mishmi village at the 19th mile stone on the

Kundil-Tezu road, where some of the villagers had actually volunteered to start a new life together in a place where better facilities for help can be afforded by the Administration. At the same time, the Administration has been careful not to impose any change in their original way of life on people who do not wish to come down from the hills. The Administration hopes that the new model village will be a success and that others of the tribal people who see it prosper will themselves wish to concentrate in more accessible community centres.

The Khamptis (5,000) inhabit the Chaukham area in the south of the Division. "To speak of the Khamptis as a tribe is to do them little justice, for there is that about the word tribe which conveys the idea of wilderness and want of culture, very far from forming a characteristic of the Khamptis, far from some of their social laws even civilised nations might take a lesson[21]", writes Cooper.

The Khamptis are tall, fair and handsome. They are good agriculturists and through their ingenuity use water power for their own advantage. In 1958 they had dug about eight miles of irrigation channels and in January, 1959, they constructed a dam across the rivulet passing through Chaukham, the biggest Khampti village in the area. The dam was supposed to provide irrigation to more than 500 acres of land thus converting the village into a food surplus area. The better class of Khamptis indulge in the 'elephant' hunt, a sport which consists in isolating and lassoing a young animal. They unlike other groups have no scruples about the drinking of cow's or buffalo's milk. They eat the flesh of every animal, but as Buddhists, they do not like to kill an animal with their own hands. They practise polygamy but very few have more than two wives. Among them the gam, or village

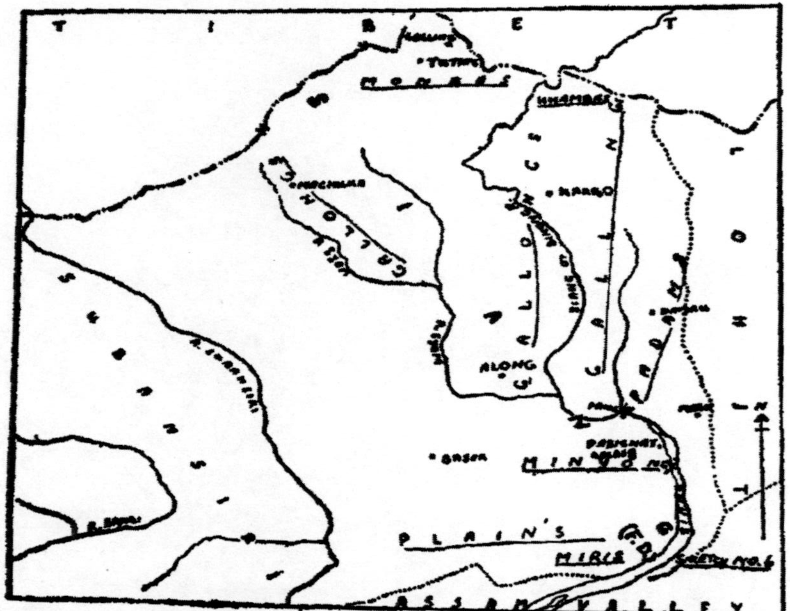

SIANG FRONTIER DIVISION

chief, commands their respect but certain aristocratic families have more influence and prestige in the community than he has.

Padams (3,000), a branch of the Adis, who will be described under the Siang Frontier Division, inhabit the south-western portion of the Division. A few hundred families have come down to colonise a couple of villages on the Kundil-Roing road.

The Singphos (500) who have been described under Tirap are next-door neighbours to the Khamptis.

Siang Frontier Division

The Siang Frontier Division is said to be "a sleepy hollow in which appear to be crystallised the civilisation of Tibet and the customs of Bhutan in a modified form[22]." It is in this Division that the Tsangpo river—'one of the noblest rivers of the world'—after making a sharp bend to the south enters India from Tibet and assumes the name of 'Dihong' or 'Siang'. The Siang Frontier Division is the largest of all the Divisions of NEFA. There was once a proposal to reorganise it into two divisions with separate and independent headquarters, one at Along and the other at Pasighat. The Dihong river forms the geological boundary between Siang and Lohit; the hills on the left bank are more prone to landslides than those of the right bank. As in Lohit so in Siang road construction, on account of loose soil, torrential rain and instability of the hills, is difficult.

Pasighat, a Sub-Divisional Headquarters, was, previous to 1950, connected by a motorable road with Assam. The Inner Line restrictions previous to independence were liberal and many of the non-tribals—the Marwaries, Nepalis and Biharis—came and permanently settled down in

Pasighat. They added variety and interest to the life of the town. Foreign Christian missionaries also came and opened a religious centre. They translated the Bible into the Adi language, the language of the people, written in Roman script. Under the present policy of the Government the missionaries are no longer there but they have left their influence among the inhabitants. In addition various State officials visited the town and persuaded the people to adopt modern methods of agriculture. In 1933 the first agriculture inspector came to Pasighat and pointed out to the people the benefits of permanent cultivation. The people, who had been noticed by Needham[23] in the 1880s planting orange trees, listened to the advice and experimented on it. They succeeded. The impact of outside influence, the missionary work and the interest of the State in developmental activities had a beneficial effect. After centuries of static life the people moved. Unfortunately the Second World War broke out and India diverted her energies towards its prosecution. Pasighat became a routine problem, but the people kept up the tempo of progress. The War ended and India attained independence. With the new era the Inner Line restrictions were tightened and the NEFA Administration started development work behind this artificial barrier undisturbed. Nature grudged the progress and the 1950 earthquake caused colossal damage to life and property. It wiped out the old road thus isolating Pasighat from the plains. Up to August 1959 it was accessible from Dibrugarh by air.

Along, like Pasighat, was linked with Dibrugarh by air. It was also connected with Pasighat by a footpath running along the right banks of the Dihong and Syom rivers and passing through Pangin, an administrative centre twenty miles east of Along and a meeting place of the two tribal groups—the Gallongs and the Minyongs.

The Division has established important administrative centres at Machuka and Tuting in the north, at Bassar in the south and Damru in the east; each centre is connected by porter tracks constructed by the CPWD. A jeepable road has been constructed to connect Bassar with Along. In due course it is planned to connect Bassar with North Lakhimpur by a motorable road, thus extending the Assam North Trunk Road to an Administrative Headquarters in Siang.

The Adis (69,000) are a proud and freedom loving people. They are suspicious of outsiders and they never allowed the Monpas and Khambas of the north to come down to the plains of Assam. The word Adi covers a number of tribal groups, the main ones of which are the Minyongs, the Padams and the Gallongs.

The Minyongs inhabit the territory west of the river Dihong extending up to Pangin. They are intelligent, industrious and dignified. The men have taken to trousers or shorts and shirts, while their women dress in a petticoat and a jumper like the Burmese. They have given up the use of earrings and beads and they cut their hair short. Their mainstay is agriculture and they practise wet cultivation of rice, where possible. In 1954 in the Balbek—six villages of more than 250 families—the area under permanent cultivation was 400 acres, but in 1959 it was 1100 acres. During the winter of 1958/59 the group produced 11,000 mds. of surplus rice which was sold in the market. They also plant fruit trees. One is amazed to see the plantations of citrus fruits, bananas, jack fruit, pine-apples, mangoes, pears, plums, guavas, betel nuts, peaches and leechees. Here the forests are also rich in edible fruits.

Whenever there is a scarcity of rice the people live entirely on jack fruit which grows wild in abundance. They live in village groups, each village being connected with the other by bridle paths well maintained. Bamboo pipes have been laid to bring clear water to the villages for drinking purposes. They have started constructing separate latrines, but in the absence of alternative arrangement pigs and fowl continue to do the work of scavengers. The villages are administered by 'Kabangs' (Panchayats), one in each village, the deliberations of which are held in 'Mosup'—the boys' dormitories—and are open to men only, though women may attend them as witnesses. On account of cultural influence of outsiders the people living in the foothill area have abolished the 'Rosungs'—girls' dormitories. These dormitories still exist in the interior in Minyong and Padam villages. In a village group the representatives from each village form a 'Bongo' to decide inter-village feuds. 'Bongos' and 'Kabangs' are democratic institutions and have potentialities of developing into local-self Government. The NEFA Administration is introducing such bodies in areas where no village government or authority of the people exists.

The Minyongs are divided into various exogamous clans, and marriages are arranged by parents of a prospective couple outside their respective clans. In the foothills polygamy and divorces are discouraged, but they are still practised in the interior. The family life is happy, stable and contented. The Minyong have a religion of their own. They acknowledge and adore one Supreme Being as the Great Father of all and believe in a future state, "but on this question their ideas are undefined, and it is probable that some of them are derived from the Hindu. I have heard them speak of judge of the dead,

A MINYONG COUPLE FROM BALEK

GALLON GIRLS FROM PANGIN

but as they gave his name as 'jam', they were no doubt thinking of 'yama' of Hindus[24]."

The Padams, the Bor Abor or 'Great Abor' of the Assamese, are concentrated amidst a net-work of rivers. The area is bordered by Dibong in the east and Dihong in the west. During the rainy season the area is completely cut off from the rest of the Division. This isolation has made the people physically stronger and less sophisticated than the Minyongs; therefore socially and culturally they are the same.

The Gallongs inhabit the Syom Valley and its surrounding area. Unlike the Minyongs their men and women do not cut their hair short. The men wear cane hats and the women dress in Mekhla (an improved form of petticoat) and Eri (silken) chadar like their Assamese sisters. Apart from slight differences in marriage customs, construction of houses and dialects, the Gallongs resemble their cousins—the Minyongs and the Padams.

Pasighat is the social and cultural centre of the Adis. It is situated on the western bank of the Dihong against a background of green hills and blue sky. Here the river debouches from the hills to enter the plains and adds to the beauty of the local landscape. Pasighat, on account of its moderate and healthy climate was rightly selected as the training centre for NEFA services; here doctors, agriculturists, village workers and other specialists attend refresher courses. Till 1958 Pasighat High School was the only school in NEFA where children of all the tribals of the Agency were educated. Now that the institution has been raised to the status of a multipurpose school, it will still continue to attract students from other parts of the Agency. This gives the institution the prestige and the students are proud of it. In fact their pride has made them restive. Social and cultural contacts with other students of the country will widen their outlook and transform their activities into that sobriety which is so essential for intellectual maturity.

Subansiri Frontier Division

This Division is named after the river Subansiri which roughly forms its eastern boundary. The Division is cradled in the Himalayan ranges which are geologically of recent origin. Its main entrance is from Kimin, an outpost of the Administration in the foothills fifteen miles from North Lakhimpur. The Division gained importance during World War II when the Government of India realised that it was politically and strategically unsound to leave a power vacuum on the frontiers of India. Slowly and gradually administration was introduced into the region. This entailed the necessity of establishing communications both by air and by land. Dropping zones and landing grounds were constructed at suitable places to link the Division with the country for supplies and other official requirements. The Government endeavoured to supply the Division by land, but the nature of the terrain, loose soil and heavy rainfall distributed throughout the year proved too difficult to permit the construction of a motorable road, although that would have helped in bringing down the cost of material imported from the plains. Up to the 1940s road construction in the area was considered as impossible, but the Army Engineers at the cost of 18 lives—1 officer, 1 jco and 16 OR—constructed a jeepable road (on dry days one ton Land Rovers can also run on it) connecting Zero with Kimin from Jan, 52 to May 58.

The road, just after leaving Kimin, enters the hilly

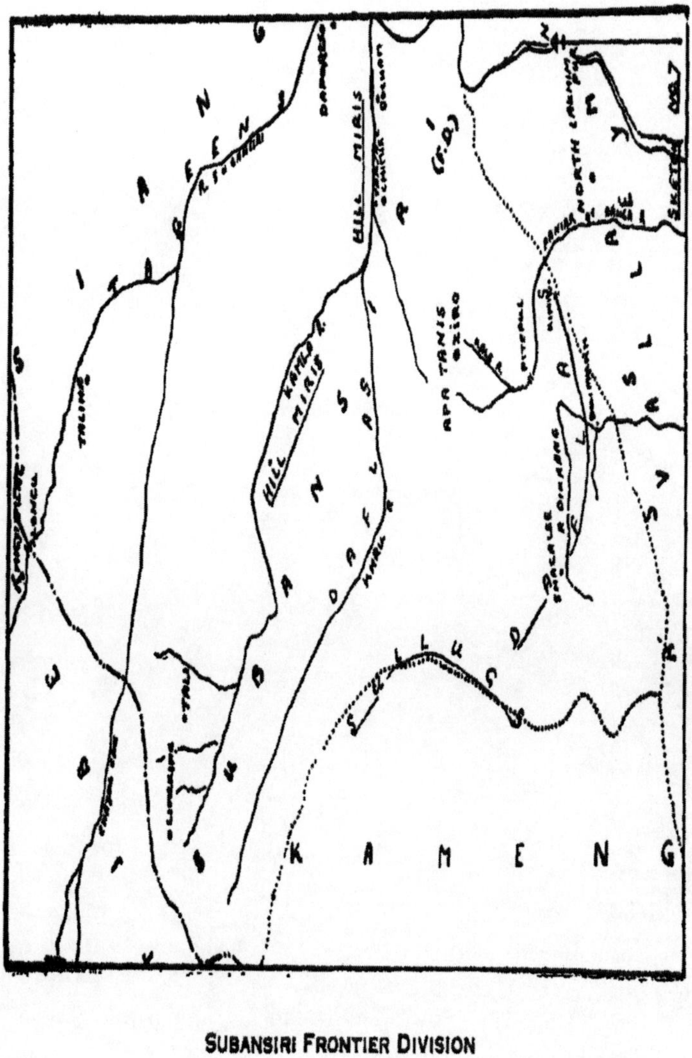

SUBANSIRI FRONTIER DIVISION

tract and after about four miles reaches 'India Gate'—a point named by soldiers. From here the road runs down-hill to the Ranga (Panior) valley and after crossing and recrossing the river enters into a region of steep gradients and virgin forests. From the 10th mile the notorious Ranga gorge commences and solid rocks wall the banks of the river continuously for more than two miles. This is the portion which claimed most of the army casualties and which must have been a death-trap to the road builders. Along this stretch the visitor notices stone after stone set up on the rocks on which the names of the deceased soldiers are engraved to remind the visitor of the immensity of the task performed by the Army Engineers. The driver's narrative of the accidents that caused the heavy loss of life creates respect and affection for the Army in the heart of the visitor. After the 12th mile the traveller arrives at an open piece of land where a camp is located. The visitor starts thinking that the worst is over. After a couple of hundred yards' drive he is disillusioned. From the 13th mile the driver still in low gear, 4-wheel drive, and the vehicle starts creeping up and up turning bend after hair-pin bend on a steep gradient continuously for about two miles. The driver heaves a sigh of relief. He has driven through the most treacherous portion of the road where overhanging boulders dangerously loose threaten danger. After the 15th mile, except for steep gradients, the road is reasonably safe and the vehicle runs monotonously along the southern bank till it reaches the 27th mile where it finally crosses the river by a bridge named 'Pite Pul' 8. The scenery changes from the 31st mile and the climax of its beauty is reached when the traveller approaches 'Zoram Hill'—nine miles short of Zero. The visitor continues to enjoy the landscape for about two miles after which the vehicle enters a belt of dense forests and finally emerges to enter the Apa Tani plateau, a drained-off swamp at an average height of 5,000 ft. studded with terraced rice fields well irrigated by an intricate system of channels. The monotony of the plateau is broken by islands covered with bamboo and pine groves peculiar to the region well nursed and lovingly looked after. The plateau looks like an extensive farm where nothing has been left to chance and where every inch of ground has been brought under the control of man for his own use. The people who have attained this mastery over nature and have made this plateau an oasis of beauty in the wilderness of Subansiri are the Apa Tanis.

The Apa Tanis (9,000), also called the Ankas, because their faces are tattooed, live in seven villages located on the plateau. The very fact that such a large number of tribal people are concentrated in this small area and supported by only twenty square miles of cultivable land indicates that the Apa Tani is industrious and intelligent. He is always busy whether he is in the fields or in the village. He lives not only for today but for tomorrow also. He plants bamboo and pine groves for his children and grand children. For his other needs he has reserved forests on the periphery of the plateau. He claims that his forefathers came from the north and brought the bamboo and pine to the region. There seems to be some truth in this, because these trees are seen growing in abundance in the colder regions of Kameng where the Monpas reside. The Apa Tani values everything of Tibetan origin specially the 'devghanti' (dev means god, ghanti is a bell), the 'evthali' (godly salver) and the 'beads'. He wears his hair long and ties it into a knot on his forehead. A male Apa Tani is distinguished from the other tribals of Subansiri by a red tail of plaited cane which he habitually wears round his waist; while an Apa Tani woman can easily be marked from distance by the wooden nose plugs worn in each nostril. A tattoo mark on the chin of an Apa Tani also distinguishes him or her from the other tribal people.

The Apa Tani is energetic and business-like. His mainstay is agriculture and he produces enough rice* to buy himself mithunes, pigs and other luxuries of life unknown in the Division. In spite of his complex and intensive system of cultivation he has not taken to bullocks and ploughs. His villages are planned and streets orderly. Polygamy is not banned among the people but very few have more than two wives. Their women share equally in the out-door work in fields with their men and have substantial freedom in running the home. Apa Tani youths are good acrobats while the women love to spend their leisure in weaving.

It is strange that the Apa Tanis surrounded by warlike people survived and developed a civilization of their own. They neither have village chiefs nor very often listen to their elders; they are too individualistic and do not like to be told what is good or bad for them. Then who leads them and what is the structure of their society?

---

* Haimendorf writes (Himalayan Barbary p. 60): "On the former the stubble of the previous year's crops sprout in the spring. and the same plant bears fruit in two or three successive seasons". This is not so. In Subansiri only one crop of rice is sown and reaped every year. Stubbles are left in those fields which are not very productive and need manure. The stubbles serve as manure. However, they are also removed when their purpose is served. I have consulted agriculture experts. They pointed out that the yielding of more than one crop by a rice plant in Subansiri is neither possible nor ever heard of. Apa Tanis also show ignorance about the fact stated by Mr. Haimendorf.

Apa Tanis are divided into two endogamous classes, one the 'Mite' or upper class, and the other the 'Mura' or lower class ; each class is again vertically divided into exogamous clans ; every 'Mura' clan is attached to and dependent upon a 'Mite' clan. The villages and their streets have been laid clan wise, each clan occupying its own quarters. The clan representatives known as 'Buliangs' form the village government which has the social sanction of the community. If there is a feud between two individual this body does not interfere. But as soon as the feud takes a form which might disturb the peace of the community the village government intervenes and makes sure that the conflict is settled to the satisfaction of all. This indicates that the Apa Tani, though an individualist, lives for the community. The community is the centre round which he lives and dies. On the same principle every boy and a girl becomes a life member of a 'patang' (club) from earliest childhood. This gang works in the fields of individuals who provide the members with meat and drink. Thus an individual who has very few helpers gets his work done by the 'patang' at a nominal cost. In this way the Apa Tanis have survived and remain progressive.

To this the Daflas and other tribal groups of the Division present a complete contrast.

The Daflas (5,000) inhabit the west and north-west of the Division. They have always been known for their turbulence and very often used to raid villages in the plains. During the British rule punitive expeditions were sent against the Daflas as a reprisal for their depredations. Their villages of Zoram, Lika and Tale invariably used to be the objectives of these expeditions. The Daflas though short in stature are physically the strongest of all

A GROUP OF APA TANIS

SULLUNG GIRLS

A Hill Miri Woman of Tameng Wearing a Small Petticoat Made of Filament Extracted From Cane

the tribal people of the Division. They are virile, self-reliant and love out-door life. They are short tempered and seldom accept the decisions of their elders for the settlement of feuds. They are pastoral and live on forest products and herds of mithunes. They are slowly taking to agriculture, in fact those who live in villages near the Apa Tani plateau have taken to terrace and wet rice cultivation. Like the Apa Tanis they also claim to have migrated from the north. The Daflas are not contour minded and negotiate a crest by marching straight up to the top. Their villages are small but cleaner than those of the Apa Tani's and are located on steep slopes. They have forgotten their dances if they ever had any and have no special aptitude for art. They love to attend weekly bazars in the plains and they march down in large groups. They are expert in cane work and build durable cane bridges across the rivers that criss-cross the Division. Among the Daflas polygamy is prevalent and it is not uncommon to see a man having more than four wives. The women population does not appear predominant and there is no practice prevailing in the community of destroying male children. Probably the balance of population of both the sexes is either maintained by polyandry which is said to be in vogue among the poor or by youths of poor means not marrying at all. Age is no bar for marriage and the more prosperous the man is the more wives he collects. This has created a serious problem in their society. The children of unwanted wives and deserted husbands are the worst victims of this cruel practice. They find it beneficial to declare themselves as orphans, because, with such pretensions they are entitled to admission in Government schools where they are assured of free accommodation, rations, clothing, education and also humane treatment. The percentage of such orphans in Subansiri is the highest in NEFA.

The Daflas as a whole are not united, but groups of villages form loose alliances and unite in times of danger. Their village councils give judgment in local feuds. Generally the decisions are not strictly executed and the aggrieved parties approach the Administration for final settlement. Therefore, one notices the Administrative Headquarters always crowded with Dafla litigants. The Administration is encouraging the establishment of 'Kabang' type bodies to settle local feuds among the Daflas.

The Sullungs (600), locally known as Chulus, inhabit the north-east corner of the Division. They are said to be the original inhabitants of the Division. They, on account of their small number, used to be harassed and often taken as slaves by the aggressive Daflas. The introduction of Administration from India has benefited them most and now they are gradually becoming free of the bondage of their masters. Except for their social status they resemble the Daflas and probably in due course they will be assimilated by the latter.

The Hill Miris (3,000) also known as Onka Miris, inhabit the area east of the Apa Tani plateau along the Kamla valley. Angus Hamilton[25] considers that 'Hill Miri' is a misnomer, but in the absence of a better term it stays. Many of the Miri families have social relations with the Assamese resulting in an admixture of blood and race. This has softened the features of many and some of the Miris are very smart and handsome. Generally the Miri women are fair and charming. They wear their hair long neatly combed and parted in the centre and hanging down their backs in two carefully plaited braids. They wear a small petticoat made of filaments, extracted from cane, and woven together. The Miris are very fond of wearing enormous quantities of beads made of porcelain. Like the Daflas they practise polygamy and polyandry. They are agriculturists and plant fruit trees. The Miris are the only people in Subansiri who perform community dances in their festivals. They speak a dialect similar to that of the Abors but do not differ much from their cousins—the Daflas—in many of their social customs and habits. The Miri country lies off the beaten track, therefore, very few people visit them. Capt. Dalton[26] visited the Hill Miris in 1845 and then we heard of the Miri Mission[27] in 1912 which reached up to the Khru valley. Haimendorf[28] and Col. Baites[29] were the last British officers to visit them, in the last decade of this century. The Hill Miris were never known to have harassed the plainsmen though they never allowed the northerners, the Tibetans, to come down to the plains. They live in small communities under hereditary chiefs. Sometimes a family gains sufficient influence and prestige in the community to *ipso facto* assume the powers of the chief. These people have recently come under the Administration proper and a Base headquarters has been established at Tameng on the western bank of the Kamla river. Tameng has great possibilities of developing into an important communication centre; here the tracks to Taliha, Daporijo, Gocham and Zero meet.

The Divisional Headquarters was established at Zero in 1949. In 1959 it was to be shifted to Habuli in the southern corner of the Apa Tani plateau. The Administration is handicapped by the fact that the supplies and material required for development schemes still have to be imported by air and so are expensive. The pressing need of the Division is a good motorable road connecting the Administrative headquarters with the plains. The present jeepable road needs improvement. It is up to the Army Engineers either to construct diversions where considered necessary and possible or to connect 'Pite Pul' by a new road with Dui Mukh, an administrative centre west of Kimin.

Sub-Divisional headquarters have been established at Daporijo and Nyapin in the interior; these headquarters have sent outposts to Tali, Taliha and other places in the north near the Indo-Tibetan frontier. Every administrative centre is connected by porter tracks with the Divisional Headquarters. The further development of these tracks into jeepable roads remains to be accomplished.

Kameng Frontier Division

This Division is the western half of the Balipara Frontier Tract and is named after the river Kameng which flows through it and at places forms its boundary with Subansiri. The Kameng Frontier Division suddenly came to prominence on March 31, 1959, when the Dalai Lama made his entry into India. The Division is accessible from Misamari, Rangpara and Tezpur railway stations. Foothill, an outpost of the North-East Frontier Agency about twenty five miles from Rangapara, guards the entrance to Bombdi La, the Divisional Headquarters. The Indian Army Engineers constructed the Foothill-Bomdi La Road up to the 45th mile and handed it over to the CPWD in 1958. Since then the Assam Rifles Pioneers and about 1500 locals representing every tribal group in the Division have completed the remaining portion of 25 miles and connected Bomdi La with Foothill. The road passes through favourable terrain and is likely to develop into a national

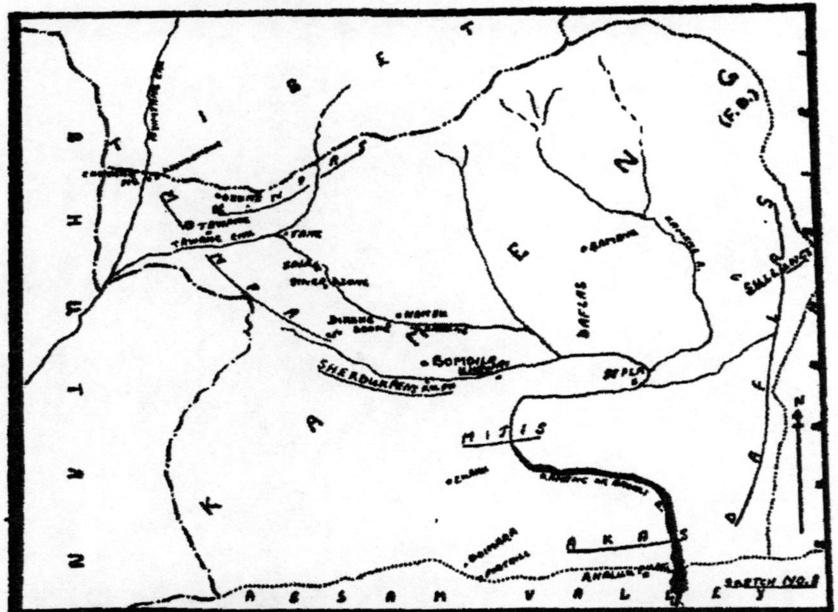

KAMENG FRONTIER DIVISION

highway at least up to Senga Dzong, about 40 miles from the Divisional Headquarters on the way to Tawang. When fit for vehicular traffic it will help in bringing construction material for the development of Bomdi La, which is already a communication and trade centre of the Division, into a first class hill station of Assam. At present Defence requirements are such that the development of the Division cannot be delayed. In fact the Division is already considered to be the best developed unit of the Agency and is prepared to hasten its material progress. Kameng has three sub-divisions known after the names of their headquarters, viz., Sep La, Bameng and Tawang, each administered by an APO. On account of political developments in the border areas and the prosperity of the Division one cannot be too sure of the administrative set-up or of the rank of the POs in charge of the sub-divisions.

Sep La is situated on the western bank of the river Kameng about 75 miles east of Bomdi La. Its climate is hot, moist and unhealthy. On account of heavy rainfall and loose soil, road construction is difficult and the use of animal transport is gradually being introduced into the area. Further development of communications both by land and air will mitigate the hardship of foot slogging over a primitive track of about 75 miles.

Bameng is located in the north-east corner of the Division at a distance of 80 miles from the Divisional Headquarters. The topographic and climatic conditions of the sub-division are slightly better than those of Sep La Bameng is connected with Bomdi La and Sep La by porter tracks which are capable of further development.

Tawang is the proudest of all the sub-divisions of Kameng. It boasts of the biggest monastery in the whole of the Buddhist India constructed a few years after the birth of the sixth Dalai Lama in a nearby village. It accommodates more than 600 Lamas. On February 12, 1951, Major R. Khating, the then APO, brought the region under regular Administration and established a sub-divisional headquarters. Slowly and gradually Tawang developed into an important administrative centre on the slopes of the northern bank of the Tawang Chu which flows east-west across the sub-division. There are three tracks in the sub-division that lead into Tibet. Two of these cross-pass at more than 18,000 ft. which remain closed from January to May every year. The third passes through Chutangmu, a frontier checkpost, located near the Indo-Tibetan boundary about 45 miles from the sub-divisional headquarters in a river valley at a height of about 5,500 ft. This route is open for traffic throughout the year. It was by this route that the Dalai Lama made his entry into India. Tawang is connected by a good bridle-path (up to August 1959) which runs along the Gangri valley in its initial stages and the Tawang Chu in the final and passes through Rahung, Dirang Dzong, Nykma Dzong, Senga Dzong—villages in a picturesque setting against the background of green fields and snow covered mountain ranges—and Se La (14,500 ft.), the beauty of which is enhanced by the presence of two lakes embedded in the lap of the pass itself. Human habitation in the sub-division is seen up to 11,500 ft. beyond which the hills are clothed in the green and white garb of firs and snow. The climate of the region is temperate and the soil fertile.

The Monpas (34,000), commonly known as Bhotias in the Assam Valley, inhabit the Dirang Dzong Valley in the centre and the Tawang area in the north and north-west. A trek through the Monpa country reminds one of the Central Himalayan scenery where oaks, multi-coloured rhododendrons, pine, and fir trees greet the eye; animal transport, local labour, dry soil and stones (the mean annual rainfall of this part is about 40 inches), and noisy rivulets are a familiar sight. As one approaches a Monpa village he notices the Man-ne, the Kakaling—the village gate—, the prayer wheels and flags, stone-built houses, the village monastery located outside the village, yaks and Dzos—a cross between a yak and the domestic cattle—well-cultivated and irrigated fields, bridges and well-kept bridle-paths.

The Monpas are tall and fair, with Mongoloid features. They dress in loose robes of scarlet colour that fall in folds around the waist. They are a simple and mild people who keep sheep and goats for wool, and yaks and and ponies for transporting merchandise. Like other places in the Himalayan regions the yak, which yields milk, butter and meat for local consumption, is a very useful animal for the people. The Monpas are prosperous and have a zest for life. Their staple food is tsampa (barley sattu) and they drink China tea mixed with salt and butter. They respect authority and show indifference to non-official visitors. Their women are plain but look prosperous. They are fairly good artists though their mask dances tend to be monotonous. They attend winter fairs at Udalgiri, Devangiri and Godam in the plains for trade. Their chief domestic implement is the famous dao of NEFA which is seldom used as a weapon.

A Monpa village is administered by a council of elders who are generally elected after specific periods differing from locality to locality and from rank to rank. For instance, in Senga Dzong the village chowkidars who are members of the village council are elected after every three months while the Gambura's term is one year; these periods may differ entirely in other villages. The council holds its meetings in the village Dzong (or fort) built and maintained by the village community. The Monpas are disciplined people and obey the commands of their councils cheerfully. Marriages are arranged by parents and are generally successful. Polygamy is prevalent among the well-to-do classes but none has more than two wives. Polyandry is in vogue in some of the border villages where people of Tibetan extraction reside. Monpas have adapted Buddhism to suit their convenience. They eat meat but do not kill an animal. This has created the butcher class which is considered of lower social status in the Monpa society.

The inhabitants of the Dirang Dzong—Namsu area are also called Bhotias and in fact they are Monpas differing, on account of the warm climate, from the people of Tawang in dress only. The clothes of the former are of silk and cotton, while those of the latter are of wool.

Sherdukpens are mainly concentrated in Rupa, Jigaon and Shergaon in the Daphla Koh Valley. They are Buddhists and observe many of the Monpa social customs. During the winter season they migrate to Doimara, a settlement in the foot-hills. From their dress, social and religious habits we can assume that they come from the Monpa stock. Unlike the Monpas their 'pams' (plots of land prepared for cultivation, and equivalent to the 'chhana' of the interior Garhwal or the 'chhanni' of Kumaon) are always located at long distances from their villages. The hard struggle for existence has made the Sherdukpens clever and business-like. Sherdukpens used

MONPA LADY STUDENTS OF CIPTC

WANCHOO EMBROIDERY WORK

A DAFLA WARRIOR FROM THE WILDS OF EASTERN KAMENG

AN AKA AND A MIJI YOUTH
(Not easily distinguishable)

to hold Khawas as their slaves, but now this practice has ceased.

"The tribes on the border of Durrung are generally called 'Paschim' (Bangni) or Western Daflas, and those on the border of North Lakhimpur, 'Tagin Daflas'[30]." Even today the Daflas (50,000) of Kameng prefer the name of 'Bangni' and the people of the Upper Subansiri Valley (3,000) that of 'Tageens'. The Daflas have already been described under the Subansiri Division. Sullungs who are in an insignificant minority have also been dealt with. In addition to these, the Akas, the Khawas, and the Mijis also inhabit Eastern Kameng.

The Akas who trace their pedigree from the Asura kings of Ancient Assam are akin to the Daflas differing only in dress and dialect. Mijis are the next-door neighbours of the Monpas, the Daflas and the Akas. They are more refined than the Daflas; they try to dress like the Monpas and intermarry with the Akas. Because of the resulting admixture of blood it is very difficult to distinguish an Aka from a Miji. The Khawa population is about 500 spread out in five or six villages in the vicinity of Rupa. This tribe has benefited immensely by the introduction of the Administration.

The people of Kameng are very co-operative and are taking full advantage of the institutions established by the Government for their welfare. In fact there is a growing demand for such institutions and as a result the Middle English School of Bomdi La has recently been raised to the standard of a High School. The credit for this 'will to progress' can be attributed to the Monpas who on account of their culture and prosperity are respected and imitated by the rest of the people of Kameng. Though the children of the Monpas, who are Buddhists, begin schooling very late, yet they show a keenness for learning unmatched in the Agency. They are little gentlemen and are worthy to be the future leaders of their community. It is surprising that in this age of greed and competition the Monpa children are not very much enamoured of government employment and generally want to go back to village life after finishing their school education. It is a good sign for the economic stability of the community and the Division. How the present stress will affect the Monpas will be interesting to watch.

The above description entails the inescapable conclusion that each Division has its own characteristics. It will serve very little purpose to lay a uniform policy and similar priorities for all the Divisions to develop simultaneously. The need of Tirap is food and more food, and food production should be given top priority. In Lohit the Mishmis are encouraged to migrate to allotted areas. Capt. Dalton, in 1845, also tried to persuade the Mishmis to come to the plains to colonise selected tracts of land, but he failed. There are more chances of Mishmis not leaving the hills—however rugged, barren, and unstable they may be—than of their coming down to the plains. In that eventuality a vast area of forested land lying unoccupied should be utilised for the advantage of the nation*. There are a few Gorkha families living as far as 18 MS on the Kundil-Tezu road and there are others who are cultivating the land on the left bank of the Lohit in the Khampti area. Either the number of these colonies must be increased or the Inner Line be

* It is pointed out that in the Brahmakund area—about 5×2 square miles—there are fruit plantations which give a clear indication that up to very recently the region must have been colonised by Sadhus or by those who seek solitude.

pushed inside to pass through Roing, Tezu, Parasuram Kund and Namsai and the area so set free be handed over to the State for reclamation. In Siang the Adis are a well-organised community. They are prosperous, intelligent and progressive. Their 'Kabangs' and 'Bongos' are quite capable of further development into regional self-government. The area of responsibility of these institutions may be widened to embrace an entire community of Minyongs or of Gallongs or of Padams. The Adi youths are already showing signs of unrest. They feel that they are the most intelligent, prosperous and progressive of all the people of NEFA. Their claim may not be far wrong. However they should be brought in contact with their brother students outside to give them a better sense of proportion. Siang being a frontier Division, is a sensitive region and yet full of possibilities. At this stage it may not be feasible to give the Adi youth training in handling fire-arms by raising a NCC battalion, but some opportunity must be given to them to creditably exhibit their achievements to the outside world. This will offer them better standards for competition and progress. Including them in visiting parties for Republic Day celebrations is not enough. Coming to Subansiri and Eastern Kameng, the problem is not very complicated. Welfare centres have not yet been established in the upper Kamla valley and the Khru valley for want of porter tracks. Lack of communications is holding up the progress of the Division. Therefore construction of roads and airfields will be welcomed by the people of the tract. Western Kameng is fortunate to have the Monpas as its inhabitants for they have an interest in life and are as keen as anybody else in India for more and more of economic and cultural development.

1. Pt. Nehru's Speeches Vol. III p. 458
2. F. M. Bailey p. 16
3. The Adults' American History by Baldwin—1955 p. 30
4. JASB 1845 Vol. IV Pt. II p. 329
5. PASB 1869 and p. 78
JASB No. 79 July 1838-47
Capt. Hanney p. 452
6. JASB 1872 p. 17
7. AR Vol. XVI 1828 p. 338f
and JASB 1900 Lt. Col. Waddel p. 39
8. Sketch of Assam by Butler p. 80
9. JASB 1845 p. 478
10. AR Vol. XVII p. 316f
11. JASB 1837 p. 327
12. The Geographical Journal Vol. 34 December 1907 p. 365
13. JASB 1845 p. 486
14. 10 Years' Progress in NEFA. A Brief Account of Administration and Development Activities in North-East Frontier Agency Since Independence. Independence Day, 1957.
15. Dr. Elwyn 6. 21
16. Ibid
17. Cooper p. 183
18. Ethnology by Dalton p. 23
19. Dr. Elwyn p. 21
20. Report on the Province of Assam by A. J. Muffat, Appx. J ixxv
21. Cooper p. 145
22. MASB Vol. V Pt. II—Abors and Gallongs p. 87
23. JASB 1900—The tribes of Brahmaputra
by Lt. Col. L. A. Waddel, IMS p. 15
24. Ethnology by Dalton p. 25
25. Angus Hamilton p. 84
26. JASB 1845 Vol. XIV Pt. I p. 250f
27. Angus Hamilton—The Abor Jungles p. 69
28. Himalayan Barbary by Haimendorf
29. The Hidden Land, by
Ursula Graham Bower
30. North East Frontier by
MacKenzie. 26 January 1884 p. 97

CHAPTER VII

SOCIAL HABITS AND CUSTOMS

"In studying communities in Mexico (or India) it is important that the anthropologist should become a student not merely of the single community but of the region and the nation as well. The anthropologist must be sufficiently versed in the more important historical, geographical, economic and cultural characteristics of the region and nation to be able to place his community in relation to each of them, and to indicate just what the community is representative of in the larger scene[1]."

McKim Marriot

For the general public, NEFA has been a ghost to be dreaded and this trend is continuing. We are told that if the tribals are photographed then their religious susceptibilities would be disturbed, while Col. Waddel[2] was surprised when he was asked for a few coins after photographing some Abors during the close of the last century. I myself did not find any tribal unwilling to pose for a picture. Then we are told that we should not refuse drinks offered by the tribal people. When Capt. Dalton[3] visited the Hill Miris in 1850s he flatly refused the drink offered to him and the Miris were not only not offended for the refusal but they took it with good grace. Anyway the practice of offering drinks, in spite of the patronising attitude of some of the visitors, is fast dying out. Similarly much has been written in recent times about the social habits of the tribal people so as to give the impression that they form a special group of mankind subject to peculiar and primitive practices. I have not studied any literature written by a non-Assamese or non-Indian where the social and religious practices of the tribals have been shown as the natural and evolutionary rituals of the hillmen in general and of the Assamese in particular. I have studied this matter in detail and have come to the conclusion that the tribal people of NEFA are similar to their brethren of the Himalayan States and of Assam, if not of the whole of South-East Asia. Because of this conclusion, their social habits and customs have been discussed as evolutionary traits rather than as isolated instances prevalent only in this forbidden land.

The tribal people of NEFA, in their social behaviour, are the Ahoms of yesterday and their development runs parallel to the rulers of Assam. In spite of differences in minor details many of their customs and traditions are common throughout NEFA. Each tribe is endogamous and is divided into various clans i.e. they are communities within a community. Their society is patrilineal and polygamy is in vogue among all the groups. Polyandry is also practised among the Daflas, the Hill Miris, the Gallongs and the tribes bordering India and professing Buddhism. Though caste does not exist among the people, the society is divided into nobles and commoners among the Nagas, the Apa Tanis and the Monpas, and into slaves and freemen amongst the Mishmis, the Adis, the Daflas and the Hill Miris, neither class marrying into the other. A 'Mite', or patrician among the Apa Tanis, will not marry a 'Mura' or plebian. There is no untouchability in NEFA and no sweeper class exists there. The people are fanatically attached to their land and forests. Generally their index of wealth is the 'mithune'. In marriage they pay a bride price, and they pay fines in the settlement of crimes and local disputes. At one time all the groups practised slavery and even today this social curse is not completely obliterated from tribal society. Lastly each tribal group conducts trade with its neighbouring states, the Wanchoos and the Tangsas with Burma, the Mishmis, the Abors and the Monpas with Tibet in the north and Assam in the south, and the tribals of the foothills with the plains of Assam.

Once polygamy was in vogue amongst all sections, except the Christians, of the country. It is discussed here in conjunction with Assam so that polygamous practices as prevalent in NEFA may not appear peculiar and primitive to casual readers. Shahabuddin[4] in 1662 wrote that in Assam polygamy was in vogue and women were sold. Major Vetch[5] confirmed that women relatives were sold and Cooper[6] thought that amongst the Assamese marriage was not binding and divorces were easy to seek, although of course, adequate provision used to be made for the children before the divorce. There was laxity in marital relationship and both sexes exercised equal freedom in such matters. Pakhari Gabharu, the wife of Jayadhwaj, had the distinction of becoming the chief consort or mistress of three Ahom Kings. Under these circumstances polygamy among the tribals is not a peculiar custom, but it is creditable to them that both the sexes maintain absolute fidelity after marriage.

Polygamy as a harmful institution is prevalent only among the Mishmis and the Daflas. Among the former its ill effects are not very noticeable to the casual observer. Probably a Mishmi weighs his financial position thoroughly before he enters into a matrimonial alliance and after marriage he tries to make it a success. This is not the case with the Daflas. Among them marriage alliances are loose; wives are neglected by husbands and vice versa. On the least pretext a cleavage between a husband and his wife occurs, resulting in misfortune for the children. Agreed that freedom exists for both sexes to separate but woman being the weaker of the two suffers more than the man, and the Administration and the people themselves are aware that there is an agitation among Dafla women against the atrocious treatment meted out to them by their men. Even thus, so far no attempt has been made to ameliorate the condition of the woman. Many women have left the Dafla country and may be leading a miserable life in the plains. The Government has prohibited the removal of boys and girls up to the age of 20 years from the tribal areas. If that ban were lifted today then quite a number of youths would find their way to the plains. Children are a national trust and primary consideration should be given to their welfare rather than to the older people. Half-a-dozen schools and a restricted number of free-studentship for the declared orphans will not solve the problem. The evil is suicidal for the community and it should be terminated immediately. Complacency in this matter is not only suicidal to the Daflas but it is also harming the national interest. It is strange but true that the political jamadars (junior officers) and interpreters, all tribals, are the worst offenders in misusing the practice of polygamy. Some of them have ten wives and aspire for more. Such polygamous government servants are never found on duty. They are always busy in attending their ailing wives or children; this is quite natural in a large family. Apart from neglecting their duties, which are proverbially nominal, these people are setting a bad example to their fellow tribals. It might have been political expediency to continue to keep such degenerates in government employment in the past, but now the Government, being in a stronger position, is dispensing with the services of polygamous government servants elsewhere. Expediency must be replaced by a sense of justice and fair-play for the weaker sex.

Slavery is another common practice the existence of which in a Free India appears not only primitive but criminal. Its form may not be that of industrial labour imported into the Southern States of U.S.A and other production centres in the Atlantic or Pacific in the past, and its hardships may not be as severe as described in such novels as 'Uncle Tom's Cabin', yet it is not comfortable to be a slave in the North-East Frontier. Here one would not mind the practice if he happens to be the owner of the serf, because he is supposed to receive, according to tribal beliefs and superstitions, the same number of slaves in the next life as he has in the present one. A perpetual luxury! The unyielding and unproductive terrain of the Himalayas induces one to want such a luxury, and it is no wonder that NEFA is afflicted with this social disease. Two examples will illustrate the fate of the victim of slavery and the official attitude towards it.

1. The father of Chulu-La, a Sullung, was the slave of the father of Taba Poa, the gambura of Sekh village about 30 miles from Kimin. Both the old men died leaving Chulu-La (CL) as the slave of Taba Poa (TP). The latter bore all the expenses for the former's marriage. Five children were born to the married couple, out of whom three duaghters survived. After some time CL died and his entire family became the slaves of TP. According to the statements of two grown-up daughters—Chulu Yemi and Chulu Yagmu—their mother along with their youngest sister had been kidnapped from the house

of TP by a Sullung from the interior and they, the older girls, were then given a beating by TP. The girls left the village and after crossing a thick belt of virgin forest in the foothills, were on their way to an unknown destination until they were apprehended by the Assam Police at 23 MS on the Assam North Trunk Road and sent back to Kimin. After a week's waiting, the PO arrived and restored the girls to TP in accordance with the current policy, with the instruction that he would withdraw the girls from the guardianship of TP if they were cruelly or unjustly treated by the latter. TP won the case and was naturally happy. Were the girls happy? Among the Daflas girls generally get married or at least engaged by 16 years of age, but these Sullung girls, though of proper age, were not even engaged.

2. Tassar Yuga was the slave of Tassar Tir, a Hill Miri Yuga was married and had a son and a daughter. After the introduction of Administration he gave a few mithunes to his master and thus bought his freedom. As a free man he along with his family moved to a hut outside the village. One day he was attacked by Tassar Tir and other Miri villagers. He and his wife were beaten and his children kidnapped. He and his wife went to appeal to the PO at Zero about 35 miles from the village. The PO was out on tour. The couple returned to the Base Headquarters at Tameng. Unfortunately the Base Superintendent was also out on duty and the couple had to return to their hut 9 miles from Tameng, disappointed. Later on I was told by the Miris themselves that Yuga might have to give a few more mithunes to get back his children. If he could not, then the mother would continue weeping over her lost children.

There are innumerable instances of the kind—some of

which have been quoted by Dr. Elwyn—among the tribal groups of the Northern Tract. No matter what arguments are advanced to uphold the practice or the indecision over taking steps for its abolition, it is high time that Government of India took up the cause of slaves and helped them to regain their freedom. In NEFA there is a public fund for the restitution of the slaves but progress in securing the liberation of these unfortunates is very slow. It needs to be accelerated.

A tribal will never commit murder for material gain. Constant association with nature, and segregation from the progressive section of Indian society has made him suspicious, short tempered and short sighted. He is sensitive and has pride in his traditions. Any remark which he feels is a slight against him or his traditions may invite his fury and in his unbalanced state he might commit murder. The Abors murdered Noel Williamson and Dr. Grierson in 1911, because a Miri interpreter aroused the former's suspicion against the latter's designs; the Tagins massacred more than 70 troops including one Major of the Assam Rifles in 1853, because the party intruded into the Tagin area without sufficiently notifying the purpose of their visit. There are other instances when a few tribal individuals threatened Government officials with violence on the suspicion of a foul play. The Administration is cognisant of tribal whims and fancies and tries to avoid introducing measures which may arouse suspicion among the locals.

Regular Administration has been functioning in NEFA since 1947 and now the tribals have grown to appreciate the Indian point of view also. I talked to many tribal people and I invariably found them comparing their views with plainsmen's views on any subject. It is surprising that in spite of continued segregated living the tribal is quite an intelligent inhabitant of the Himalayas. His power of expression and discussion of a subject is remarkable and he is not incapable of appreciating another man's point of view. He understands the times and their requirements, and it is gratifying that not a single shot has had to be fired by the Assam Rifle jawans in bringing these remote areas under regular administration. In fact in many cases the tribal themselves invited the Administration to open its headquarters in their territory. Up to 1948 the Wanchoo area had not been brought under the Administration. The locals requested the authorities to extend medical facilities to their area. The request was acceded to and then, for the facility of the medical services, administrative personnel were increased. Wakka an interior Wanchoo village was the last to come under the Administration. The same thing happened in Tawang area. It is said that the Monpas were not happy under the local administration because the officials insisted on 'oola', or free work levies and the people resented this degrading and unprofitable custom. To avoid heavy tribute and many exactions with little benefits the Monpas requested "British India to rule" them.

Therefore, crime, in the sense that we understand it, against outsiders is unknown in the tribal society. It is the misdirection of their judgment, feeling and intelligence which makes them commit crimes. The Administration also treats their acts of violence with leniency. The culprits of the 1953 massacre were awarded light punishment. Some of them are already working for the social uplift of the people and I was told others may soon be out of jails to work for and with their own people. There is another instance :—A Miju killed a 'munim' (a bania clerk) at Hayuling a few years ago (the exact cause of the murder is not known to the public). The murderer escaped to the upper Dibong Valley and is said to be living in an Idu village. Tacitly he has been excused.

A tribal has two standards of morality—one for outsiders and the other for the tribe. What is true for one may not be true for the other. Profit has never been the motive behind crimes against outsiders in the tribal areas. But this cannot be said of crimes committed by a tribal against his own kinsmen. A women or a slave is an economic unit and the private property of a local. Dispossession or acquisition either damages or benefits the owner or the usurper materially. This involves a sense of profit whether in this world or in the next and causes friction and many a times violent conflicts between the contending parties. In the past retaliations and counter-retaliations followed suit and feuds were persistent. Head-hunting and hand-hunting expeditions and local warfare could be traced to the stealing of women and slaves of one group by another. Since the advent of Administration, the intensity of these violent outbursts has tremendously decreased and attempts are being made to impart quick justice for the aggrieved party. But it is wrong to believe that such internal feuds are extinct. So long as the emancipation of women and freedom of slaves is not accomplished such feuds will remain a headache for the Administration. Land, many a time is another bone of contention in local feuds. Traditionally a village knows its land and forests. Any encroachment against these also brought various groups into conflict. Yet another cause used to be trade. As said before all the tribals were at one time traders of some sort and naturally they were open to petty businessmen's weaknesses. The

Apa Tanis being the cleverest of all the tribals of Subansiri, bought mithunes from the Daflas and the Hill Miris, and some times bought goods from the latter groups. In these transactions many times the Apa Tanis did not keep their word and so provoked their neighbours. The outcome used to be continued hot or cold war between the two—the Apa Tanis and the Daflas or the Hill Miris. In fact during the 1940s the hostility of the Apa Tanis against the Daflas was the cause for the former to extend an invitation to Haimendorf to come and stay in the Apa Tani plateau. Tribal history is full of such instances where one party invited others to settle local feuds developed because of the dispossession of the property of one by the other. In the past, feuds were decided by the jungle law of force; now they are decided by administrative officers summarily. These feuds are growing complicated, requiring reorganisation of the executive and the judiciary branches of the Administration. At present, the tribal interpreters are not free from party or group influences, bribery and corruption. If the trying officer is not thoroughly conversant with the local language there is every chance of miscarriage of injustice. Of course if officers are conversant with the local dialects then what is the need of interpreters?

Emotional and sentimental disturbances also impel a person to commit crimes. The chief of Khela was enamoured of a local girl and wanted to marry her. Another chief was against the alliance for some personal reasons and the result was that the Khela chief lost his head. Then another tribal interpreter cut off the head of his wife because he was constantly taunted by his friends and relations for her moral lapses. When he was tried before his APO he produced a mass of congealed blood from his bag as a proof of his love for the dead woman, the blood mass being hers. The culprit was fined and let off. Apart from murders and serious crimes, minor offences like thieving, cheating and betraying the interests of one to another, are also on the increase. In Garhwal, Kumaon and Nepal there are agencies, apart from government administration and police, which serve as humanising influences. Such agencies do not exist in NEFA, at least in such a way as to guide the people to new values of life. It will take a long time for the locals to produce their own leaders to lead them to modern social and spiritual values, though Dr. Elwyn maintains that the POs, the Medical Officers etc. are teaching the people their respective subjects and also inculcating loyalty towards India[8]. In democracy this should be the task of social workers and national leaders and these are conspicuously missing from the NEFA society. Times are changing fast, so are the values of life. Even Indians, who have always had leaders—religious, political, social or educational—are finding it difficult to adapt themselves to new values. How then can one expect the tribals to adapt to changing conditions without capable leaders ? To estabalish a jail here and a jail there in the NEFA area will no doubt inculcate a feeling of 'oneness with the territory' among the tribal convicts and probably their stay in jail will not give them an inferiority complex, or feeling of inadequacy, but it will not help much in teaching them the broader values of life which are so essential for them if they are to integrate themselves into the larger society of India. That can only be done by multiplying the area of association and contact with the outside world and not by keeping them within their own narrow circle. They have had enough time to overcome the after-effects of the intoxication under the influence of which they were supposed to have been asleep and now they are ready for a new life.

At present the POs and the APOs have wide criminal and civil powers and under Assam Frontier Regulations they are exercising these. The number of litigants is increasing day by day with the result that local administrative bodies as described under Chapter VI, are losing authority and initiative. The Administration is planning to introduce Kebang type Panchayats in every tribal area, but the success of such bodies greatly depends on the success of Panchayats elsewhere in India. This system is still in its infancy and under trial among the Indian rural population who are slightly better educated and better informed than their counterparts in NEFA. In this age of scientific development, centralisation of power is inevitable and how this decentralisation of administration will work is not certain. Even if it succeeds then it is bound to perpetuate the rule of those who so far have led the society. Panchayats, as has been proved from recent elections held in different rural areas, are bound to make the hands of the existing ruling class stronger and keep the gulf between the higher class and the common man as wide, if not wider, as it ever was. This is contrary to our declared objective of classless society. Therefore, under the circumstances the picture of Panchayat Raj in India appears to be bleak. If this is the position in the rest of the country, then what can we expect in the tribal society where the social position of village elders and chiefs is much stronger than that of India's petty landlords and namberdars in the rural India. However, if the Panchayat Raj succeeds in India then the tribals may look forward for the development of democratic institutions within their own territory, otherwise hopes of the tribals managing their own affairs in the near future are fraught with disappointment.

Some social habits and customs are peculiar to a particular group and if any of them are common then they differ in their broad details from group to group. Head-hunting is one of these customs.

A great deal of hullabaloo has been raised about head-hunting and writers have commented adversely about the cessation of the practice among the Nagas; doubts have been expressed, that the Nagas would lose their virility unless alternative channels were discovered so that their energies, so far devoted to head-hunting, could be diverted to some constructive purposes. J. P. Mills writes:

> "The suppression of head-hunting, though necessary in any area which is fully administered, has probably not been for the benefit of the tribe. The very fact, that far from being an honour, it is a disgrace to be killed in war, makes all Nagas very careful of their own safety, and their wars were singularly innocuous affairs. In a war between two big villages each side might lose one or two men a year. The number of lives saved by the suppression of the practice is therefore negligible, and is far more than balanced by those lost through the spread of the disease made easy by safe travelling everywhere. In addition to this there is a very real loss in virility and keenness. Unbroken peace is no better for Nagas than it is for any other race[9]."

Expressing a more sensible view, Peal in the closing years of the 19th century observed that head-hunting was a "deep-rooted fashion, and by no means a necessity like 'jhuming'[10]." Col. Waddel considered the so-called Naga wars as cold-blooded murders.

> "The keen desire for heads is kept up by the horrible fashion which demands that no youth is permitted to wear the badges and ornaments of a man until he has taken one or more heads. And as any head counts, it is usually the head of some helpless old woman or child, treacherously waylaid and slain on the outskirts of the village when fetching firewood or water. Few of the heads are taken in fair fight. And strange to say, although these heads are mostly obtained by the sacrifice of women, it is the young women of the tribe who goad on by their jeers the young men of the village to this cold-blooded murder, at the expense of women and children of other villages[11]."

Probably Mills's figures of one or two killed per village in the so-called Naga wars may be correct, but when the cumulative effect of the casualties of an area is studied the statistics are not healthy reading. "A fairly safe estimate—judging by the skulls in the Morangs—would give about 12,000 murders, in about 40 years, in an area roughly 20 miles square[12]", observed Peal. "Among many tribes it has been given up, and where it is still in vogue seems largely due to the young women chaffing the young men who are not tattooed, or otherwise distinguished as 'Braves'. But inasmuch as at least half the heads taken are those of women and children, this decoration, as a test of bravery, is now heavily discounted by all parties and a very little pressure by the paramount power would put an end to a custom which there is good reason to believe, is already unpopular among the rising generation[13]", writes the same administrator. The tribals, specially the youths, realised the necessity of giving up this abominable practice during the fading quarters of the last century. The young people of the 1870s or 1880s are dead and if anyone now talks about skulls or head-hunting, he is stared at with a contemptuous eyes by the Nagas. During the Miri Mission in 1912 the Naga porters took to head-hunting. Probably a desire to collect enemy heads as souvenir of their personal exploits in the alien territory rearoused the old custom. The Nagas had been warned to desist from the practice, but it is interesting to note that they were not punished for their defiance of orders or instructions though the advance of the mission was stopped by the stiff resistance offered by the terrorised and resentful locals.

Agreed that the Nagas of Tirap are known to have offered a few captives as human sacrifices to their deity in 1915 and to have taken away the head of the chief of Khela in 1953, yet such instances are isolated and are no more common than reports of human sacrifices at the instigation of a witch doctor or a sadhu or even a pandit elsewhere in India. Head-hunting ceased in the beginning of this century and it is utterly foolish to pretend to lament it; the Nagas are still virile and active which shows that they have found an outlet for their energies which they used to spend in committing cold-blooded murders of women and children. "It is true that the suppression of head-hunting, which was closely inter-related with many aspects of Naga culture, will mean an inevitable decay in certain types of dance, personal ornamentation and tattooing, wood-carving and funeral ceremonial[14]", writes Verrier Elwyn. If there was any inevitable decay in the so-called Naga culture then it must have come and gone, and by now the people are adjusted to the newer, happier circumstances. At the present moment they cannot be said to have deteriorated in their culture.

The Nagas may not have made the same social progress that some of their compatriots made in the State, but the Ahoms and others also had similar barbaric practices. "Capital punishments extended to the whole family of a rebel; parent, sister, wife and children, and it is probably from these sources that the rafts are supplied, which are frequently seen floating down the Brahmaputra, past Goalpara, covered with human heads[15]", writes Hamilton. Barbarous punishments ceased in Assam and so did head-hunting from the Naga society. Head-hunting was a remnant of human sacrifice which had been practised in ancient times. "The Persians were, perhaps, the only nation of ancient times who did not indulge in human sacrifice[16]." H. G. Wells writes: "And it is a very remarkable thing that throughout the world wherever there is sowing and harvesting there are still traceable the vestiges of a strong primitive association of the idea of sowing with the idea of a blood sacrifice, and primarily of the sacrifice of the human being[17]."

Similar to head-hunting some of the groups performed a hand-hunting ceremony. Haimendorf[18] witnessed the ceremony of 'Ropi' in which the hand of an alien woman was exhibited in the Apa Tani worshipping place—Nago—and then was burnt with great rejoicing. Since the establishment of Divisional Headquarters there has been no report of 'Ropi' being performed by the inhabitants of the plateau. The Daflas also celebrated a similar ritual. "When an enemy is killed the head is usually cut off but is not carried away, but the right hand is severed at the wrist and taken to the raiders' village, where it is attached to a tree, palm upwards, by means of cane thong. The raiders then gather round and discharge arrows at it[19]." The period when the Daflas gave up the practice is not known.

Among the Nagas of Tirap head-hunting provided the basis for the Naga dance. The practice has ceased but the dance continues though with less vigour and privacy. It is possible that a day may come when the head-hunting dance will be obsolete. A new trend is noticeable among the Noctes—Vaishnavism is taking roots in the society and the people are taking to 'kirtan' (singing of devotional songs of which Lord Krishna is generally the subject) and 'bhagti' (devotional dances depicting various episodes in the life of Lord Krishna with his lady-love Radha) dances. This change may also infect the rest of Tirapians.

Dance, whether individual or collective, is an art and a sport for the enjoyment of the performer. But how many people in NEFA perform community dances? Individual dances are unknown in the tribal society. The Mishmis, the Daflas and the Apa Tanis, if they knew any folk dances, have forgotten them. The Abors and the Hill Miris have their own colourful dances; the Noctes and the Wanchoos also perform them during community feasts which usually fall on tribal festival days or are arranged by the village chiefs' machinations to settle private feuds between two quarrelling parties within the tribe. Since the introduction of Administration such dances are arranged and staged for government officials. This artificial formality and dictation has robbed the tribals of spontaneity and initiative. Now the community dances are a matter of official shows which have to be rehearsed and practised with all the mannerism suitable for a particular exhibition. The Monpas perform religious dances, and like their own slow and monotonous life, their dances are devoid of mirth and agility. One frequently sees pictures of a Minister or other official with his arm around the neck of a tribal belle, and a professional smile on his face, evidently trying to give the impression that he and the girl are doing a tribal dance. The actual realities, however, are quite different. Apart from these well arranged exhibitions, there is very little mirth and rejoicing among the people. Further, the dance, whether individual or collective, without vocal and instrumental music, has very little chance for development. Musical instruments do not exist in the tribal society. Vocal music, if it exists at all, is not up to such a standard as to attract the attention of the government officials for patronage, and, without musical instruments it has no chance for future development.

During the Second World War, concert parties were organised and troops entertained in the field. I attended, on many occasions, dràmatic performances arranged by government staff and I always observed that the locals enjoyed the shows and showed a real keenness to stage such performances themselves. The Padams of Roing for instance staged a drama depicting the war they had fought against the British and they were absorbed in the show. These people are said to have an abundant capacity for the enjoyment of life, and let us help this capacity to grow.

'Morangs' are club houses or dormitories where tribal youths are trained in civic duties. The Monpas have similar institutions called 'dzongs' and the Assamese have 'kirtan ghars' which serve as the village meeting place. Akin to these houses, those tribal groups which lead a congregated life in big villages have village community meeting places; the Nagas, the Adis and the Apa Tanis have them and among the first two they are called 'Morangs'. In 'Morangs' youths of the village gather every evening and inform the gathering of the day's happenings. Important meetings are attended by elders of the village. Tribal guests are also put up in the village 'Morang' for the night. If the village is in danger and the youths are to be mobilised for the emergency, then instructions to act are given from the 'Morangs'. Among the Nagas and the interior Abors these 'Morangs' also serve as places for the young people to meet and select their marriage partner. The custom of courtship and marriage through the 'Morang' was not a universal practice in the Agency and in a few years it will no doubt uniformly die out. The disappearance of the function may cause a temporary dislocation of moral values among the tribal youths concerned, but it is too late to check the inevitable. They will have to learn that, although the 'Morangs'* will stay in NEFA, they will remain only as Community Halls, and not as marriage bureaus.

The tribal folks have a knack of celebrating festivals with a mounting crescendo of activity. Generally these festivals are connected with deaths, marriages and the sowing and harvesting of crops. These are the only occasions when the people drink rice beer in such large quantities as to become intoxicated. The Assamese brew rice beer as do the tribals. Among the former it is consumed secretly behind closed doors but the tribals drink it as a

* Rangbhangs (youth clubs) among the Bhotias of Kali and Dhauli Valleys in UP have similar functions as those of 'Morangs'. They are still used as marriage bureaus. I believe similar institutions also exist in Western Nepal.

tribal custom. However, they have voluntarily begun to give up its use, and tea is replacing rice beer.

In NEFA two types of alcoholic drinks, the distilled and the fermented, are consumed. 'Ara', a distilled liquor extracted from rice or millet is used in the colder regions of the Agency. The Monpas and other people at the fringe of the Indo-Tibetan border distil and drink 'Ara' throughout the year. At lower altitudes and in the foothills, the fermented liquor is consumed. The liquor passes by different names in different Divisions, but for an outsider it is the 'lao pani' of Assam or the 'madhu' of Bengal or the 'chang' of Tibet or 'apong' of Siang. Many writers have described its preparation in various tribal monographs, but the fact is that the method of its manufacture is known to only a few families in a tribal group. Cakes of indigenous yeast can be bought in any weekly bazar of Assam but the basic constituents of the cake itself are a trade secret. 'Lao pani' contains about 2½ per cent of alcohol and cannot be termed as an alcoholic drink. "The Apong (beer) of the Adis has been studied by the Department of Anthropology which has found that, while the alcohol content is small, it enriches the nutritive value of the Adi diet approximately by 10 per cent of calories, 5·5 per cent protein, 5·3 per cent of calcium, 11 per cent phosphorus, 29 per cent of iron and 8 per cent of niacin, with the result that it has been found superior to the food of the average Indian peasant in all important nutrients[20]." The Tirapians may have a scarcity of rice during the rains but not of 'lao pani'!

Rice beer if taken as a beverage and a food, seems beneficial to the consumer, quite in contrast to the wide spread habit of using the terrible drug of opium.

Hamilton[21] in 1820 and Muffat[22] in the middle of the 19th century observed that Assam was growing enough opium for home consumption. Maniram Diwan*[23] in the 1850s recommended that 5 per cent of opium cultivation should be interdicted every year. If his recommendations had been implemented the Assamese would have escaped from its baneful effects by the 1870s. But evidently the prohibition of the use of the drug or its cultivation was not introduced. Cooper in 1872 argued for a cautious policy in the matter. "I have heard many clever and thoughtful people observe that the use of opium should be put down with a strong hand, but while concurring with them in the wish that the use of the drug should be extinguished I cannot agree with them that it should be forthwith prohibited, and for the reason, that those who have been accustomed to it cannot leave it off without dying from want of it[24]." The present day policy of the Government is to respect the tribal views and not to hurry the introduction of measures for their cleansing the area of this evil against tribal wishes. As a result, 88 years after Cooper's remarks, the tribal views on the subject have not changed and the use of opium is more wide spread than ever. "The general tribal view is that, while the older men must be permitted to continue their opium smoking, for otherwise the loss of 'this disease which cures all diseases' will be intolerable, the younger men should at all costs be saved from it, and that poppy-cultivation should be *gradually* reduced and its introduction into areas where it is not known, such as the Dibong Valley, should be prohibited[25]", writes the ATA. (Italics

* Maniram Diwan's suggestion was more specific than presently suggested.

are mine). However, the smuggling of this drug flourishes on the Indo-Burma border.

In India up to very recently this drug used to be consumed by a fairly large number of people of respectable class but it is now a thing of the past. The tribals because of adverse climatic conditions, like other hillmen. used it to forget the hard realities of life and quickly became addicts, and to give a respectable guise to the habit of opium consumption the British Political Officers carried opium stocks with them on tours to be distributed to the tribals, as rum used to be issued free to the Garhwalis by the touring officers. Because of its social sanction, opium came to be used as a 'political gift' by the official class and as a currency among the tribals to buy wives and mithunes. The Digarus, the Mijis, the Singphos and the Noctes are the affected tribal groups and as a result have become decadent communities. In fact the Singphos have degenerated to the point of extinction, and it is feared, if new population does not migrate from Burma within the next twenty years, the word 'Singpho' will remain but not the tribe. There is still time to save the Mishmis and the Noctes from the impending disaster facing them because of their fondness for opium smoking and eating. A vigorous and active policy of prohibiting the cultivation and consumption of the drug is long overdue and it must be implemented, the earlier the better. The NEFA Medical Department can detect and hospitalise the hopeless addicts while the crops are rooted out thus saving the young generation from contact with the drug.

The tribal people have a profound respect for the dead. This feeling of reverence for the dead is also prevalent throughout India and Assam. Here in NEFA the dead person in some groups, is still considered as a member of his family for a considerable period after his death and his departure from this world to another is made less painful and more comfortable, so the people believe, by burying his belongings and earning along with his dead body for use during his journey. The family tie is kept strong by burying the remains of the deceased under the protection of the house. Among the Noctes a dead body is kept in the house for three or four days and bathed every day. It is placed on a platform constructed over the fireplace. When the body is charred and the obnoxious smell of decomposition has subsided it is removed to an allotted place either inside or outside the village and kept over a 'chang' (a raised bamboo platform) for a year after which the remains are buried under the house. During the year the family considers the deceased as a living member of the house and his share, whether of food or of drink, is daily set apart and placed by the side of the coffin. The Wanchoos offer similar treatment to their dead with a slight modification here and there. The Adis, like the Ahoms, bury their dead along with the personal effects and wealth of the deceased. In 1958 the Political Jamadar of Roing, a Padam, died. Rs. 3,000, his own saving, were buried along with the dead body. If any one should be tempted, by the large amount of wealth to rob the grave, he would certainly be asking for very serious trouble.

Man has always been very conservative and sensitive in showing respect to the dead and this is more so among the tribal people. Any jeering or a slight remark against the manner for the disposal of the dead may cause serious resentment resulting in a display of force. The Banferas of Ninu murdered Holcombe and wiped out his entire party in 1872, because a few Gorkha troops showed disrespect to the dead body of their chief who had died a week earlier. The tribals have become more tolerant and such an exhibition of violent revenge may not be repeated, but still all outsiders are advised to refrain from such lapses of respect for the sentiments of the people.

Except for the Tangsas, the Singphos, the Khamptis, and the Monpas who are all either Buddhists or have a leaning towards it dispose of their dead in a manner not very different from that of the Hindus, all the tribal groups bury their dead in postures differing from tribe to tribe depending upon the cultural influence the particular tribe is subjected to. The Mishmi funeral rites display a change in the common practice of burying the dead. The poor classes among them either burn their dead or throw them into a river. The rich keep the dead body on view for some time and then cremate it. Then, they, whether poor or rich, observe the anniversary of the death to appease the spirit of the departed soul.

To the Army has been handed the responsibility of defending the Indo-Tibetan border. Regular army units may not immediately move into NEFA territory and the battalions of Assam Rifles may continue to carry on all defence duties, but construction engineers, whether mobilised or semi-mobilised, are bound to go to NEFA in the immediate future. On account of lack of leisure time and perhaps administrative restrictions, social contacts between the locals and the newcomers may not be too frequent, but the very presence of the canteens, rest camps, depots and headquarters that come with the Army are bound to bring a change in the daily habits of tribal people. The change is unavoidable, but it will be gradual and natural. The tribal is bound to go the way that the

Garhwalis, the Kumaonis and the Assamese did. He may start the use of tea and milk; he may be encouraged to produce crops surplus to his requirements; he may develop a taste for ghee (boiled butter) and may start wearing shoes, he may cease colouring his teeth and may improve his personal hygiene and may even develop a sweet tooth, but these new habits will be in keeping with the manners and customs of the Society in which he has eventually to live and move.

PART II.—LIVING CONDITIONS OF THE PEOPLE

The tribals, considering the general standard of living in the country, are a fairly well-fed and sturdy people. Hunger is unknown throughout the Agency and scarcity of food is unthinkable in the Northern Tract. Nature so far has been able to keep a balance between production and demand and survival has not been a problem.

The mainstay of the majority of the people of NEFA is agriculture and they have been carrying on the primitive method of 'Jhuming' (Shifting cultivation) for food production. 'Jhuming' is practised in some parts of Nepal, Sikkim, Bhutan and throughout the Eastern hills of of India and Burma. Up to the 1930s the Kumaonis also practised it. Mr. George William Trail, Commissioner for the affairs of Kumaon, described this practice as periodic cultivation. He writes: "This consists in cutting down the forest, and clearing patches of land along the summits of the ridges: the trees are left for a few months to dry, and being chiefly pine, are then easily consumed, and the ashes used for manures. As the declivity of these spots is usuallly too great to admit the use of the plough, the land is prepared with a hoe. Only one or at most two crops are taken from each spot, after which it is abandoned for another, and not again touched till after the lapse of from six to twelve years according to the nature of the soil; such land is termed as 'Kala Pahar'[26]." With slight modifications, according to the climatic conditions and the duration of rotation, the same definition is appropriately applicable to 'Jhuming' in NEFA. The Kumaonis practised 'Jhuming' ('Ijra or Katil' in the Kumaon dialect) for opening new land for terrace cultivation and now, however, they have given up the practice and they are not sorry for it. Peal[27] observed the destructive consequences of 'Jhuming' among the Nagas of Tirap of the 1870s. According to him the population had utilised the maximum of land for 'Jhuming' for food production. Would there be any surplus of land available now for 'Jhuming' in Tirap after 90 years and would the productivity of soil be the same? Forests retain water and are the chief source of supplying fuel in NEFA. The Wanchoo country in Tirap is denuded of forests and a constant scarcity of water and fuel prevails; people have to march for miles from their villages to fetch drinking water and fuel for daily consumption. Peal fought for the removal of this ill-advised and evil practice but failed to move the authorities to action. Recently the Commissioner for Scheduled Castes has written: "The urgent need for weaning away the tribals from this primitive form of agriculture by settling them permanently on land and teaching them modern methods of agriculture has been engaging the attention of the Central and the State Governments ever since the country embarked upon special programmes for the welfare of the Scheduled Tribes[28]." The report further continues: "It is an accepted fact that due to pressure of population on the area available for shifting cultivation, the 'Jhuming Cycle' is gradually reduced and this causes a progressive decrease in yield as well as denudation of forests. Thus the people living on 'Jhum' gradually approach a state of crisis in food supplies if they persist with this type of cultivation alone[29]." Therefore, the task of the Agriculture Department in NEFA has been to introduce permanent cultivation where possible and simultaneously to "improve jhuming-cycle to ensure that forests are not permanently denuded[30]." The attempt to make 'Jhuming' a science, or improve it will remain a myth. Jhuming can only be replaced by 'terrace cultivation' though this method has its own evils and when carried out in steep hills, will not check soil erosion. NEFA is a peculiar country. Here torrential downpours, constant grazing, deforestation caused by 'Jhuming' and soft soil have combined to accentuate soil erosion. One has only to visit the Dafla Hills in Subansiri where there are miles and miles of barren hills, spotted here and there by a couple of mithunes grazing, and the Mishmi Hills which are geologically unstable, and the Wanchoo country where a cluster of trees is as unknown as a wild tiger in Delhi to witness the baneful effects of 'Jhuming' in the mountains and in tropical belt of NEFA. Dr. Elwyn has discussed the problem of 'Jhuming' and is of the opinion that whether 'Jhuming' is replaced by permanent cultivation or whether it is improved, the process would not increase productivity; for every solution he has tabulated a corresponding drawback. He concludes: "The introduction of wet rice cultivation also raises its own problems. In the foot hills of Lohit, it has been successfully introduced in a number of villages, and the people are delighted with bigger crops they raise—but wild elephants, which never damage the 'Jhums', threaten the level fields. In Pasighat the switch-over to concentrated rice-production has not every where given the people more to eat. They are more prosperous, certainly, but they sell their rice and the neglect of jhums has meant a loss of gourds and vegetables they formerly got from them[31]." Elephants are more important than man, and people should remain satisfied with gourds and vegetables rather than produce surplus rice! How long are the people of NEFA to be kept behind an artificial curtain, divorced from the plainsmen? When welfare measures reach these people, and they must, the population is bound to multiply at a rapid rate in consonance with the rapid developments of communications. Will gourds and vegetables then be enough to satisfy the needs of all the people? Who will be the sufferer? The tribal people, of course. Mr. C. G. Helme I.C.S. writes about the Lushais in 1931: "It may be said in general that contact with civilisation has made little or no difference to life in an ordinary village. For the important purpose of trade the Lushai Hills are not really in effective contact with civilisation at all. They produce very little that has any exchange value and difficulties of communications (there are no motorable roads in the Lushai Hills, only bridle-paths) make the marketing of surplus produce practically impossible. Thus the ordinary effects of contact with civilisation—the stimulous to produce, the ability to exchange, the rise in the standard of consumption are almost entirely absent[32]." In 1958-59 in the Lushai Hills the rarely flowering wild bamboo bloomed in great profusion. Rats which feed on this bamboo-seed multiplied astronomically and having finished the seed turned ravenously to the rice fields and destroyed the entire crops. Warnings of famine had been given by the village elders to the State authorities when the bamboo began to bloom, but the warnings were not listened to. Later, faced with the reality of starvation in the Mizo villages, sufficient food could not be imported because of non-existent roads. Thanks to Mr. Helm and to those who acted on his advice! Thus the Lushais could not be provided with enough foodgrains in time to avert the famine of 1959/1960. According to the Chief Minister of Assam "about 1,60,000 out of a total of 2,40,000 people were affected[34]." The Mizos will not forget this famine for years to come. In the Lushai Hills only the Mizos suffered, but if a tragedy of this kind visited the NEFA area, specially the Northern Tract, it would not only be felt by the people but it would have far reaching effects on the defence problems of the country as well. Therefore, the inevitable should be faced boldly and difficulties overcome. This cannot be done by sermonising on the defects of civilisation. It is too late to challenge science and keep civilising influences from entering into any backward area, let alone NEFA which is an important frontier tract.

So far the Monpas, the Daflas and the Mishmis are living on the forests and trade. On account of Communist discouragement of the Indo-Tibetan trade the Monpas have stepped up their trade with India and have more or less made up the deficiency caused by the cessation of trade with the trans-Himalayan people. The economy of the Daflas was linked with that of the Apa Tanis. The latter produced rice while the former reared mithunes.

But now the Daflas have started taking interest in agriculture. The Mishmis were reputed to be keen traders and they had trade relations with the Tibetans. Since the occupation of Tibet by the Chinese the prospects of the Tibeto-Mishmi trade have considerably dimmed and the Mishmis are finding it difficult to carry on their age-old vocation. Mithunes which supplemented their family economy are not proving adequate for the survival of the already depleted race. Therefore the Mishmis must take to agriculture or perish. Briefly, in the very near future, all the tribal groups will depend on agriculture to provide them enough for meeting their increasing requirements of life. Therefore, the process of persuading them to adopt modern methods of food production and the use of manure, the plough, and good seeds should be accelerated.

Tribal houses are constructed of bamboo, timber, leaves and grass. They are long and raised considerably on posts of cleft timber. They are indiscriminately constructed on the top or side of a hill, but the level of the floor is well preserved and maintained. The partition of the house depends on the social customs of the tribe. The Nagas have two rooms, one for the men and the other for women; the rooms, is have as many rooms as the number of wives of the chief of the house and a corridor connecting them: The Apa Tanis and the Hill Miris each have only one long room. There is a varanda behind the house with a hole in the floor used for sanitary purposes; pigs, dogs and fowl act as village scavengers. The houses are comfortable and are provided with fire places to keep them warm. It is, therefore, not wrong to say that every man in NEFA has a roof to sleep under.

In NEFA, previously clothing was an art, it was decoration and used to signify the rank of the wearer.

Now it has attained utilitarian values, and one buys the clothes which one's pocket permits. I have seen one Naga chief covering his body with a black coat and another with an olive-green bush shirt to escape the cold. Dress in tribal regalia is reserved for ceremonial occasions only.

The Khamptis and the Singphos are clad like their cousins across the border in Burma; the Monpas dress like the Bhutanese or the Sikkimese; the Akas, the Mijis, and the Daflas, in fact all the tribes of the Northern Tract, dress according to the climate and the environment. The Noctes and the Wanchoos when they come to the plains dress like Hindus, but in their villages they have started wearing Lungis and Chadars. The educated, whether they are from the Eastern Tract or from the Northern prefer trousers and shirts rather than any other form of dress. School boys dress like any university students in the rest of the country and they look very smart. The Administration tried to discourage the wearing of Western styled clothes but evidently the attempt completely failed. The student in NEFA, in matters of dress, copies his school masters and Agency officials who are generally dressed in a coat and a trouser with a tie wound around the neck and dangling on the chest. In like manner Indians also aped the British in spite of Mahatma Gandhi's and Gurudev Tagore's disapproval.

In matters of food, housing and clothing the tribal is much better off than his compatriot, the Indian villager. This is not so in respect of his longevity (mortality figures of the NEFA population were unfortunately not available). The mortality rate differs form village to village and is very high. There may be various causes for this, but the attitude towards medical science and hygiene is an important one.

The Administration encourages the institution of tribal doctors, and advocates that it should be a supplementary agency to the doctors trained in the Western methods of medical science. "A wise doctor in NEFA will make friends with the local priests, invite them to visit his hospital and let them offer prayers and make sacrifices for his patients, explaining that his own way of treatment is supplementary to their's[34]", writes Dr. Elwyn. I hesitate to write that there are very few such doctors in NEFA! The result of this principle, "of working through the local institutions and not in rivalry to them[35]" is that the tribal maintains a blind faith in his priest-cum-doctor and sticks to him, in case of illness, to the very last. The poor allopath receives the patient in the last stages of the disease. With an ill-equipped Operation Theatre, instruments lying idle and a half-trained staff, he is expected to perform miracles. Obviously he fails and the tribal laughs at modern medical science. The doctor also soon becomes disappointed and frustrated. Why was he brought to such an undeveloped area to waste his first class professional knowledge and experience on people who are not encouraged to take advantage of the benefits? He blames the Administration and the tribal sympathisers blame him. The position of an allopath among the tribals is like that of a heavy tractor in an Assamese marsh.

It is not that these allopaths have come to NEFA only. Nearly 500 Indian doctors have gone to Burma and I met many of them living in the Burma border areas, but there they were happy and satisfied. In Burma they were allowed ample opportunities to utilise their talent and fill their pockets too, because their clients were prosperous. If the Administration believes in the principle of gradual and natural development according to the genius of the people, then the obvious thing was to send Vaids and Hakims, medical experts nurtured through the evolutionary processes of the Indian society who believe in chanting mantras or other magic verses, playing of *dholes* and burning of agar, to the tribal areas. These people would have had opportunites to conduct their researches on herbs and would have at the same time enriched their own knowledge of enchantments. The allopaths so saved from these positions could have easily been absorbed elsewhere where they were needed most and where their knowledge could have benefited people who have reached such a stage of development as to appreciate the benefits of modern medical science. It is not understood why this has not been done. If the Administration is anxious to give the best to the tribal people, and obviously Vaids and Hakims are not considered as the best, then why is the policy of encouraging tribal witch doctors maintained ?

Among the Himalayan people there is much to be desired in improvement of personal and public hygiene, and the tribal people of NEFA as such cannot be made an exception. Climatic conditions and the scarcity of water are the causes of this neglect of cleanliness. The Nocte and the Wanchoo villages are perched on the tops of hills where even drinking water, let alone water for washing purposes, is hardly available. The Mishmis, Daflas, Apa Tanis and the Akas see no reason to be very clean hygienically. It is the influence of the Bihari labourers and contractors, and of the Marwari shopkeepers of Siang and the Assamese cultivators of the North Lakhimpur district which has brought about a change for the better in personal cleanliness among the Adis and the Hill Miris ; still there is much room for improvement. The tribals in general are not concerned about taking a proper bath, though they do wash the exposed portions of the body—face and legs—whenever they happen to cross a river or a stream on a warm day. Disposal of human secreta is always a weak point with the residents of the Inner Himalayas. One has to pass through a U. P. border village, where there are no private or public latrines and no scavengers, either human or animal, to clean the village lanes, to guess the standard of cleanliness among the people. This is not so with the tribal villages. Pigs, dogs and fowl keep the villages fairly clean. The curse of the larger villages in NEFA is mud, slush and filth. For instance Apa Tani villages are well laid-out but they lack a proper drainage system. This is not so essential in a Dafla village for two reasons—(i) it comprises only a few houses, and (ii) the slope of the ground is steep and does not let water stagnate. In Naga villages, one would not find stagnant water, but the village scavengers are not sufficient to keep the village free from the filth which breeds flies and infectious disease germs. Under these conditions it becomes very difficult to control an outbreak of an epidemic in the Naga country. Among the Wanchoos smallpox has always been a dreaded scourge. It has many times claimed hundreds of victims and wiped out village after village in the past. Probably that is how nature was able to keep a balance between the growth of population and the limited land for food production in the Wanchoo country.

In a land where people have not developed proper notions of personal hygiene one cannot expect the standard of public hygiene to be very high. Even so the large tribal villages can boast of better hygienic conditions than many of the towns of Assam where a drainage system is usually conspicuous by its absence and swarms of mosquitoes and flies dismay the visitor.

The tribals attend weekly bazars in the plains but their sojourn is usually of very short duration. The plainsman does not enter the tribal area, and those who reside in NEFA administrative camps are medically free from contagious diseases and are protected against the infectious ones. Thus there are few chances of a contagion or an infection entering the tribal areas from the plains. Such diseases, if any, are of local origin and their prevalence cannot be accidental. The origin might be traced to past generations.

In spite of liberty in sex relationship before marriage and the ignorance of girls on the subject, prostitution is unknown in the tribal society. There are instances of this profession being practised by a few women of Tibetan extraction living in villages often frequented by Tibetan traders in the Tawang area. Apart from such isolated instances, a Tribal girl does not surrender her body to any man for money. As a result, VD and allied diseases are unknown among the people of NEFA. Recently a few cases have been reported from Apa Tani plateau, probably because of the increasing contact of the Apa Tani with the plainsman. VD is a familiar disease among the people of Tibetan stock but these are very few and are confined to a couple of notorious villages near the Indo-Tibetan border.

The drinking water of Assam, and also of NEFA, except that from a waterworks, tastes like distilled water and is devoid of essential salts. Medical research at the Pathological Laboratory at Pasighat, is making a deep study of goitre, dermatitis, tuberculosis, and leprosy, and how far drinking water is responsible for the incidence of these diseases can only be confirmed after the results of this enquiry are known. Goitre is generally a disease of the hills and is caused by iodine deficiency. Although rice beer, the fermented beverage, is supposed to provide Vitamin B, still dermatitis is very common among the people. Tuberculosis and leprosy are not a menace in NEFA as they are in some parts of the country.

In NEFA the staple food of the people is rice and meat supplemented by forest produce. A vegetarian substitutes vegetables and lentils for meat, and with this combination the locals seem to be free from intestinal diseases.

Whenever and wherever the tribal rests he must have a fire and a roof, be it of hurriedly collected leaves or of grass to sleep under. Both protect him from the evil effects of moisture, and the smoke from his fire drives away mosquitoes and other insects, and the tribal however, is not immune to various fevers, pneumonia and malaria, which take a steady toll of human life.

Depopulation, though not from disease, is noticeable among some of the tribal groups. In the absence of any planned and proper census it is difficult to say whether it is affecting other communities or not, but it is fairly noticeable among the Singphos and the Lohit Valley Mishmis. Although both these groups still practise polygamy, their population is not showing an upward trend. Almost all writers and investigators of them have subscribed to the view that the deterioration of the Singpho population is attributable to the habit of smoking and eating opium. In the case of the Mishmis opium is said to be one of the main causes for depopulation; other causes may be poverty, lack of recreation, strenuous work and isolated living.

1. Village India by McKim Marriot p. 147
2. JASB 1900 Vol. LXIX Pt. II p. 13
3. JASB 1845 Vol. XIV Pt. I p. 259
4. Ibid. JBORS
5. Major Vetch Report 1794
6. Cooper p. 101
7. The Hidden Land by Ursula Graham Power p. 145
8. Dr. Elwyn p. 190
9. Census Report, 1931, Assam Vol. III Mr. J. P. Mill's Report.
10. JASB 1894 Vol. LXIII Pt. III p. 26
11. JASB 1900 p. 63
12. 13. JASB 1894 Vol. LXIII Pt. III p. 26
14. Dr. Elwyn p. 225
15. Hamilton Hindustan Vol. II p. 714
16. JASB No. I to IV—1876 Vol. XLV Pt. II Rahendra Mitra p. 88
17. A Short History of the World by H. G. Wells p. 51
18. Haimendorf: Himalayan Barbary p. 47
19. JASB Vol. II 1836 Article No. 4 p. 28
20. Dr. Elwyn p. 742
21. Hamilton Hindustan Vol. II p. 742
22. 23. Muffat Appx. B iv and Jixvi
24. Cooper p. 104
25. Dr. Elwyn p. 241
26. AR Vol. XVI p. 181
27. JASB 1872 p. 25
28. 29. 1957-58 Pt. I pages 70 and 72
30. 10 Years' Progress
31. Dr. Elwyn p. 86
32. Cens. Report 1931
33. The "Pioneer" of 19 February 1960.
34. 35. Dr. Elwyn. pp. 177, 187

CHAPTER VIII

Farce of Inferiority Complex

"I want to stress that we must cease to think our being different from the so-called tribal people. This vicious idea and superiority complex must go. Many of the tribal people have reached a high degree of development. In fact, I found that in some places the tribal people are better educated and disciplined and lead a better corporate life than the caste-ridden society that we suffer from[1]."

Jawaharlal Nehru

Dr. Alfred Adler, the Psychologist, gave us the phrase 'Inferiority Complex' which means more than the feeling of inferiority which is conscious. It means a galaxy of unconscious ideas characterised by a sense of insecurity and inadequacy which is intolerable and of which the subject is not aware. The effect of such a complex is that the subject continuously strives to prove the suppressed misgivings as false, and in doing this his behaviour is affected and at times it becomes dictatorial. The subject loses faith in himself and creates barriers, as a protection, which debar ideas, liberal and contrary to his own, to penetrate his conscious mind; he develops unsocial behaviour and imagines things which in reality do not exist. He becomes a nuisance to himself and to others as well. This complex is not particular to individuals for nations also develop it. Much of the present day political conflicts between nations, or groups of people, can be traced to an 'Inferiority Complax'. The complex is developed through fear, continued disappointment and frustration. It is a mental trait and cannot be eliminated completely though its growth may be retarded and effects minimised. In the case of tribals this depends on the people who deal with them or who are likely to come in contact with them.

Dr. Elwyn very often quotes instances of the white man's behaviour towards coloured aborigines (mostly Africans) in order to reach a conclusion from which he can make a generalization, and then writes, "Transfer this to India and it will serve as a serious warning as to what may happen in the tribal areas here[2]." The Doctor forgets that India is neither England nor America, and that the Tribal area is not Africa. He further forgets that times have also changed. The white man was an explorer and an adventurer and a trader; he came with a desire to expand at the expense of the colonials and to dominate them mostly for economic gain, or for imagined prestige amongst the other Western nations. This power-mad, glory-hungry delusion of grandeur came to be known as "Imperialism" or "Colonialism", or the cultural outlook of the colonist was entirely different from that of the indigenous people who were considered as a subject race and who needed guidance, or some times force, to make them march on the road chosen for them by their white masters. Those who resisted force and refused to abide by the new tenets suffered and in some cases were annihilated. There were a few white intellectuals who were genuinely concerned about the fate of the coloured aborigines or tribals. However, in contrast to the old white colonialism, when an Indian goes to the Indian tribal areas he goes to his own countrymen who are a member of the larger community—the Indians—without whom the tribals can neither live peacefully nor stabilise themselves as a community. The white man could not assimilate the natives because of colour prejudices, but the Indians and the tribals are of one colour. Then Dr. Elwyn tries by quoting examples of the tribals of CP during British days to teach a lesson to present day Indian Administrators. Here also he is not in tune with the times. During the British regime, Indians fired on Indians for activities which could not, by any stretch of imagination be termed as violent. and exploitation of man by man went on unabated in the name of "Law and Order". Can such things happen now? Yes, but things are different now. During the pre-Independence era the interest of the ruler never coincided with that of the ruled. Now the interest of Government should generally coincide with that of the people, when it does not, firing is resorted to. But a free people can now ask questions in their own Parliament. Times have changed and so have the people. These outmoded examples and sermons only confuse the issue.

However Dr. V. Elwyn has listed a few desirable qualities to be inculcated among the Agency officials. They are:

i. Personality—A warm, generous, affectionate, positive, but not too effusive, character is the best.

ii. Hard working—The tribals admire promptitude and punctuality in others even if they do not practise these themselves.

iii. The tribals like to feel that the officer is a person of position, authority and dignity, but at the same time they expect him to mix freely with them on terms of equality: they expect him to be easily accessible.

iv. The tribals appreciate any genuine interest in their customs and traditions and respond readily to expression of admiration for their textile and other arts.

v. Patience and an even temper are qualities admired even by the most warlike tribes.

vi. A married officer is most respected.

vii. An officer is to be quick and should fulfil his promise.

viii. Very important to tribal psychology is the love of truth and a belief in justice. This is why sincerity in an officer is more important than academic or technical qualifications.

ix. The tribals have no use for a puritan*. For puritanism is a cowardly approach to life; it is afraid of happiness; it will not let boys and girls dance together etc[3].

This is an elaborate, exhaustive and impressive list of qualities that an officer is required to have. These qualities cannot be cultivated in a man in a year or two. Mature officers are posted direct as POs and APOs and it is presumed that these qualities must be inherent in them, for the NEFA Administration cannot culture these attributes in its officers through short term courses. Army Officers are quite familiar with these requirements, which are the basic essentials of any good administrator and they are trained in them. That is why most of the administrators of senior rank in the NEFA are Army Officers. Troops in

*Dr. Elwyn is not very clear about the word 'puritan'. If he is hinting at the Hindu, 'Puritan' POs then he would be surprised to know that I met two Hindu POs who were literally 'Puritans'. These gentlemen were respected and nick-named as 'Mahatma Gandhi' or Lamo so and so by the locals. If the Dr. means the Christian 'Puritans' then also he is wrong. Christian 'Puritan' POs are as popular and respected, if not more, by the people as their Hindu colleagues.

the Indian Army are generally raw youths from rural areas and are not very much different from the tribals in emotional and educational make-up and the Army Officer, because of his mastery of the art of management, finds no difficulty in commanding respect from the tribals. Undeniably when such a mature, experienced Army Officer is posted to NEFA and endowed with unlimited administrative powers, he is bound to prove a good administrator.

In NEFA this question of tribal inferiority complex has assumed an importance which can not be ignored. Doctor Elwyn quotes examples[4] of a couple of youths who felt slighted both when they were addressed as monkeys and when they were confronted with the palatial buildings of modern towns. No matter what the officers may do for them, the tribals will continue to feel inferior in the presence of those of their countrymen who hail from the advanced sections of society as long as their experiences through education and social contacts are not widened. As long as they are kept behind the "Inner Line" curtain as museum pieces for research Scholars or Officers, "Interesting specimens" for VIPs and 'Becharas', "Unfortunates" for administrators, their future does not seem to be bright.

Now let us study the employment open to tribals, because, the manner of their employment may redeem their social position. They are employed as Political interpreters, peons and porters and a few Abors have joined Assam Rifles. During the Ahom rule their status was better, and they were recruited in the Ahom Army. The British also recruited about 3,000 Nagas in the Labour Corps for service in France in the First World War. Will his present employment relieve the tribal of his inferiority complex? It is not likely. If the present rate of development continues can the tribals hope to become POs and APOs within the next ten years? The outlook is doubtful but a few may. If education and modern science are popularised among the tribals and firm steps are taken to accelerate the rate of their economic progress then their waiting period before assuming the responsibility for administering their own territory may be very much reduced. Even if after a few years some qualified tribals are available as Administrators would it not be advisable to post them to other States to give them the national bias?

NEFA Divisional Headquarters are picnic spots for VIPs. There at the centre every thing is available and a good show can be arranged in the Army manner for the visitors, but conditions in the more remote administrative centres are not made known to the public. Officers are encouraged to bring their families but what arrangements are made for the latter's welfare? One class II Officer, (Mr. X), who was a Brahman brought his family to a Sub-Divisional headquarters in the Wanchoo area. There was a hospital, but there was neither lady doctor, nurse nor cook. A male Doctor occasionally visited the place as the local doctor had been mobilised for road construction work. A child was born to Mrs. X. Mr. X could not call a Dai (Midwife), or a sweeper to keep his wife's room, and bathroom clean because none was available. The officer had to serve as nurse, sweeper, and midwife to his wife. A tribal woman could not be called to help with the menial work because it might give her an inferiority complex. At another place, I visited a newly married doctor whose wife had also received nurse's training before her marriage. When I reached the house they were sitting idly on the otherwise empty Varanda.

They welcomed me. On enquiry I was told that there were no patients in the hospital and the only company for the doctor was his wife. I asked them why they could not visit the tribal villages. The Doctor's reply was humourous and convincing. "My wife wears a saree, and if she goes to tribal huts dressed like this she is liable to inculcate an inferiority complex among the tribal people. She is not prepared to discard her conventional clothes and the tribals are not ready to start wearing proper clothing. How can the two meet?" The NEFA policy in this respect is that "our officers—and their wives—adopt certain elements of tribal dress, they not only fit better into the landscape and come nearer to the people, but they help to counteract this unhappy type of mental depression[5]." I quote another example in a Padam village. I visited the family of a primary school master who was an Assamese. He called his three children who were playing in the village with other children. The youngsters in keeping with the company were stark-naked. Unfortunately the teacher was not a Rousseau and he took the children inside a room and dressed them properly so that they might appear presentable. But within a few minutes the children discarded the clothes and ran away to the village. There is nothing wrong in this but the question crops up: Should the people from outside themselves revert to the tribal ways or should the tribals progress enough to adapt to the new ways? At present it appears that the administrators are expected to adapt to the tribal ways. The employers (The Indian Government) naturally take the example of Christian missionaries and their selfless devotion to the cause of man and expect their servants to work with missionary zeal without caring for material benefits.

The example is laudable, but the advocates of the notion do not ponder over the problem deeply. Everyone has basic wants according to his standard of living, and he wants to satisfy them. In addition he desires that his family should be able to live according to the same standard of life to which he is used. He does not like to be told how his wife or children should dress and live, unless the advice is practicable and for better living. Besides, there is something more than these basic requirements. Every individual has an ideal and would be happy if he could pursue it freely without any detriment to the fulfilment of his basic desires. Sometimes incentives for bettering the prospects of satisfying his basic desires may accelerate his efforts to achieve the ideal. As the individual has an ideal so have different organizations, for organizations are made up of like minded individuals. This is specially true of non-profitable private ones. For instance, the ideal of the church is to gain as many converts as possible to faith in Jesus Christ as Saviour and Lord. There are many individuals who have the same ideal in life. Such persons willingly and voluntarily join the missionary programme of the church. Thus the ideal of a missionary coincides with that of the Church and his contribution to service is direct and intensive. There is an ideal—the spreading of Christianity—before him and this ideal is not only his own but is also the ideal of the organisation within which he works and which sees that lack of basic necessities and modern conveniences does not force him to fall back to primitive, exhausting and inefficient, and time consuming ways of doing things.

"The Christian missionary occupies a unique position in relation to these groups in that he devotes himself whole-heartedly to their advancement, and his supporters in the civilised countries are interested in increasing his efficiency[6]", writes Smith, a missionary himself. The missionary sends his children to the best schools available, usually outside the backward areas and he can usually find faithful servants amongst the local people. His work gives him happiness and satisfaction because he sees his ideal being fulfilled. His measure of success is the spread of the gospel of Christ, perhaps accompanied by an increasing number of converts. It is perhaps wrong to say that he is selfless, for his self interest lies in his work for Christ and as he carries that on, he thus fulfils his personal aim. Coming to a Government servant and his relation to the NEFA Administration, however, it may be said that the ideal of the one may not coincide or may not be in consonance with the other. For instance, suppose the ideal of a certain Government servant is to spread his own religion or to uplift humanity, while the declared objective of the Administration is the emotional integration of the tribals with the people of the rest of the country. Inherent in the ideal of this government servant is the presupposition that he stands at a higher level of civilization than the people among whom he is employed, while the latter ideal accepts the people as they are. The two ideals are at variance. The employee is faced with a conflict—whether he should foster his own ideal or the ideal of his employer. Since he is a servant and has joined this particular service to fulfil his basic material requirements he suppresses his ideals and resigns himself to look after his own material interests, which is usually the attitude adopted by any normal government servant anywhere in the world. In his frustration his contribution to service becomes passive and indirect.

But even in respect to his material interest also he finds himself in a disadvantageous position. No doubt, monetarily, he can afford to live his own life according to his own notions and he does send his children, if he is an officer of class I or II cadre, to schools of his own choice, but he is told how he and his family should dress and how they should behave in order to keep the tribal people from developing an 'Inferiority complex'. In other words he and his family are not free to live their own lives according to their own traditions. In Tirap I was told that the government officials are debarred from observing, in public, festivals pertaining to their own tradition and culture, lest the locals feel inferior and "Left out".

Although the ideal of the employee may not coincide with that of his employer, yet the government servant, as duty bound, works to satisfy his master. If he finds that he is successful in his work and is approaching the objective set by his employer his efforts will be accelerated. But what is the NEFA Administrator's standard for judging success? If there is any such measure or standard it is at best vague and indistinct. Just to say that the tribal people have been won over is not enough. And how can one justify the validity of such a statement? Is there any method by which one can, specially in peace time, judge the loyalty to a country of any individual or group? In NEFA the prospects of the government servant feeling the joy of work 'well done' are not bright, and therefore he lacks that incentive or motivation to pursue his work. His only motivation then is to work for money, for his own material benefits and for a higher position in the world. Regarding the ideal of the Administration itself, this, as things in India have been and are existing today, is the ideal of every

State in the country, namely to integrate the people of that State into the nation as a whole. But that is not a strong enough motive to infuse drive and zeal into the Administrative machinery. It is regarded as a routine ambition which needs no special efforts to achieve. Therefore, the obvious conclusion is that the government servant, in absence of an ideal worthy of the name and in the face of the standard adopted for judging his success in achieving this so-called ideal, is discouraged from working selflessly. Give the government servant an idea, which is concrete and dynamic, and he may be encouraged to work like a missionary.

In this discussion it has been presumed that the government servant, has at least his limited desire of receiving a handsome salary fulfilled. Consider the fate of class III or class IV servants whose salaries are meagre. The education of their children remains uncertain. They cannot afford a double establishment—one in the plains and the other in NEFA itself—therefore their children must live with them. As a consequence the youngsters receive an education which has no market value. It is true that the pay of these so-called class III or class IV officers is more than they would receive in the plains. But outsiders do not realise the hardships that these unfortunate individuals are subjected to. Their financial circumstances are so much strained that they cannot visit their relations in the plains, and thus they are cut off for all practical purposes from their community. A government servant living in a sub-divisional headquarters near the Indo-Tibetan border was called by his ailing wife in the Punjab. In those days the only means for him to reach the plains was to trek on foot, and he had to hire at least two porters to carry his personal kit. He took eight days to reach the nearest motor road and then three days and three nights by rail, III class, to reach the Punjab. He could not reserve a sleeping berth because he could not find the date of his journey in advance. He had scarcely one week at home and then had to make the same journey back again to his lonely forsaken outpost on the border. By any mean calculation it would cost him from Rs. 200 to 300 for the journey. He cannot, as a subordinate, afford such a luxury even once a year.

Plainsmen see members of the NEFA staff driving jeeps and staff cars and they grow jealous of such lavish use of government transport. If they were to investigate further they would find that the jeep occupants are POs and APOs who are entitled to the use of such vehicles. These officers are fortunate and some of their children study in Shillong Public Schools or in other good schools elsewhere in the country, and a few of them do combine duty with personal work, but this is not the case with class III and class IV officers. If the Government would agree to enlist the co-operation of a social organisation such as Ramkrishna Mission or the Medical Association of Assam to work in NEFA as a complementary body to the Administration then it would serve a dual purpose—that of accelerating the development work for the people and of improving the local environment for the benefit of the children of subordinate grade government staff thus lessening the worries of the latter. From such an organisation the public would be quite justified in asking for missionary zeal and probably they would not be disappointed. Further, such an organisation would not be interested in creating such circumstances so as to cause an 'inferiority complex' to develop among the tribals. Agreed that the purpose of social work would be defeated if so-called reforms were allowed to penetrate these areas in an individual capacity. But an organisation wedded to the welfare of humanity should be allowed to function in NEFA to help both the tribals and the staff.

I have attended community feasts in the Divisional Headquarters and in the tribal villages, but I have never yet seen a tribal interpreter or a school child sitting comfortably near his superiors. Generally the tribal sits as far as possible from the government servants; and when, at officially arranged parties, the tribal chiefs were given special attention, even then they were unable to behave in such a manner as to show that they consider themselves equal to the well-paid officials. This is only natural. If by chance any tribal acts in his natural, carefree manner in a social gathering of high officials then he at once becomes an object of curiosity, and is regarded as a freak—an object of patronising pity. Once in Subansiri a tribal continued to smoke his pipe, which was only natural for him, while talking with the then Governor of Assam himself. The Governor was greatly amused at the unsophisticated old fellow's behaviour, and had a picture taken of this great curiosity. Even today this story is told to visitors as a great joke. No wonder the tribals shrink from contacts with the officials when they are gawked at as curiosity and their most natural actions and habits are made the subject of such great amusement amongst their 'superiors' and overlords. Only the economic and cultural emancipation of the people will enable them to rise above their rustic and primitive behaviour patterns which make them laughing-stock of thoughtless outsiders. Only so can they escape an 'Inferiority Complex'. The ordinary Indian officers, who have day to day contact with the tribals, find much in the actions of the tribals to remind them of their own childhood stages of growth, and so are more understanding and patient with them. The stages of development that the hillmen of other parts of India passed through will also have to be passed through by the tribals of the Agency. The length of this period can only be lessened through education and economic development and not through treatises and sympathetic lectures.

The army has gone to NEFA and anti-national elements or intellectual snobs may argue that the troops will themselves cause the tribals to develop an inferiority complex. This is far from the truth. This is not the first time that the army has gone into NEFA. Army Engineers operated in Subansiri and Kameng from 1951 to 1959 and the locals are used to soldiers. Secondly, the training of the army personnel is entirely different from that of civilian officers. An army officer, even a Lance Naik is an officer of some grade, has learnt to value the man because that is normally his chief tool ; he respects the man and loves him. In fact in the army, the self-respect of a man is carefully nurtured and maintained, and an army man can be expected to treat tribals the same way. Thirdly, because of the nature of the terrain, sparsity of population and certain administrative restrictions, contacts between the locals and the armymen will be rare. Therefore, the army will have little influence psychologically on the tribal people ; if the soldiers do influence the tribals, then that influence should definitely be wholesome for the latter. Apprehensions about the results of the army's presence in NEFA have been created in the public mind unnecessarily. They can only be removed when the plainsmen comes to understand the tribal. The army will definitely befriend the tribals and thus will give the lie to the myth that it will create an inferiority complex among them.

1.	Pt. Jawaharlal Nehru's address Dec. 4, 1954	p.. 459
2.	Dr. V. Elwyn	p. 144
3.	,,	p. 140f
4.	,,	p. 140f
5.	,,	p. 187
6.	The Ao Naga Tribe of Assam by W. C. Smith	p. 225

CHAPTER IX

Religion of the People

"......and in Assam the Christian religion which these missionaries have brought has stood not only for a change in the social and intellectual habits of life and thought, but has also, unfortunately, in its effects, made for political alignments of an almost anti-national nature[1]."

Sri Prakasa

"The Mongoloid contribution is not so extensive or deep but nevertheless it is there, in the history and life and culture of Nepal, of North and East Bengal and of Assam; and through Brahmanical Buddhism this contribution has got to some extent a pan-Indian implication as well. The impact of a composite Brahmanism (and of medieval Buddhism) on the Mongoloid peoples has its special appeal for the student of Indian religion and culture as a whole[2]."

Dr. Suniti Kumar Chatterji

While returning from Mebo to Pasighat I met a crowd of Assam Rifles troops among whom there were a few Garhwalis. Some of the Garhwalis who had been trained in my Regimental Centre at Lansdown and who recognised me invited me to a feast which was being held at the time. The troops were playing on a drum and were enjoying themselves with Pandav* and other dances. There were many Abor boys in the crowd. On enquiry I

* Garhwali folk dance in which only men take part.

was told that they were observing the day for the god of the woods; the god is worshipped by the Abors, though the Garhwalis and the other Central Himalayan troops were also enjoying the festival and paying their veneration to the god. Quietly the Central Himalayan people and the Abors were becoming one group. This is not peculiar to Pasighat. The tribal youths are attracted to the Army where their adventurous and independent spirits find full expression and their beliefs and spiritual values receive a welcome among the troops of other States. As a consequence they are joining the Assam Rifles and the Assam Regiment in ever increasing numbers. The process is natural and not new, for it existed during the Ahom rule and is in evidence now also; it is not deliberately encouraged by any section of the society and it will be foolish to dub it as a manifestation of Hindu Imperialism.

Hinduism is not only a religion, it is also a way of living and a movement and is moving on slowly but surely, adapting itself to the needs of the time. Unlike Christianity and Islam which are revolutionary, in the sense that they dissociate their converts from the past, and are intolerant of other faiths, Hinduism is evolutionary and accommodating. Before the arrival of the British the tribals of Assam were gradually, and peacefully being assimilated into this civilisation or culture. Islam could not penetrate into the tribal areas and Hinduism was and will never be in a hurry to claim them to itself. It is said that the border line between Hinduism and animism (the basic religion of the NEFA people) is very vague, for Hinduism manifests itself according to the mental development of its recipients. This vague barrier between Hinduism and animism was, through the ages, being dissolved. "...... that the Brahmaputra Valley was known to the Aryan invaders of India at a very early period, and the process of converting the aboriginal tribes to Hinduism, which is going on before our eyes today, commenced long before the time of which we have any authentic record[3]", writes Gates. The British discouraged the flow of tribals coming into the Hindu fold. The Census Report of Assam, 1881, in no uncertain terms condemned the conversion (in the real sense it is assimilation or integration and by no means conversion) of Cacharies to Hinduism: "......and their conversion to Hinduism certainly more strongly to be deprecated, in as much as they possess at present many simple virtues of great price (truthfulness, honesty, simplicity, straightforwardness of character and conduct etc.) and have not as yet had all the manhood crushed out of them by a vicious one-sided civilisation[4]." What a sweeping statement by a Government document! The historian Macaulay "believed, mistakenly, that the spread of English would result in the conversion of Orientals to Christianity[5]." According to Census Report as late as in 1931 recommendations were made to spread Christianity where it had not claimed converts so as to make them into a majority community. The missionary programmes were encouraged in the early 1920s—the years when the national struggle for freedom was gaining popularity among the Indian masses. "The progress of Christianity in Assam during the last decade has thus been extremely rapid and there is no reason to suppose that it will not continue at the same rate during the next ten years. The Manipur Hills, the Garo Hills and the Naga Hills are the three hill districts in which the number of Christians is still comparatively small and these districts offer probably the most fruitful fields in India today for growth of Christianity[6]." Whether the

Naga has "mental outlook and mental processes far more consonant with those of the European than has the ordinary native of India, whose thoughts for generations have been stunned by the cumbrous wrappings of caste and Hinduism[7]", or has lived "untouched by higher civilisation for thousands of years[8]" or is "thoroughly primitive and independent of religious professions[9]", he was considered a suitable subject for missionary activity. Government aided schools run by missionaries were established and the Nagas were taught to live at peace with their neighbours. These efforts bore fruits and the Aos, the Lotse, the Semas and the Angamis took to the new religion. However, some difficulties soon arose. "An Animist puts his village before himself. A baptist himself before the village[10]", wrote Mills in 1931. Here the conflict starts. Among the Nagas, religion plays an important part in every ceremony and that religion has never been Christianity. Therefore, the Baptists shunned every ceremony and some times refused to contribute their shares for village festivals which were to them Pagan. This attitude created disunity in the tribal village. The Christians became a misfit in their own country and lived the life of strangers in their own villages. They forgot their past and did not or could not equip themselves for the future; and in their misery they started blaming the plainsmen and wrongly thought that complete independence and their own State would bring them economic aid from foreign countries, ushering in prosperity to the strife ridden and unproductive Naga Hills. Economically backward and uneducated Nagas, mostly non-Christians, did not agree with this idea. They knew that with the present state of development and education they would be left behind in the race for material prosperity and would fall further behind the

Christian elite. Such people, who form a majority in NHTA, supported and still support Government development activities. However, the Government has now acceded to the demand for a separate Naga State. It is unfortunate that this solution to the problem had to be resorted to, for politically it weakens the State and so the nation. These people were dreaming of a Christian State on the Eastern Frontier of India and their hopes now seem to be approaching fulfilment. When fully matured and developed this State will be entitled to receive foreign aid from the United Nations, so the people of NHTA believe.

Buddhism is another religion to be discussed in connection with NEFA. The advantage of this religion is that its religious teachers need not be imported from outside the territory. The preachers of Khampti and Monpa area could spread Buddhism among their neighbours if they so desired. But previous history belies any such expectation. The Mishmis have been next-door neighbours of the Khamptis for the last two centuries on one side and of the Burmans on the other but they have never accepted Buddhism. The Abors have always been antagonistic to this religion and they will not accept it. The Tagins and the Hill Miris are similar to the Abors. The Apa Tanis are concentrated in a small area and are well organised; they are prosperous and are too busy to effect changes in their existing social and cultural order. Buddhism is too mild a way of life for the independent and war-like Daflas. The only people who may be influenced by the religion are the Akas and the Mijis, but they are very few and would not affect the religious picture of NEFA.

Coming to Hinduism Dr. Verrier Elwyn points out that the gentle figure of cow stands between this religion and the tribal people. He also lists the caste system which the tribals will not accept.

> "I doubt if the NEFA people will accept Hinduism in any organised manner. Between them and that great religion stands the gentle figure of the cow. Yet there are many things which should attract them in popular Hinduism: the same belief in a supreme deity ruling over a host of spirits; the same sacrifices; the same colourful festivals; myths and legends of a rather similar pattern. But the tribal people, even the educated ones, will not give up their mithune, beef and beer; they are likely to reject caste system, the new and unfamiliar taboos, the prevailing puritanism[11]."

In dealing with Hinduism, one should not ignore Vaishnavism which is the cult of the majority of the Assamese. Vaishnavism once solved the religious problem of Assam. Can this Sect meet the requirements of the people of NEFA without uprooting them from the past and can it implant in them firmly the shape of things to come in future?

Beef eating is not a serious bar to becoming a Hindu. In ancient times beef was deemed as an absolute necessity by pious Hindus in their journey from this world to the next, and a cow was invariably killed to be burnt with the dead[12]. Economic necessity and the impact of Buddhism on the Indian society brought disrepute to cow-killing. With a desire to respect the sentiments of their Buddhist neighbours beef eating was given up by that generation of Hindus and was declared to be an act of Mlechhas (non-Arayans). "Work which lead not to paradise, and are condemned by public opinion, should not be performed. Thus, the slaughter of large bulls and large sheep for

Brahmans versed in Vedas, though duly ordained, should not be done, being detested by the public. Further, the rule, let a cow fit for offering to Mitra and Varuna, or a barren cow, or one that has ceased to bear after first calving, be sacrificed, is duly ordained; still such sacrifice being opposed to public feeling, should not be performed[12]", quotes Rajendralal Mitra from scriptures. This public spirit induced the Mohammadans of Hyderabad and Eastern Bengal to abstain from beef eating. There are hundreds of Hindus, even high caste ones, who take beef when visiting the West, but they give up the practice in India because of the respect of others' religious sentiments. Moreover, since the Independence, by-laws have been enacted by local governments prohibiting cow slaughter, and the measure in many cases is welcomed by the Mohammadans for the amity between the two major communities it produces. This shows that the problem of beef-eating is not difficult of solution on a voluntary basis. After partition in misguided zeal some Pakistanis started killing cows to show their spite against Hindu religious sentiment but the State soon realised the danger of scarcity of milk that would prevail if the destruction of cattle continued unabated and was not checked in time. Soon Government machinery moved and restricted the destruction of milk-yielding wealth. China has not got much cattle wealth and so has difficulty in providing milk to infants and their mothers. NEFA's case runs parallel to China, and where there are no cows there the problem of beef-eating does not arise.

The people of NEFA do not eat beef as ordained by their customs of religious beliefs, they do not consume it deliberately to injure the feelings of those who are culturally or socially opposed to them either. As they consume other meat so they consume beef. They neither have a special social sanction for it nor do they relish it as a delicacy. In order to enjoy the benefits of belonging to the large family of Indians they must be expected to voluntarily give up beef-eating. As far as the eating of mithune is concerned, that will not bar the tribal people from enlisting themselves as full-fledged Hindus. The Newars of Nepal eat buffalo's flesh yet they are considered to be a branch of Hindu society. And a buffalo for an ordinary Hindu is similar to a mithune.

Before analysing the flesh eating habits of the NEFA people, let us take note of an observation made by Capt. Butler in the 1870s about the Angami Nagas' abstinence from meat. "Some have told me that they believe that if they have (according to their light be it remembered) led good and wordly lives upon this, and abstaining from all coarse food, and specially have abstained from eating flesh, after death their spirits would fly away into the realm above......[13]." Even today a teetotaller and a vegetarian is respected by the tribal people. Though as a general rule the people have no objection to the eating of meat, their ideal has always been vegetarianism which entitles them to a better life in the next world. Regarding the eating of flesh itself, the tribals are not very rigid about it and it can be modified to suit the new circumstances. The Noctes and some of the Wanchoos do not profess to eat beef, and it is quite common for the Nocte women to be strictly vegetarian. The Mishmi women are forbidden to eat the meat of domesticated animals, and there are few wild animals left in the Mishimi Hills to add to the Mishmi diet. Even if the Mishmi wife is fortunate enough to be provided with meal of a wild animal she is debarred from eating it before the birth of a child. Coming to Mishmi menfolks, they abstain from flesh-eating in presence of senior relations from their wife's side and they being polygamous generally having more than four wives, (ten is not an unusual number) have many such relations in the village. As a result they seldom get a chance to eat flesh. Thus the Mishmis would not miss beef if they were accepted in the Hindu fold. The Adis abhor the use of beef. The Apa Tanis and the Daflas are the only people who may take some time to overcome the difficulty; even they, on account of increasing association with the plainsmen may learn to resist the temptation to eat beef. The Akas, the Mijis and the Khawas are few in number and they are already influenced by the teachings of Hinduism and Buddhism and most probably would spare the 'gentle cow' from their table. Therefore, if the tribals decide to embrace Hinduism the cow should not prove to be an insurmountable barrier between them and this religion.

The caste system and untouchability are other stigmas against the Hindu society which could stand in the way of tribals becoming Hindus. Examples of Manipur Nagas who are said to have been absorbed in the sweeper caste are quoted to discourage the simple people from thinking of becoming Hindus. It has been observed and confirmed by many Western and Eastern writers and social workers that although the caste system does prevail in Assam yet the orthodox tenets of Hinduism as practised in Bihar, Bengal, and Uttar Pradesh are not strictly observed (in Assam, the sweeper class is conspicuous by its absence), and even Mahatma Gandhi accepted the fact that the virus of untouchability, as prevalent in Southern India has no place in Assam. For a casual observer, communalism among the Hindus and the Muslims also does not exist and the taboo against the latter cooking food for the former is practically ignored. Under these conditions the caste system and untouchability are not likely to prove an impediment or prevent the tribals from entering Hinduism. This caste has not affected the social status of the Rajbansis of Goalpara, Cacharies of Cachar, the Miris and Mikirs in other parts of Assam, the Newars and Lachhavis of Nepal, or the Ban Rawats in Kumaon. and there is no reason why it should affect the people of NEFA adversely. Some of the Naga, Abor, and the Dafla girls have been married to Hindus and they have been absorbed into the caste of their husbands. There are innumerable instances of Hill Miri girls marrying the plains Miris and being absorbed into the latter's society. In fact Assam is the only Province in India where this fusion of tribal people has been going on smoothly without caste difficulties, and it has been going on for centuries. This is mostly due to the cult of Vaishnavism which has already taken thousands of hillmen and dwellers of the jungles into its folds.

In Assam the term Hinduism connotes very little and is not understood by religious teachers. The Sattradhikari of Dakhinpat, one of the chief Sattras (Vaishnav worshipping centres) on Majuli island, enquired of my religion. I replied that I was a Hindu. He wanted a further elaboration of my religious belief; he wanted the name of the deity whose temple I frequented. I told him that I worshipped and visited the temples of all Hindu gods and goddesses. He was surprised. He knew of Lord Krishna, Siva and Kamakhya and the respective sects of Vaishnavism, Saivaism and Saktaism; for him Hinduism was restricted to these three sects only. Vaishnavism, the worship of Vishnu or Lord Krishna, is known and is popular in the rest of the country, but in Assam it needs special mention. Worship of the female principle, the power of nature as manifested by personified desire is Saktaism.

> "O Adya! the five essential Elements in the worship of Shakti have been prescribed to be wine, meat, fish, parched grain, and the union of man with woman. The worship of Shakti without these Elements is but the practice of evil magic[14]."

Parallel to Saktaism is Saivaism, with a difference that in the latter the male principle rules the tenets.

Because of social advances in society and changes in social values and the misunderstanding about Saktaism itself, this religion is not preached in public and its outworn, medieval and erotic practices are not openly talked about; if they are performed then they do not come to the notice of non-Saktas. But it does not mean that Saktaism has decayed in Assam. One has only to visit the temple of Kamakhya and see for himself how much the goddess is venerated throughout Assam.

Swami Shankar Dev (1449-1557), the founder of Vaishnavism in Assam, is venerated as a reincarnation of God. He was a great reformer and a nation builder, and he had a personality to match the task of uniting the Assamese. Before Shankar's birth the religion of the Assamese was Saktaism or Tantraism; Tantric Buddhism also prevailed in the foothills of Northern Assam. Tantric religious practices, human and animal sacrifices at the altar of the deity, and the worship of innumerable gods roused in him a fervour for religious reform and he revolted against these cults existing then in the Hindu society. He used to recite:

> "Pouring of water at the root of a tree causes

> the branches, leaves and flowers to thrive, but if you pour water on the leaves and the branches no part of the tree will thrive. To sustain and nourish the limbs and organs of the body you have got to satisfy your hunger by eating but if you fast and wear ornaments on every limb you feel no satisfaction. In the same way he who worships the supreme deity appeases the minor deities also but if he worships any one of the minor deities he pleases none[15]."

Briefly: "There is one God; there is only one devotion; there are none but one.[16]."

Therefore he preached unqualified Monoism. Shankar's cult is comprised of four main principles—(i) comprehension of Param Brahma, the all pervasive Supreme Being in the form of Vishnu as extolled in the Vedas, (ii) undivided devotion to the Supreme Being in the form of Lord Krishna, (iii) Sat-Sanga (Association with godly people.) with pious divines as enjoined by Bhagvat Purana, and (iv) Kirtan, chanting of hymns, prayers and holy names of the Lord. The last principle has been interpreted by Muirhead so as to throw more light on the religious bent of the Assamese.

> "But although this new idea seems to offer at first sight something quite opposed to the Sakta with their diversity of deities and images, his (Shankar Dev's) instructions are couched in such phrases as to lend themselves easily to different interpretations according to the belief of the devotee. For example, in order to convey to his followers exactly what he means by the highest type of devotion to Krishna; he says it should be like the love of Radha, the gopi-girl, for Krishna, the

cow herd. But there is surely no fundamental difference between this comparison and that of the Saktas, who say that the blissful state of the worshipper, who is finally through prayer and meditation united with Siva, is akin to the ecstasy which Parvati feels in sexual union with Siva, her husband[17]."

It means whether it is Vaishnavism, Saktaism or Saivaism the same current of earthly realism pervades all the three sects of Hinduism of Assam; and the Assamese are more realistic than philosophical; for them Krishna Lila (episodes of Krishna's life) is more significant than the philosophy of Vedantaism.

Shankar Dev was against the caste system. He was a Kayastha (second highest caste in Assam.) and was married to a Hari (low caste) girl and his Sattradhikaris (head priests) and Atas, deputies to the former, were from every caste and creed—Madhav Dev was a Brahman, Anirodha a non-Brahman, Narottam a Naga, Parmananda a Miri, Ramai a Cachari, Purnananda a Kaivarta, Haridas a Baniya, Chandsai a Muslim and Damodar a Bhotia—and they preached Vaishnavism throughout Assam including the tribal areas. After Shankar's death casteism crept into Vaishnavism and three or four religious centres of different sects were established in the State.

At present the Vaishnavs of the Assam Valley can broadly be divided into the Mahapurshias and the Bamunias or other 'Vaishnavs'. The former will accept a Sudra (low caste) as a religious guide, worship none but Krishna, and are uncompromising in their hostility to idols. The latter will recognise only a Brahman as their Goswami (Head priest of Vaishnav temples). They permit the adoration of other deities, such as Siva and Kali, in addition to that of Krishna and allow sacrifices to be offered in their honour. A Brahman can become a Goswami in either sect, but a non-Brahman can be a Goswami only amongst the Mahapurshias. The ordinary member of either sect can be of any caste. There are four main Sattras in Majuli-Garamur, Auniati, Dakhinpat and Kamlabari—, the Sattradhikaris of the first three are Brahmans while that of the last a non-Brahman, but thousands of Miri devotees throng the former, and high caste Hindus are not wanting in the list of Kamlabari disciples. Similarly in the vicinity of Nazira and Dibrugarh there are various Moamari (low caste) Sattras but non-tribals also attend Kirtan in their namghars (the prayer halls or the Kirtan Ghars). The redeeming feature of Vaishnavism in Assam is that in the Mahapurshia Sect, low caste disciples are allowed to eat pigs, fowl and the flesh of game, and the Bamunias are also more liberal in their diet and eat goat, pigeons and ducks.

Therefore, Kirtan in namghars, a liberal sanction for consumption of beer, port, and fowl, a simple way of living, a tolerant Monoism, a place for sacrifices to various gods and goddesses and an almost casteless society, it is felt, should appeal to the tribal people of NEFA more than any other religion. Vaishnavism will strengthen the tie connecting their past with the present and the new followers of this faith will not feel isolated from their past beliefs, practices and legends.

Dr. V. Elwyn has analysed the tribal religion elaborately; his analysis is academic and philosophic. He agrues that the human mind is incurably religious and science will fail to destroy religious faith. On this basis he adds: "Tribal religion, developed and reformed from within, is thus not bound to be destroyed by science[18]." Who will develop the religion? Where are the tribal religious leaders ? Will the world allow a small society to wait for the birth of leaders who may guide them to religious progress ? These are questions which are bound to disturb the minds of those who are interested in the emotional integration of the tribals with the rest of the people of the country. Dr. Elwyn optimistically concludes : "It is worthy of preservation ; I believe that it contains seeds of growth[18]." It will certainly grow provided others will let it grow. What happened in the Naga Hills, Lushai Hills, Jaintia and Khasi Hills and the Garo Hills ? According to the Doctor two of the great religions have developed from humble beginning. Correct. But under what surroundings ? Do the same conditions apply in India ? In this century for a religion to be growing it requires, if not ever-increasing number of its adherents, at least quite a substantial number of followers so that its devotees may feel at home and confident and may be able to hold their own amidst the followers of other faiths. Is it possible in NEFA ? The population of NEFA is not more than 3 Lakhs comprising more than thirty main tribal groups, each group having its own beliefs and religious notions ; they are surrounded by the followers of Buddhism and Hinduism, religions of far advanced and developed concepts of nature ; under the circumstances the tribals cannot hold their own, though at present, as long as they are isolated from their neighbours, their religious beliefs meet all of their spiritual requirements. It will be futile to analyse their religious faith. Martin describes the religion of Kochs as : "The Koch offers sacrifices to the sun, moon and stars, and to the gods of the woods, hills and rivers ; and every year, when they collect the first crops, they offer some of the first fruits and a fowl to their deceased parents, calling to them by name, and clapping their hands[19]." The Kochs are now Hindus but this depiction of their religion during the last century is an appropriate description of tribal religion in NEFA. There may be minor differences here and there and the names applied to various gods may also differ, but in gist it remains the religion of the Nefaites. Some would name it as Animism, and if that is so, then the Hindus are not far from it.

The Noctes of Tirap are Vaishnavites and the Goswami of Baraghar Sattra, 3 miles from Nazira, visits them annually. He has established about five temples in Namsang area and according to him the Wanchoos are also keen to join his sect. The Tangsas and the Singphos are Buddhists of some sort, and the Khamptis are full-fledged Buddhists though their religion has been influenced by tribal gods and Hindu deities. Recently Sri C. Gohain, MP from NEFA constituency, built a temple dedicated to the god of woods. Mr. Gohain is a devout Buddhist. The Mishmis, the inhabitants of a tract where once Aryan civilisation flourished and where Temeshwari Mai* was being worshipped up to the middle of the last century, and who were the rightful claimants of the offerings of Parasuram Kund or Brahma Kund, believe in Majeedagrah, the god of destruction and an equivalent of Siva or Mahadev. Basu[20] tells us that the Mishmis are the descendants of Brahmans and their religion is the religion of the Aryans. The Abors and the Hill Miris believe in a future state, and have an indefinite idea of a god who

* Lt. Rowlatt (JASB 1845 Vol. XIV Pt. II page 479) recorded that the Idu priests of the temple were living in North Lakhimpur in 1840s and that the practice of human sacrifice had been in vogue up to 1825.

presides in the region of departed souls; they call him 'Jam' probably a corruption of the 'Yama' of the Hindus. The Apa Tanis may not and need not change their way of life. The Daflas of Subansiri gather round the temple of Basudev, founded at the confluence of the rivers Rangapjan and Kachikata in the native village of Madhav Dev in the district of North Lakhimpur, and their interest in Vaishnavism is increasing day by day. Raja Tagi of the Akas after his return from Gauhati in 1832 introduced amongst his people the worship of Hari (Vishnu) and since then Vaishnavism is not an unknown cult among the Akas. The Mijis have matrimonial alliances with the Akas and it is only a question of time when they also may take to this religion. A new trend among the Akas has recently been noticed; they have started flying prayer flags and erecting *man-nes* like the Buddhist. Of course, the Monpas are ardent Buddhists and need not transfer their loyalty from Buddha to Krishna.

When the Ahoms arrived in India they had not been converted to Buddhism. Their religion was the religion of the tribals of today. Because of their non-Aryan character they were not favourably inclined to the caste system, though the Brahmans wove mythological stories about them and declared them to be equivalent to the Rajputs. They were attracted towards Saktaism which suited them and their habits of flesh-eating, wine drinking and of performing elaborate ceremonies. "It seems that Saktaism was more in keeping with their own racial traits and habits of life. Meat-eating and wine-drinking, hardly hill-men as the Ahoms originally were, they naturally took to a creed which offered a good scope for the continuance of their old practices, though in a modified form[21]." Later some of the Ahom Kings patronised Vaishnav temples. The Manipuris also accepted Vaishnavism and they are proud of their religion and the art that emanates from it. Therefore, Vaishnavism is the natural religion of the people of NEFA and in due course they will take to it without impairing their old traditions.

"One thing is certain. The people of NEFA, and of all the tribal areas throughout India, are making rapid progress in material prosperity, but this prosperity may be positively dangerous unless there is a parallel spiritual and ethical revival[22]", writes the ATA. The country sooner or later will have to provide for the spiritual needs of the people of NEFA. A religious vacuum is a favourable hunting ground for the vested interests of the West and the communists of the North.

1. Discovery of Assam
2. JASB Vol. XVI No. 2 1950 p. 157
3. JASB 1893-1904 Selection (Gates) p. 272
4. Census Report of Assam 1881 p. 71
5. Modern Burma by Le Roy Christian p. 188
6. Census of India, 1931, Vol. III Pt. I report by C. S. Mullan M.A., I.C.S. p. 195
7. The Angami Nagas by J. H. Hutton, C.I.E., M.A: p. 37
8. The Naked Nagas by Haimendorf p. 3
9. Sketch of Assam by Butler p. 150
10. J. P. Mills Report
11. Dr. Elwyn p. 209
12. JASB 1872 p. 174
13. JASB 1875 Butler p. 315
14. Mahanivaran Tantra translated into English by Arthur Avalon p. 63
15. Early History of Kamrup by Rai K. L. Barua Bahadur—1933 p. 311
16. Shankar Dev by H. M. Das
17. Assam Valley by R. C. Muirhead Thomson D.Sc. p. 44

18. Dr. Elwyn p. 215
19. Eastern India by M. Martin, Vol. III, 1938 p. 541
20. History of Kamrup, Vol. I by Nagendra Nath Basu p 84F
21. A History of Mughal North-East Frontier policy by Sudhindra Nath Bhattacharyya p. 24
22. Dr. Elwyn p. 222

CHAPTER X

Lingua Franca of the People

To

The Hon'ble Fred. James Holiday

Lt. Governor of Bengal.

Honourable Sir,

.... the Assamese language is the common medium of intercourse with the mountain tribes that surround the Valley. The Bhutias, the Mishmis, the Abors, the Miris, the Khamptis, the Singphos, the Nagas, and various other tribes compose a vast population, all of whom if ever reached at all, must be reached from this Valley, and through the medium of the Assamese language. From these constant intercourse with the Assamese from the days of Ahom kings, some among them can speak Assamese very well, everywhere such may be found active as interpreters, and forming a medium of communication. **It is not probable that the language of all these tribes can ever be reduced to system; and books and translations prepared for them to any extent: but through the Assamese language, as a common medium, much can be accomplished from them even at the present time.—(Bold is mine)**

The importance of this subject is my only excuse for the length and freedom of these remarks. On the decision your honour may make as to the encouragement or continued suppression of the Assamese language, hangs almost entirely the question of the more speedy amelioration of all these barbarous tribes on our frontier, the success or otherwise of Vernacular Education in this Province, and the consequent elevation of the masses around us.[1]

I have etc.,

13 November, 1854 (Signed) M. Bronson,
American Missionary,
Nowgong, Assam.

"Assamese. This is the language of the middle and upper parts of the Assam Valley. It is nearly related to colloquial Bengali, but its claim to be regarded not as a dialect of Bengali, but as an independent language, rests mainly on the fact that it possesses an important toleration, besides having several characteristics of pronunciation. Its literary style does not suffer like Bengali from the excessive use of Sanskrit. The literature goes back to an early date, is varied in character, and specially abounds in historical work. Assamese cannot be said to have any real dialect."[1A]

A. A. Macdonell

On Friday the August 7, 1959 a PTI message was published in the "Pioneer" according to which Pt. Nehru told Mrs. Mufida Ahmad in the Lok Sabha that Government recognised the importance of teaching the Assamese language in NEFA and was examining the question of encouraging this language as a medium of instruction. This decision was long over due. In fact, from all historical and other evidence it was a foregone conclusion that the Assamese language should have been the medium of instruction in the NEFA schools, but the Government was advised wrongly and a period of 12 years was wasted in wild goose chase. Since 1947 the tribal children have had to undergo the tremendous strain of learning different languages; first they were taught in Assamese; then in Hindi; and now, it is said, they will be taught in Assamese. In formulating their educational policy, the authorities completely ignored the tribal group psychology and in many cases imposed alien dialects on the unwilling learners. This benefited neither the locals nor the government. The advocates of Hindi and the local dialects were the only beneficiaries, because, they could sustain their lucrative appointments in the NEFA Education Department, though the general public in Assam and in NEFA itself never became reconciled to the measure. The favourite argument of the tribal parents was that by learning the Assamese language their children could freely communicate with the Assamese, and by learning Hindi they could secure employment under the Central Government Departments, but what material advantages could they gain by learning the dialects of other tribal groups with whom they had never been on friendly terms? For instance the Namsanghias and the Bordurias are both Noctes and are next-door neighbours, but they speak different dialects and each group is jealous and suspicious of the other. It was considered futile by the Bordurias to learn the dialect of the Namsanghias and vice versa. This is not an isolated instance, it can be applied everywhere in NEFA. It is an accepted fact that natural barriers disintegrated the tribal society into innumerable groups and kept them isolated from each other for centuries thus giving rise to equally numberless dialects. The saying that 'barbarism creates languages, civilization destroys them'. was discarded and attempts were made to keep alive the dialects of influential groups irrespective of the number of people who used them. Mackenzie collected the non-Aryan languages of the Frontier Tract into only four linguistic groups (i) Aka, Dafla, Miri, Abor, and Mishmi, (ii) the Shan language, (iii) Tibetan, and (iv) the Naga group[2]. According to this classification the first could widely be applied in the Northern Tract, the second on the Tract's northern fringes, while the Shan language could be encouraged among the Khamptis and the Singphos ; and the fourth in Tirap only. Contrary to this, more than 50 tribal dialects have been recognised and the NEFA Education Department has produced books for primary classes in 27 dialects. At present the NEFA philologists "are devoting themselves to the preparation of Grammars, Dictionaries, and phrase-books to help officers to learn the local languages, and to supervise the translation of school text-books, so that education at least in the primary stage can be carried on in the mother-tongue ; and to building up a written and printed tribal literature. A substantial collection of the myths and legends of NEFA, many of unusual interest has been published. At present it is in English, but I hope that in time local versions will be prepared and will help to preserve many of fascinating stories full of poetry which may otherwise be forgotten[3]", the ATA informs us. How long will it take to build a literature of this kind in every tribal dialect ? Will the publication of the myths and legends help the tribals and Assam at all ?

The only people of the Northern Tract who have a script of their own are the Monpas of Kameng and their cousins residing on the northern fringes of Subansiri, Siang and Lohit. The script is of Tibetan characters. Whether the script will be of any material benefit to the people, only time will tell. Since the occupation of Tibet by the

Chinese the prospects of the Tibetan script have tremendously dimmed. The language may continue to be locally popular but, as a provincial or regional language, it is hypocritical to say that it will flourish along with other Indian languages. If the literature of this language has to be built up for the happiness of the people of Kameng, then let the people themselves take the initiative in the direction, or let the Indian universities shoulder the responsibility. In the Eastern Tract the Khamptis have a written language. The arguments which apply to the Monpa language are also applicable to the Khampti script of the Shan origin. As regards the remaining tribal groups they speak dialects which have no scripts. The Abors have a profound respect for education and idealise it but even so, they are devoid of any script. After 1912 Christian missionaries introduced the Roman script among the Abors but now through disuse it has gone into oblivion. The Abors now in matters of a written language are in a similar position to the rest of the people of NEFA.

It is not realised in responsible circles that material benefits play an important part in learning a language in this country. In spite of sentimental harangues and exhortations, non-Hindi speaking provinces are not enthusiastically learning the national language. Proficiency in English enables one to secure lucrative appointments and this language in spite of its alien character is learnt and respected by the Indians. Let us take an example of commercial link to language popularity. Ahoms had a language and a script of their own. They ruled Assam for six hundred years and their language, being the language of rulers, was popular throughout the State. The Ahoms went out of power in 1835 and the language, in spite of such a long standing use, disappeared from Assam, because it no longer had a commercial value—the new ruling class did not use it. Now nobody, outside Assam, would believe that even today Ahom records written in the Ahom character, are available. Will it benefit Assam or India to revive this language? When this is the case of a language which had a literature of its own and has been given up by the people, it serves no purpose to start evolving a literature in those languages which never even had a script. Will it pay the country if attempts are made by the Government to appoint a special staff to conduct research on the Garhwali or Kumaoni literature? After all the Garhwalis and the Kumaonis are also sentinels on our border areas. Further, agreed that Hindi is an old literature, and it is rich and varied but it lacks reference books, specially of the Muslim and the British periods. When, after centuries, Hindi has failed to produce a broad-based literature, how many centuries will it take for the little known man of NEFA to translate his dialect into a script and then to build a literature of some value? Lastly will the tribal people materially benefit by the venture? A few Hindi scholars, ignorant of English, may get a few good jobs here and there through their personal influence, otherwise their market value is not going to be very high for decades to come. Of course, it is no use dealing with the narrower aspects of culture if one is educated only in one language. The tribal people of NEFA in order to bridge the gulf existing between them and the advanced sections of society will have to be educated in more than one language, up to a fairly good standard in order to be able to handle the languages learnt with the ease of an expert. In this, no spoon-feeding or undue patronising will help them. At the same time basic principles of child psychology should not be ignored. It is the birth-right of every child that he should be taught in his mother-tongue, at least, in the primary stage, but when he grows up and reaches the higher standard he should be taught in the language of the community in which he has to live. A Garhwali child may be taught in the local dialect in the primary stage but to prolong its teaching beyond this stage is to make the child unfit for his future life in the community. Similarly a Borduria child may be taught in the local dialect in the primary stage but to continue his education in this dialect beyond the primary stage is to prolong the agony of his backwardness. Every explorer, administrator and missionary has observed that the Assamese language is the lingua franca of the tribal people of NEFA; it is the vehicle through which the ideas of one group are passed to the other, therefore, even if not today, it will, in future, have the same status as Hindi in Kumaon Division, provided aggressive propaganda is not carried on by the propagandists of the Roman script. It is logical therefore, that the medium of instruction in the NEFA schools should be Assamese language and none else, unless, of course the Administration is thinking of closing all the doors of NEFA leading to Assam and establishing special devices for the tribals to have direct communication and social contacts with Hindi Provinces, in which case Hindi should continue to stay as the medium of instruction in the Agency. If emotional integration of the tribals is considered most essential and desirable for consolidating and strengthening India then it is unavoidable that national pride in a tribal child should be inculcated step by step—he should be proud of his area first, of Assam next and then of the country. If attempts were made to short-circuit the process by dropping out the intermediate stage then there is every possibility that the child may develop anti-Assamese feelings and be encouraged to form extra-territorial loyalties. Suggestions of learning the Assamese language in Hindi script will not be accepted by the State, and the introduction or encouragement of Roman script will weaken Assam and will create anti-national feelings in NEFA. It is interesting to note that the Chinese are planning to encourage the Roman script in Tibet and if Nefaites are also taught the same then the common affinity may disturb the political loyalty of the latter. Modern thinkers may consider this idea as ridiculous, because for them national boundaries strengthen nationalism, an anarchic force, which impedes the development of science. "In a great many respects national boundaries have become a technical absurdity, and further advance demands that they should be ignored[4]", writes Bertrand Russel. In India, in fact in the whole of Asia, "Nationalism is immensely strong" and it cannot warrant abolition of national boundaries for decades to come.

Examples of Russia are quoted by Dr. Elwyn in support of the present policy of teaching languages and dialects to the tribal children. He quotes Pt. Nehru to support his argument.

> "In the Soviet Republic we have the example of a country that has adopted such a policy with success. Lenin and other leaders in his time were exceedingly wise in this respect. Regardless of their ultimate objective, they wanted to win the good will of the people, and they won it largely by their policy of encouraging their languages, by going out of their way to help hundreds of dialects by preparing dictionaries and vocabularies and some

time even by evolving new scripts where there were none. They wanted their people to feel that they were free to live their own lives and they succeeded in producing that impression[5]."

In considering this quotation one has to realise that in Russia, revolutionary rather than evolutionary methods, are applied even in the cultural sphere, and that includes education. "Every Union republić is a sovereign socialist state having the right of free secession from the union[6]." Is it true? Such free unions were organised first and then smaller groups were merged into the larger ones and a regional written language given to them. "In the USSR, books are published in 84 languages[7]." If every group's identity was recognised then the number of languages would be much larger than 84. Further, in how many scripts these books were written is not known. "The Turkmenian tribes speaking in dozens of dialects, did not have their own languages[8]." Statistics of attainments are given but nothing is mentioned about the script and the number of dialects to which the original ones were reduced.

From every angle the evolving of more than two dozen new written languages cannot be upheld in areas which are politically sensitive. At the best we can take Mackenzie's classification, and divide the tribal languages into four groups. We can concentrate our energies for building a literature on these 4 groups and thrust this down the throats of the tribals in the communistic manner. Otherwise common-sense dictates that the Assamese language which has always been the lingua franca of the Agency should be made the medium of instruction in the NEFA schools at this stage with the aim of developing it into the mother-tongue of the tribals. Assam is already experiencing difficulties in making Assamese the official language of the State. Let us not over-burden her with more worries. In Russia a union may be anything on paper, but in practice it cannot afford to raise its voice against the Central Administration. In India the creation of new unions and the evolving of new written languages for them will give birth to a chain of difficulties which will not be easy to surmount by democratic means.

1. Correspondence Relating to Vernacular Education in the Lower Provinces of Bengal No. 749 p. 151
1A. India's Past by A.A. Macdonell p. 247
2. Mackenzie p. 547
3. Dr. Elwyn p. 277
4. The scientific outlook by Bertrand Russel p. 204
5. Dr. Elwyn p. 202
6. The Community of Soviet Nations. p. 16
7. " " p. 37
8. " " p. 35

CHAPTER XI

Policing the Nefa Territory

"Of the honesty of the hill people, too much praise cannot be given."

George William Trail

The police as an agency for investigating crimes, bringing offenders to book and maintaining law and order within the territory were not much needed in the past in the Himalayan districts. Revenue officials were vested with police powers in the Western and the Central Himalayas. With the expansion and the development of communications the influence of modern civilization accompanied by its necessary evils and resulting in an increase in crime is making inroads into the hill districts, thus necessitating the establishment of kotwalis (Police stations) or Thanas at selected places. Minor offences such as theft, swindling and fraud are on the increase and heinous crimes such as murder and dacoity (robbery committed by five or more persons, and it is generally accompanied by violence or at least by show of force) are not uncommon, specially along the national highways. So far NEFA is free from minor offences, and crimes are of different kinds than those that we are acquainted with. However, the tribal has displayed violence against foreigners. As a preventive measure against such violent outbursts and to safeguard the interest of the State a special force was required in the Assam Frontier areas. Very often the peace of the tract was disturbed by inter-tribal feuds resulting in bloodshed. These internecine wars, for the peace of the tract, had to be suppressed. The nature of terrain and the vastness of these scarcely populated areas required a highly mobile police force. The Assam Rifles supplies all of these requirements. "The task of pacifying and humanising these primitive hill people would have been impossible had there not been at the command a trained and armed force which could be employed in small detachments, could be rapidly set in movement and could make shift with a minimum of transport", writes Sir Bomfield Fuller.

It is a well known fact that the inhabitants of a border area, be it in India, China or any other part of the world, always have dual loyalties, and NEFA, under the white man's rule, was very much prone to this. To have a watch over the recalcitrant elements in these border areas, units of the Assam Rifles served as an efficient checking agency and guarded the checkposts established on all the passes along the Indo-Tibetan border in the NEFA territory. The chief function of the Assam Rifles was to maintain law and order within the territory. Defence against foreign aggression was never the responsibility of the force, though up to August 1959 such a contingency never arose. During the British period, Tibet was a buffer State and the Indo-Tibetan border was quiet, in keeping with the calmness of the snows. Since the Chinese incursions into the Northern Tract the responsibility of the Assam Rifles has also increased. The extra burden of defending the Sino-Indian border has been handed over to the Army; still Assam Rifles is the main co-sharer in the task. Now Assam Rifles has come under the operational command of the Indian Army. This is in addition to its normal duties of peaceful mission for which the force was raised in 1830 under a different name; the force has always been commanded by

Officers of the Indian Army who opted for service with this organisation from the very day of its raising. The force was given the entire charge of policing the Frontier in 1880/81 and for this increased task five separate Military Police Battalions—Lakhimpur, Naga Hills, Lushai, Garo and Cachar—were raised. After the partition of the country the Indo-Pak border added to the mileage of the frontier in Assam, and as a consequence the number of battalions had to be increased. Now because of the Chinese incursions in the North the Assam Rifles' jurisdiction has been extended to Sikkim.

The Inspector General of the Assam Rifles, a Military officer of Major General's rank whose services are loaned to the State, is the Chief of the force but, for its unified and co-ordinated control he takes directions from the Adviser of the North-East Frontier Agency. This has been a sore point with the Army. Probably the new developments on the Northern border and the increase of the authority of the Inspector General extending upto Sikkim will provide a change for the better. The I.G. will probably come under the Operational Command of the Army. This will raise the prestige of the Assam Rifles which it so eminently deserves.

Regarding recruitment to the Assam Rifles from outside Assam, the British confined it solely to the Gorkhas, not because they were hillmen and akin to the tribal people but because the Gorkhas were foreign troops and the rulers wished to keep and develop NEFA as a 'Crown Colony'. Now the National Government has changed the policy and the recruitment of hillmen from other parts of the Himalayas is also open. In recent times, the Garhwalis, and Kumaonis are coming forward to serve in the Assam Rifles in increasing number. As long as the

Gorkhas predominated in the force, the locals were not really exposed to any outside influence, because the Gorkhas themselves hailed from an equally undeveloped country, but now, as the character of the force is changed, the tribal people will have a wider circle of individuals of a higher civilisation to mix with and it is hoped that the result of these contacts will be desirable.

Units of the Assam Rifles have rendered commendable service to the Agency. In the Second World War, one of the Assam Rifles Battalions fought a heroic battle at Kohima and saved India from the subjugation to the Japanese. The Battalions, for service, were not confined to Frontier areas only. Some of them saw over-seas service in World War II. After Independence the Abor and the Mishmi Hills were devastated by the 1950 earthquake; but for the local battalion, the relief work would have been nearly impossible. The force also has its own engineers who worked very hard to complete the Kimin—Zero and Foothill—Dirang Dzong roads. In short the Assam Rifles is not only a mobile force valuable in the mountainous terrain, but it is also an integral arm of the Army.

CHAPTER XII

Development Work

"We are anxious to help the people of NEFA to develop according to their own genius. But it must be according to their own genius and not something they cannot absorb or imbibe and which merely uproots them. I would much rather go slow in our plans for development than risk the danger of this uprooting[1]."

Jawaharlal Nehru

Before Independence in 1947 the tribal people in the hills were left on their own, and development work was found difficult and unremunerative partly because administration and partly because the Government feared that with opening up the country political awakening might infect the people; "and partly because some of the senior officers sincerely thought that the people were happier as they were[2]." The late Gopinath Bardoloi's observation depicts entirely a different picture.

"We are really pained to learn that the former Governors of Assam and their supporters are advocating in England and in other places for a 'Crown Colony' to be formed with the entire hill regions of Assam and the Western hill regions of Burma. They tried to retain administrative hold in this part of our country even after we had thrown off the yoke of foreign domination. After going through the administrative files I have fully come to understand that the then rulers in Delhi made a plan to form such a 'Crown Colony' because they foresaw the possibility of such a colony........[3]." This settles the argument as to why the tribal people were left on their own and thereby a separatist tendency inculcated in the tribal mind.

The separatist tendency started taking shape in the early thirties of this century when the Chinese pushed the Inner-Outer Tibetan boundary west to about 100 miles East of Lhasa which included Chamdo in Sinkang, thus bringing the Chinese Frontier contiguous to the Abor and Mishmi Hills. This local adjustment of the Sino-Tibetan border presented a threat to the integrity of India. This was a signal for the present Sino-Indian border trouble. Political upheavals brought about Stalin's National communism and Hitler's National Socialism and the struggle for national freedom within this country, were some of the important factors responsible for a new British interest in resurveying the political situation of the Himalayan region.

Nepal was the first Himalayan State to attract British attention. She had been granted independence, and her separate identity was recognised and confirmed by 1934 when she sent her first ambassador to London. Similarly NEFA's seclusion was confirmed and strengthened by the Government of India Act of 1935 which incorporated more stringent provisions for converting the backward tracts into areas of total and partial exclusion. To safeguard the separate identity of the Himalayan region, Great Britain appointed her representative, as a reaction to the presence of the Chinese Commission in the Tibetan capital, to the Lhasa court. This measure also ensured that the political status of Tibet as a buffer state between India and China was maintained. If the security of India was in view then certainly compartmentalisation of India into secluded and partially secluded areas was misconceived and misdirected. Probably political expediency or the imperial interest dictated the policy, but the policy now is encouraging fissiparous tendencies based on racial, linguistic, religious, social and economic differences. It will be very interesting to watch the political developments in NEFA where there are 27 recognised dialects and innumerable religious beliefs.

During the first half of this century the defence of NEFA against the Chinese weighed heavily upon the Government and defence requirement dictated the objectives to be attained by the British rulers. As a corollary to this the maintenance of peace in the plains of Assam fringing the foothills of the tribal areas was considered essential. Military outposts were established and occasionally punitive expeditions were despatched to the interior to punish the lawless elements for raiding villages in the plains. The Social welfare of the people of NEFA was none of their concern. After Independence, the administrative machinery changed from being largely a law and order concern to a welfare agency.

The First Five Year Plan for NEFA made provision for an over-all expenditure of Rs. 300 lakhs while Rs. 201·22 were expended under the following headings:—

Five Year Plan	*Plan provision in lakhs of rupees.*	*Actual expenditure in lakhs of rupees.*
Agriculture	32·00	32·77
Education	41·81	19·07
Medical Public Health	65·00	46·06
Forest	20·00	22·86
Cottage Industries	6·19	9·91
Communication	135·00	70·55
Total	300·00	201·22

After the experience of the First Plan, the Second Five Year Plan provided an expenditure of Rs. 950·50 Lakhs, split into the following major heads :

	In lakhs of rupees.
Roads	197·43
Airstrips	30·00
Power	13·00
Agriculture	61·00
Medical and Public Health	90·00
Education	60·00
Community Project/National Extension Service	76·27
Forests	35·00
Industry	18·48
Research	13·30
Access Roads by Army Engineers	344·00
Miscellaneous	11·92
Total	950·50

The NEFA Administration did not think it wise to raise the over-all scope of the Plan beyond this figure for several reasons. "These are mainly, the shortage of technical personnel and material in the fields of engineering, agriculture etc., the need to avoid large scale diversions of tribal people from their main activity of agriculture, non-agricultural activities and the need for caution in the introduction of large number of subordinate staff[4]." For a cautious approach the Administration "Phased the original programme of the Second Five Year Plan over a period of ten instead of five years[5]."

The objectives of the plan were "To promote the all

round development of the tribal people of the Agency; secure their great participation in the development activities, both in the planning and the executive stages, to bring about a feeling of oneness between them and the rest of the country and, finally, to help them evolve a pattern of life which will retain the inherent good qualities of their character and, at the same time, utilise the benefits of modern science for better living", and to attain these objectives top priority was given to communications, followed by agricultural development and then the rest. Health services, including water supply, education, development of tribal languages and cottage industries. "The essential thing, however, in the successful execution of any development work is the initial approach to the people which will win their confidence, because if this is not done and their suspicions are not removed, no amount of subsequent planning will be of much avail. Therefore, selection of the right kind of Government personnel for the Agency would claim the biggest priority[6]." This is quite logical, but opportunities for the staff to work in favourable conditions are equally required.

In NEFA, except in the Dirang Dzong and Tawang, there are two seasons in the year, one is the working season from October to March, and the other is the non-working season filling up the remainder of the year. The tribals on any national project can work only during the working season either before or after 'Jhuming' which commences from the last week of November and terminates by the first week of January, depending upon winter rains. Therefore, all the villages cannot start work simultaneously at the end of those six weeks. Then, the tribals observe or celebrate various festivals and ceremonies such as death, birth, marriage, and other observances of religious nature and these interrupt their work. During the working season, the official machinery is usually geared to launch and execute constructional projects. What happens then? Generally VIPs from the Centre or from the NEFA Headquarters find time to visit the Agency and interfere with the tempo of the work and keep the officials tied to Headquarters.

As long as some of the Divisional Headquarters were not connected either by road or by air with the plains they were not haunted by frequent visits, but such headquarters suffered from lack of publicity. Even after the opening up of land communications, these headquarters remained in the background, because, generally* the number of visits were in direct proportion to the accessibility of the place by air. Siang and Subansiri were linked by air, hence they were favourite picnic spots for the great personalities who honoured the Divisional Headquarters frequently with their short visits.

Coming to the Selection of Government personnel, the POs and APOs were and are mostly recruited from the army. In fact army officers are the fittest persons to assume the responsibilities of administering these backward areas, and apart from their physical fitness and all the attributes connected with it, they are free from party or provincial prejudices and their subordinate staff is generally happy and contended. Much of the credit for good work in the Divisions goes to the zeal, initiative and hard work of the POs. Their capabilities and their tactful handling of the man-machinery is reflected in every work in NEFA. At the same time the Single Line Administra-

* The entry of Dalai Lama into India gave the best publicity to Kameng. Such occasions are rare, so were the accelerated promotions of officers present on the spot.

tion as working in NEFA has introduced a drawback which cannot be controlled by POs and which is so obvious that one is led to remark that 'the type of administration was an emergency measure and cannot cope up with the expanding development as envisaged by the Government'. The drawback is that when the PO is away from the Divisional Headquarters every decision and activity is liable to be temporarily suspended. It means that the word "Initiative" is a most unfamiliar term among the members of the NEFA staff. The PO is the head of the team and he no doubt creates confidence and will-to-work among his subordinates but he is not omnipotent and on account of very poor communications, and his preoccupation elsewhere, some of the minor works of far flung sub-centres are bound to escape his notice. It leads to the conclusion that the field staff members of subordinate rank are ultimately responsible for all the development works, and the 'Gram Sevak' (Village Level Worker) is the basic official on whom the whole development structure is based.

The 'gram sevak' is recruited from three categories of personnel—non-Assamese, Assamese and Bengalee, and the locals. Non-Assamese are intelligent and tactful. They invariably attend to the job when the senior officer is around, and when he is not, they are fond of fishing or shooting or creating work for temporary duty outside the Inner Line to break the monotony of their solitary living. They treat the locals decently, but that 'oneness with the tribals' hardly finds a place in their conduct. The Assamese and the Bengalees find themselves in an advantageous position over their non-Assamese colleagues in that they face the tribals directly and their language—Assamese—helps them in this task. Within a short period they usually gain the confidence of the bulk of the people amongst whom they work. Constant mixing with the locals on equal terms enables them to learn local dialects within a very short time. Invariably it is seen that wherever and in whatever village the Assamese or the Bengalees, (the latter of course very few in numbers) VLWs are found, there the locals are more lively and socially progressive. This popularity is also shared by tribal workers who have faith in science and have no racial prejudices against the people with whom they live; Again a majority of the indigeneous workers coming from advanced tribal groups like the Khamptis, the Abors and the Semas produced good results in their own areas, but they failed to work with the same zeal in other areas. A fairly good number of local VLWs were good, but there was a wide scope for strengthening their faith in the efficacy of science to improve the lot of their compatriots.

A visit to NEFA and its far flung administrative centres convinces the visitor that the members of class III and class IV grades are not satisfied with their lot. And all of their complaints are not frivolous and erroneous. Here it may be added that a medical licentiate is a class III officer. I had an argument with a doctor of this class. I said, "It is alright for everybody to grumble but the Government has got to develop the people to bring them up to the level of living and culture existing in the rest of the country." A long discussion followed and I came to know many things which helped me formulating the following suggestions, if the NEFA Administration is really anxious to develop the locals economically, socially and culturally:

1. The Government officials must make up their minds whether they will run the Agency as a separate and

independent entity parallel to a State or merge it with Assam in the near future. This will automatically lead them to frame a policy for organising the NEFA Administration on either a permanent or else a temporary basis, thus transferring the government servants to the permanent category or else discharging them from service. The present system of employing government servants on monthly or quarterly or annual contracts strikes at the very roots of efficiency and contentment. Uncertainty of employment nurtures insecurity and fear among the employees, and many of the ills among the subordinate staff can be traced to this fear.

2. Government are paying 33 per cent of the basic pay to their servants as a special NEFA allowance. It may be adequate for administrative staff, but it is insufficient for allopathic doctors who are in grade III. For the latter the allowance should be raised to 40 per cent. It should be appreciated that the doctors are technical officers and they do not have the special powers enjoyed by administrative personnel which enable them to throw their weight around and keep their ego satisfied. The doctors are government servants and their aim and ideal is remuneration which they cannot supplement with private income in NEFA. It is quite reasonable that their special allowance should be slightly higher than that of others.

3. There should be a well-regulated rotation of service. When any government servant has served for 3 or 4 years in NEFA he should be given a chance to live in a good and developed station. But the case runs parallel to the army. When army personnel or units have served in a backward area (field) the party affected is given a chance to be stationed at a place where most of the modern conveniences and amenities are available;

This is not so in NEFA. Except for the Western Kameng, all the other areas are equally 'Field Areas' at least for class III and class IV officials. At present the non-administrative staff, specially of outposts, is far from being contented. There have been a few cases of resignation and a few also have suffered from mental worries. Therefore in order to minimise such occurrences the Agency should be broadened to include some healthy districts to give a chance to the subordinate staff to sometimes be posted to these districts

4. Further, as in the army so in NEFA, when a person of lower rank has served for a few years in the defence forces and he wishes to revert to civilian status, he is not taken by civilian employers unless he is forced upon them or recommended by Government. Therefore, short term engagements of any rank are not conducive to economic stability. If a NEFA temporary officer has to be discharged or relieved of his duties from the Agency, official efforts must be made to secure him a suitable appointment under another employer.

5. There is hardly any need to emphasise that allopathic doctors are a misfit in the society and for the sake of science and progress either an effort should be made to encourage the locals to rely on government-appointed doctors or these specialists should be withdrawn and replaced by vaids and hakims as previously suggested.

The Commissioner for Scheduled Castes and Tribes recorded in his 1957-58 Report (on page 116): "During my recent visit to the NEFA it was noticed that the jeepable roads that were started 6 years back have still not been completed." And the position up to August 1959 was not very different to what is stated in the Report. In view of loose soil, absence of stones, torrential rains, geographical and geological shortcomings of the NEFA terrain and restrictions on the import of labour and contractors from outside, how could the position have been improved ?

Road communications in NEFA have been described in the chapter dealing with the Divisions. Regarding airstrips and landing grounds satisfactory progress has been made in this direction. Regarding telephonic communications Bomdi La was the first to receive a telephone line, a connection to NEFA Headquarters at Shillong in 1959, thanks to the Dalai Lama !

The establishment of the 'Border Road Control Board' of which the Prime Minister is the chairman and the Defence Minister a member will hasten the road construction in NEFA. It is surmised that roads that would ordinarily take four years to construct will be completed within one year.

Nearly all the Nefaites practise 'jhuming'. It is said to be closely linked with social customs, mythology and the religion of the people. It is considered the only method for cultivation, because the NEFA hills are steep and irrigation is impossible. 'Jhuming' is damaging to the people and the State but the social habits, mythology and the religion of the locals still need not stand in the way of adopting improved agricultural methods. The social habits and celebrations connected with 'jhuming' have been formed around the 'Jhum' land, the sowing of seeds, and the harvesting and storing of the crops. Of all these, only the customs associated with the sowing of seeds need to be changed and these changes will evolve new habits. They need not be in any way damaging to the mythology or the religion of the people. Regarding the difficulties because of the steepness of the hills, one should visit the

Khasi and Jaintia Hills which are as steep, if not steeper, than those of NEFA and see the terrace cultivation which is successfully practised there. Further, irrigation in NEFA, on account of copious rainfall, is not considered necessary. Some agriculture and forest experts maintain that in NEFA irrigation, instead of benefiting the crop, will ruin it. Therefore, since the steep hills can be terraced and irrigation is not necessary, there can be no objection to changing, in NEFA, from 'jhuming' to a settled system of agriculture and the sooner 'jhuming' is given up the better it is for all concerned. In connection with the cessation of this practice the rearing of fruit plantations on undulating tracts, and wet rice cultivation on the plain land must be encouraged. This will involve food-import into the territory till the plain land is well enough that it will produce cereals sufficient to sustain the tribal population. But this change of crops—from rice to fruit—and the problem of importing foodgrains, is greatly preferable to watching thousands of acres of valuable forests burned (to provide new jhum land) before the very eyes of Administrators every year, and what is gained by this wanton destruction ? 'Jhum' produces just enough for the people to subsist on, where cultivation is desired, and at other places it produces a better crop for few mithunes, if grazing is desired. What a colossal damage to land and forests is suffered for such a pitifully small gain ! So far no attempt has been made to discourage 'jhuming'. Unless serious attempts are made to bring about the cessation of this destructive practice, the economic future of the entire area will be irreparably damaged, and until the results of this practice are scientifically scrutinised, how can one contend that giving up of 'jhuming' would injure tribal people's economic interests ? Wherever 'jhuming' has been replaced by WRC the quantity of foodgrains has multiplied, so why not give a chance to the latter practice to produce food for the people of NEFA?

The NEFA Agriculture Department has established Demonstration Plots at every Divisional Headquarters and also distributes seeds and chemical fertilisers. Pairs of bullocks have been given to some of the people. But the people are still not convinced of these measures, though Demonstration Plots are proving a success. 23,000 acres of land were said to have been reclaimed for permanent cultivation by August 1959, but the major portion of the land was worked by Government employees. Whatever improvement there was in the yield was largely due to government efforts. The people who practise 'jhuming' are reluctant to adopt modern methods of cultivation, but what about those like the Monpas, the Khamptis and Singphos etc. who do practise permanent cultivation? By exerting a little effort they may be persuaded to adopt modern methods of cultivation. The Mishmis who have been encouraged to colonise selected pieces of land in the plains of the foot of the hills are, in spite of Government propaganda, destroying forests in the old way to obtain land for jhuming. In 1955 I travelled to Burma through the densest forests of Asia along the Hindustan-Burma road from Tamu to Kalewa and I saw within this distance of 96 miles about three newly raised villages being colonised by the surrounding hillmen, including those of India, but 'jhuming' was not at all in evidence. At the 37th MS the villagers, who were mostly Kukis and Lushais, came to see me and told me that they were happily settled there. When people can migrate to a foreign land similar to their old surroundings in order to make a better living why cannot they be encouraged to effect minor changes in their social habits to achieve the same aim—a better standard of living? Mythology and religion need not deter economic progress and a religion which is not dynamic or well-defined is bound to fade away, and the sooner the better.

To increase the yield of their land, the people should be taught the value of cattle. At present the use of bullocks is not properly appreciated by the people. They must be convinced of the right use of animals and green or animal manure. What is the use of distributing chemical fertilisers to such people?

The Agriculture Department is also taking interest in piggeries and poultry farming. I saw two Yorkshire Stud Boars in a Wanchoo village. On account of their enormous size the animals could not breed with the local sows. Lately poultry farming has brought about some improvement of the local breed and the people have been benefited by this.

Outwardly the tribal people look muscular, agile and physically strong, but their resistance to disease is questionable. Occasionally outbreak of small-pox is still dreaded by the people and no tribal is immune from the kinds of fevers that infest the Agency. Therefore, health services are as essential in NEFA as anywhere else in the country. However, the medical or the hygienical needs of the people differ from Division to Division and from group to group. For instance in Tirap, villages are perched on tops of isolated hills and there is an acute and persistent shortage of water causing filth, dirt and disease in the Naga villages. It is not likely that WRC will induce people to settle down in river valleys; if they do migrate to valleys then they would lose their agility and virility and would show signs of decay within a few years.

It is not true, as some assume, that the people established their villages there for security, but it would appear that they made these arrangements because the hilltops provided healthy living sites. Then because of the prolonged isolation and segregation so caused between the various groups, the necessity of defence arose, and since hilltops are easy to defend, the people stayed there. With the introduction of Administration the people are assured of security, but they want better living conditions in their new homes if they are to move from their hilltops. At the present rate of advance in science in the country it is not reasonable to expect that the valleys of the Tirap rivers will be transformed into health resorts in the near future.

The prospects of Naga villages shifting to river valleys are very remote. Therefore, Naga villages will stay where they are. Water can be supplied to the people in their villages by raising the water-level of a few of the perennial streams that flow through the Division by constructing dams. If the Tirap river is dammed near its source on the western slopes of Patkoi and water is stored at a height of 3,000 to 4,000 ft. above sea level then it can, without much difficulty, be pumped up to most of the Tirapian villages.* The experiment of raising the water-level has been tried in Khela though on a very moderate scale. The water is pumped to a height of about 50 ft. above its source, and the locals are quite happy about it. If the scope of the same experiment is widened to include greater heights then it would change the miserable, unhygienic life of the Tirapians considerably.

The Mishmis and the Daflas need all-round health education to make their life worth living. The Abors and the Monpas are well organised communities and they need more and more of hospitals. The Apa Tanis though an organised and prosperous community still need a lot of improvement in their personal and collective hygiene. A network of village drains is the least that the Health Department can introduce in the Apa Tani villages. The Apa Tanis have a good water supply both for drinking and washing purposes. They can be taught the proper use of water for personal and village cleanliness.

The most obvious work that the Health Department is carrying out is the running of hospitals and Government dispensaries. In the Divisional Headquarters these institutions are well equipped and many of the dogmas—'tribal ways and cooking'—are ignored and patients made comfortable. But outside the Divisional Headquarters these institutions are not very much patronised by the locals, and so have fallen into inefficiency and decay. Generally these were visited by a limited number of outdoor patients, mostly consisting of the children and wives of polygamous interpreters and Political Jamadars. The main argument advanced by the locals for not going to such hospitals was that, when they could get the same standard of food and clothing at home as they receive in NEFA hospitals why should they give up their familiar environment, and forsake the company of their families in favour of lonely living in an inhospitable hospital ward? In spite of this the outpost hospitals are encouraged to have primitive conditions of living for their patients. "The NEFA Medical Department is now trying to make things more familiar, give patients their own clothes and blankets[7]." Why should a local seek admission in one of such hospitals as an indoor patient when he is not going to be provided with any better living conditions than those he would receive at home? Who would go to foreign lands for further education if the same conditions of living, food and association as one gets in the Indian Universities at home are provided there?

In 1947 there were two Primary Schools in the Agency. Since then the strength of educational institutions has been increased to more than 100 Lower Primary Schools, about one and one half dozen Middle English Schools and five High Schools—one in each of the Divisions of Kameng, Subansiri, Siang, Lohit and a fifth at Pasighat which is a Multipurpose School. There is a Teachers' Training College at Chougloug in Tirap also. The attendance of students in MESs and HSs could be improved and there is an ample scope for its increase in the LPs. The LPs are located in villages, and at many places they serve the purpose of night schools only. Tribal children, who are working units for their families, attend schools only when free from work. The Director of Education of the Agency, in July 1959, was thinking of closing down these penny packet schools and was planning to concentrate his efforts in the bigger villages. This step if pursued would challenge the initiative of the local people and would also make the lives of the now solitary schoolmasters happier.

As in the country, so in NEFA, Basic* Education is imparted to the children. It is still too early to predict the results of this. However, if the efficacy of Basic Education in the whole country, though it has had years of trial has not been conclusively established, then how can one

* Mahatma Gandhi is said to be the originator of Basic Education. It is a Government sponsored system and it has been or is being introduced almost in all the Government Schools, at least up to the Primary Stage, in the country. Basic Education is supposed to coordinate mental activities of the learner with those of the body. The child is supposed to learn while he works.

judge the merits or demerits of the system for NEFA where its effects may remain dormant for years to come? Among these economically backward people, segregated by the Inner Line absolutely, any method for educational progress, that one wants to choose, can be trumpeted (as in the case of other reforms) as successful. The people should be the best judge of their own progress. but when they themselves need 'unnati' (progress) what judgement can they pronounce on their own educational progress, specially when they are kept artificially separate from the educationally advanced sections of the society?

Coming to the medium of instruction, the students of NEFA have already started showing signs of restiveness. The students of Subansiri High School, in 1959, forced the authorities to accept their demand of replacing Hindi by the Assamese language. The NEFA Administration would do well, for the emotional integration of the people among themselves, to hasten the introduction of the Assamese language as the medium of instructions in the NEFA schools.

The policy directing the 'medium of instruction' also controls the appointment of school staff. It is a fact which needs no emphasis that an Assamese village schoolmaster is much more successful in the NEFA Lower Primary schools than any of his colleague from other States. The Assamese teacher is familiar with the environment and so naturally his pupils will also be cheerful, lively interested in school activities. There are cases where non-Assamese schoolmasters have proved good leaders and have adapted themselves to the local conditions, but such cases are not many.

India is a welfare State, the whole of NEFA Tract must be regarded as a National Extension Block (for all-round development) in the working of which the people themselves should use their initiative to better their own economic and social condition. But the people on account of their pre-occupation with securing the bare necessities of life are not available as workmen for public works and improvements during the working season, as various celebrations and the entertainment of VIPs have slowed road construction to a snail's pace, so also they have hindered the progress of Public Works. Progress in the community Project's Programme is said to have been achieved but not to an extent commensurate with the efforts. The success of the Programme depends on communications and upon improving methods of agricultural production in order to increase the output of cereal grain so that the tribal children become surplus working units and start attending schools in appreciable numbers. Then and then alone will the community projects yield satisfactory result.

In spite of the best efforts, all development work is confined to Divisional Headquarters and their vicinities. Interior areas are still considered too difficult of access for development work to be practical. The Prime Minister on July 7, 1959, at a function in Delhi said that much was being done to improve the condition of primitive tribes in the country, yet he felt that due weight had not been given to this important task. He expressed his anxiety and emphasised that the tribals, who had been neglected for long, must get out of their present state of backwardness quickly. Later on October 8, 1959, he again dwelt on the same subject and expressed his satisfaction with the development work and revealed that "he had actually applied a brake to some of the development schemes in NEFA because, he thought, they are just going to upset the balance by too many people going into NEFA and creating some difficulties in the way of the local people[8]."

NEFA up to July 1959 was a social problem but since then it has become a defence problem as well, and the statements of the Prime Minister clearly indicate the influence of the Sino-Indian border controversy. When the prospects of peace dominate the negotiations, which are being conducted between the Government of India and the Chinese Government, the development work appears fascinating and its progress is satisfactory, but when a different trend is indicated, the Prime Minister declares: "Yet I feel that due weight has not been given to this important work." These words of the Prime Minister should be a good measure of judging the results of the development work in NEFA. The period from July 1959 to October of the same year is not much but the result of the development work changed from 'due weight had not been given' to a sense of satisfaction with the progress!

Pt. II—Arts and Crafts

Leisure is that fruit of civilization which reflects itself in the arts and crafts of a people—the higher the civilization the finer the standard of these niceties. This means that arts and crafts are dependent upon leisure and that their *development* is in direct proportion to the standard of civilization and culture of the people of that society.

Now it can safely be presumed that the people of NEFA have their own civilization and culture, and that, therefore they should have their own arts and handicrafts in consonance with their genius. As geographical conditions and environments control the way of life, so do they influence art. Availability of raw materials, frequent practice and a utilitarian motive, the presence of craftsmen and the improvement of implements, the ease of communications, the aesthetic influence of immigrants, and fashion dictated by religious factors, which properly utilized enhance the growth of art. These conditions are perhaps not yet present in toto, but they can be developed and can help art in NEFA. For instance, Nepal geographically and climatically is not very much different from the NEFA territory. Yet the Newars of Nepal have developed art to a high pitch and there is no reason why the people of the North-East Frontier cannot attain the same proficiency, if the latter are allowed to be influenced by contemporary Assamese art.

In Tirap the conditions have not been favourable to the development of art, or if they were, they only localised it and made it static. The Noctes, if they ever knew weaving have now forgotten it on account of frequent contacts with the plains from where they could easily buy mill-cloth at reasonable rates. They used to make fast colours, but chemical colours available in the market discouraged them from devoting the time and energy needed to produce indigenous ones. Among the Wanchoos. the women of noble families have plenty of leisure at their disposal and they produce exquisite embroidery, which unfortunately is of local importance only. Tangsa women show a keenness on the handloom and Tangsa scarfs, bags and lungis are quite familiar sights in the

Division. A few of the Wanchoo men practise elementary wood carving. Smithy is not much in evidence in Tirap, though it is said that double barrelled guns are made there.

Lohit is in an enviable position with respect to the development of indigenous art. It is cut off from the Assam plains by the Brahmaputra, and Sadiya bazar, on account of treacherous terrain, is not easily accessible for marketing. This encouraged the local people to rely on their own cottage industry. Availability of raw materials like ivory, cane, plants and herbs within the Division itself made them good handcraftsmen. They exploit forest plants and herbs; they poison their arrows, and they produce fast colours which they use in colouring the Mishmi-cloth—half cotton and half woollen. They are well known for their work on the handloom, and Mishmi coats, bags and shawls are becoming very popular with the NEFA officials' families. The Mishmis also make bags of monkey or bear skin which they hang across the body by a leather belt. They do not show any aptitude for wood-work or wood-carving; they are said to produce and repair their own weapons.

The Khamptis are good at ivory carving and are quite at ease with wood-work. Their women practise both knitting and weaving. They also have a passion for colours which is reflected in their daily wear.

The Adis of Siang excel the Mishmis in every art. In addition they are well known for their cane-work. The Gallong cane hats are a familiar sight in the Division and the Adi cane bridges could invite admiration even from bridging experts of industrially advanced areas. These bridges are strong and durable.

In Subansiri, the Apa Tanis show a keenness in weaving unmatched in the Division. The lack of interest in art and crafts among the rest of the people of the Division may be attributed to the nature of the country part of which is aptly descriged by Major Godwin Austin. "The Hill portion of the Dafla country is covered from base to summit with dense forest, the larger trees being clothed with thick creepers; and the bottom of the ravines are occupied by a luxuriant growth of bamboo, cane, tree, ferns, screw pines, plantations—etc[9]." Naturally the people had no leisure and incentive to practise art because most of their energies were spent in procuring the basic necessities of life from adverse terrain covered with ever-green forests. The Hill Miris of the same Division were commented upon by Dalton: "I suppose there are no people on the face of the earth, more utterly ignorant of everything connected with the arts than are the Hill Miris. ...... they have not the remotest idea of weaving[10]." Since Dalton's visit in 1845 the Hill Miris have developed an aptitude for art and their women have taken to weaving. Nevertheless, the Daflas still prefer to buy cloth from the Apa Tanis or the plainsmen. However, constant living in intimate contact with nature encouraged the jungle dwellers to master the art of construction, with commendable ingenuity, of cane-bridges across the innumerable rivers and streams that cut deep gorges in the Dafla country.

Religion does not appear to have played an important part in influencing art and handicraft in any of the Divisions except Kameng, where the Monpas make masks and decorate themselves for religious dances. Painting in India owes a great deal of its development to temples the walls of which are painted with Hindu legends and myths. Buddhists also seem to have copied the ideals of Hindu painting. In Kameng one is delighted to see the episodes of Lord Buddha painted on the walls of 'Kakaling' (Village gate) and monasteries. In the rest of the Divisions, there are no places of worship, except in the Khamti area, and hence no evidence of painting.

The art of pottery is not at all popular in the Agency. It is not that soil is unsuitable for making earthen pots, but, it appears, that there is no necessity for such utensils for two reasons—first, bamboo provides for all the needs satisfied by metallic utensils elsewhere and, second, due to the humidity, the process of evaporation to cool the drinking water is slow. Also the intense desire for drinking cold water after strenuous work is much less in evidence than in the drier zones of the country. A chhagal (A canvas water bottle) or a Surahi (Earthen water bottle) is popular in the Punjab and Rajputana but not in NEFA.

On the basis of an evaluation of the above information, the NEFA Administration has established Cottage Industries Training and Production Centres in every Division and attemps are being made to revive the tribal arts and to protect their handicrafts. In Tirap, the Noctes and the Wanchoos are taught smithy, cane and wood work. Their women attend weaving classes along with their Tangsa sisters. Attempts are also being made to popularise the Wanchoo embroidery. In Lohit CITPCs are very popular with the Mishmis and the Padams. Here cloth of colourful design is produced which fetches a good price in the market. CITPCs are equally popular in Siang and the products of these centres are gaining popularity in the whole State. In Subansiri the Apa Tanis are taking a keen interest in these centres and their women folks are attending the weaving classes in increasing numbers. In Kameng, the Production Centres are most popular and the Centres at Bomdi La and Tawang are fairly extensive, embracing many subjects of the arts and handicrafts. Monpas are the only people in NEFA among whom painting is a profession and local artists of high calibre are employed as instructors in the CITPCs. Dafla, Aka and Miji youths are trying their very best to attain to the standard of Monpa art. Here though pottery as such is not a subject for training, the making of wooden bowels, jugs, jars etc. is taught to the trainees. The outstanding thing about these utensils is that their outside surfaces are painted with beautiful and balanced combinations of colours in various designs of praiseworthy standard. Tailoring is also one of the subjects in the Kameng CITPCs.

Comparing the time, energy and money spent on the developmental schemes with the limited results achieved locally among the population surrounding Divisional Headquarters only, it would not be illogical to conclude that there has been complacency in executing the development plans and complacency, specially in the NEFA Tract which has been neglected for centuries, is not a good thing. However, responsible statements have been made encouraging the country to step up the existing developmental schemes further, but the schemes themselves are outdated and their application limited. They will have to be broadened and the administrative mechanism so fitted that the results develop a regional and national bias rather than simply a local significance among the participants. To achieve this, the Assamese and the Assam Government must be associated with all the activities directed towards the economic and cultural advancement of the people of NEFA. . A wide gulf between the hillmen and the plainsmen has been created by vested interests and their sympathisers—both indigenous and foreign—and Assam is facing disintegration to the detriment of the country. NEFA so far has not taken a part in the controversy current in the State. Either the system of Administration bars the Nefaites from voicing their views or else they have not so far developed the intellectual standard needed to form political views. Whatever the case may be, it would seem to be the course of wisdom to attempt to inculcate loyalty to the country among the people so that when the time comes they do not speak a separatist language. The example of Nagaland is not a good omen for the country, but there is still time to see that the people of NEFA develop a regional attachment, otherwise our North East Frontier will have five more small States. A strong and united Assam is as essential as the Himalayas to the security of India.

1. Message from Pt. Nehru—Ten Years' Progress in NEFA
2. Ten Years' Progress in NEFA
3. The Outlook on NEFA.
4. Ten Years' Progress in NEFA
5. Dr. V. Elwyn p. 114
6. " p. 179/180
7. " p. 180
8. The "Pioneer". October 9, 1959.
9. JASB 1876 p. 65
10. " 1845 Vol. XIV Pt. I p. 266

CHAPTER XIII

A Sealed Land

"In Australia and United States of America the existence of a white racial doctrine renders assimilation of aboriginal tribes impossible, but in India where they constitute nearly 5 millions spread throughout the country, and with whom, in some form or other, there has been contact since the earliest times with considerable acculturation on both sides, and even a great deal of mixing of blood, such however cannot be the case. Besides, complete isolation has never led to progress and advancement, but always to strangulation and death whether we look to lower animals or human beings.

On the other hand, the history of human society shows that civilisation everywhere has been built by the contact and intercourse of peoples, which has been the chief motivating power behind progress. There are innumerable instances of the borrowing of cultural traits by peoples of different countries, such as articles of food, use of metals, domesticated animals, methods of agriculture, spread of alphabet. So long as the borrowing has been natural and in harmony with the cultural setting and the psychological make up of the people, it has entirely been beneficial and even added to the richness of the culture[1]."

Dr. B. S. Guha

On October 1, 1958, Dr. Ram Manohar Lohia, a leader of the Socialist Party tried, without any valid permission

from the NEFA Administration to cross the Inner Line, to enter Tirap from Jai Rampur, but failed. Again during December, 1959 he continued his efforts of defying the Inner Line Regulations, but every time he reached the Assam-NEFA border he was arrested and brought back to Dibrugarh for release. Dr. Lohia had hit upon an unusual plan by infringing the limits of the forbidden domain of calling attention to the plight of NEFA beyond the Inner Line. On November 26, 1959, he sounded an additional note of warning—if the Government kept NEFA as a "Sealed area[2]" then like the Dalai Lama's Tibet 'It may meet its doom[2].'

It is true that the Doctor went too far when he made this sweeping statement manifesting as it does a defeatist attitude, which is probably, based on disappointments and frustration faced in the political field. But the warning concerning the backward communities being segregated from the rest of the Indians needs a deeper understanding. Prime Minister Nehru on November 8, 1948, while discussing adequate safeguards to be provided for minorities said: "It is right and important that we should raise the level of backward groups in India and bring them up to the level of the rest. But it is not right that in trying to do it we create further barriers, because the ultimate objective is not separatism, but building up of an organisation[3]." It is a long time since 1948 when Nehru objected to the keeping of the existing barriers but the barrier of the Inner Line is still in existence, on the excuse of developing the people according to their own genius behind the curtain. Dr. Lohia is the first public leader outside Assam to raise his voice against the Inner Line Regulations. Assamese political opinion has always been very sensitive over the issue. In fact a compilation of various compositions in the form of a book—'The Outlook on NEFA'—was placed by certain intellectuals and social workers of Assam before the 63rd Session of the Indian National Congress at Prayagjotishpur on January 6, 1958, to acquaint the delegates with different aspects of NEFA. The Assamese in their mild but persistent manner are continually fighting for the opening up of the Agency for cultural and social penetration. So far the Assam public has failed in this mission. There have been no signs of breaking the isolation of the tribal people of NEFA. In spite of continued public agitation the Inner Line is still considered essential to afford the tribal people " 'a measure of protection' so that they will not suffer, as similar populations have suffered all over the world, from commercial and religious exploitation, and so that they will not lose their land[4]."

For ages the tribal people have had trade relations with the people of Assam Valley, and exploitation in trade can never be one sided. There were instances when the tribals showed the acumen of keen businessmen. During the last century they were found adulterating their commodities for sale causing on many occasions, a violent exhibition of tempers in weekly markets. If there was any economic exploitation it was unavoidable, because, the more the ignorance of the contracting party in a business deal the more the party is liable to lose in the bargain. Therefore, to keep them completely divorced from trade competition is to keep them ignorant of the market trends, and this ignorance becomes the cause of their economic exploitation, if not locally in NEFA then when they go down to the plains. Probably the economic exploitation alluded to by the NEFA Administration refers to Marwaris (A business community) going to NEFA villages and settling down there for exploiting the rural population. The protagonists of this view do not take other Himalayan regions into consideration before advocating such illogical views. Probably their ideas are limited to plain's tribesmen like those of CP, Bihar and Orissa where the tribal areas are easy of access and surrounded by mandis (trade centres) and bazars. Economic exploitation of the people, as anywhere else in the Himalayas, is prevalent in the towns only. Who has seen the village bania (village shopkeeper of the Bania community) operating in Ladakh, Kashmir Valley, Riasi, Basoli, Chamba, Himachal Pradesh, Garhwal, Kumaon and in Nepal? None. Then how can one expect the bania to go to the villages of NEFA where conditions of insecurity and discomforts will no doubt prevail for some time to come. The Marwari (a shopkeeper from Marwar, a tract in Rajasthan) or the bania like anybody else needs the physical comforts and amenities of life for his living and naturally he will be attracted to township only. Further the protagonists of Inner Line protection are completely devoid of any knowledge of the organisation of Hindu society and its economic development in the preliminary stages. The economic development of Assam owes a great deal to the Marwari community the members of which have penetrated right up to Sonepura (a village on the Assam-NEFA boundary in Lohit) and beyond. It was not that the British encouraged the Marwaris to migrate, for they had been there long before the British rule*. The Marwari is

* Shri Sharma, a Marwari and aged 81 years in 1959 at Tezu in Lohit, told me that his grandfather was a priest in Gauhati in 1780 and his father moved to Sadiya in 1840 when the British were still fighting the tribals for supremacy in the Sadiya Tract. Mr. Sharma's grandchildren are running a Hindu hotel in the Divisional Headquarters.

the product of Hinduism, the only religion which worships wealth, the goddess of which is Laxmi. One would be surprised to see that every Marwari in NEFA, irrespective of the means he adopts and the amount of profits he makes, devotes a few minutes every evening in chanting 'Arti' (hymn to God). This shows that he religiously believes that it is his profession and duty to keep the business going and make profits. In Roing, I asked a Marwari the reason for his being a munim (retail shopkeeper's clerk) in a shop owned by a tribal (Padam). "The tribals cannot run the business. If they buy an article for a rupee and sell it at the same rate they consider that the rupee realised is their profit and they spend it on themselves. Therefore, to keep the business as a growing concern they employ us", said the munim. He further added, "Business is in our blood and it is our profession. We would sell an article worth Re. 1 for Rs. 1/2 and would after making allowance for our recurring expenses reinvest the whole amount in the business." There are two observations to be made here. One is that the tribals cannot be forced into business if they have no liking for it. The Garhwalis and the Gorkhas, in spite of the straightened economic conditions of their hilly tracts, and appreciating full well the rigours of economic exploitation, because they are generally the victims of this design, still regard business with contempt. The second is that the Marwari is the right person to deal with business in a primitive society in the country. He has the capital and is full of initiative. He takes risks and migrates to far flung places where he can make profits. The construction of roads in Tirap could not be completed if a Marwari was not employed to store rations for government employees and road workers; Government offices would have been closed in Lohit if the Tezu bazar had been wound up; the people of Siang would not have crowded the Pasighat market had there been no Marwari, and the bazars of Assam Duars are a good example of the popularity of the bania among the tribal people of NEFA. Therefore, a policy of eliminating the bania from the NEFA Divisions is practising discrimination against him. There used to be a bania at Walong who later on was removed. In 1958/59 another bania was removed from Zero and another from Bomdi La and this practice is said to be continuing. Barring a few small shops owned by the locals, the 'Parshads', 'Rams' and 'Lalas' (common bania names) are being replaced by 'Banerjis' and 'Sakhias' (Bengalee and Assamese names) who are running retail shops and exploiting the people, if making of profits is economic exploitation. If there are co-operatives running in Divisional Headquarters, then those who are invariably outsiders and who very often run to the plains for purchasing stores on behalf of the co-operatives, are liable to make illegal gains. Therefore, under the present system of economic development, if communistic methods are not given prefrence, the economic exploitation of the tribals is unavoidable. Then why not face the inevitable and give the tribals opportunities to cultivate a better understanding of the man and material?

> "Another greatly treasured gift of the Administration is the lifting the fear of economic exploitation. There must be few places in the world where such great pains are taken to ensure that 'primitive' people get a square deal. Land is protected, prices controlled, money-lending is checked, shopkeepers are licensed. The domination of the weak by stronger ....[5]"

Comments are unnecessary. One has to visit the bazars in the plains—Sadiya, North-Lakhimpur, Rangapara etc. to see for himself how far the tribals escape from exploitation.

The British annexed the Naga Hill District and established District Headquarter in Angami country at Samoogoodting in 1866. Regular administration began and Christianity was introduced in the area. This great religion did benefit the people materially, but certainly if it has not created anti-national feelings, at least it has nurtured separatist urge amongst its adherents. Christianity, with its emphasis on the value that God sets on each individual person, gives a man a sense of self-respect, and a demand that others also respect him, carried out in practical life he will also learn to respect others if he is allowed to keep his own self-respect. This attitude of self-respect is alien to the fatalistic caste system of India, and creates problems where there are Christians who feel themselves free from bondage to superstitions, magic and tribal rites. In a primitive society the conflict between the 'Heathen' or 'Animists' and the Christians is quite likely to assume a political colour as it has already done in the Khasi, Jaintia and Naga Hills. If the Inner Line restrictions are withdrawn from NEFA it will be open to religious reformers of every faith. If the Hindu preachers are permitted to persuade the tribals into their (Hindu) fold then there is no reason why Muslim and Christian missionaries should be debarred from preaching their faith among the 'Heathen' and the 'Animists'. And if the Christian missionaries were permitted to cross the artificial barrier and preach their religion in the tribal area then it is almost certain that foreign capital in the shape of religious endowments will flow into NEFA to claim the locals to Christian fold* and there will be every chance of the story of the Naga Land being repeated here also. A theocratic State within a secular country! Therefore the entry of religious reformers and teachers into NEFA may remain restricted. On the other hand to keep a spiritual vacuum among the people of NEFA is also dangerous specially when the philosophy of materialism is knocking at the northern doors. Religion is a sure bulwark against Communism the baneful influence of which can only be neutralised by broadening the religious outlook of the people. Anyway isolation is the negative solution of the problem and is fraught with danger. It is left to the Assamese how to overcome this problem. However, they can render a useful service by taking a keen interest in the social welfare of the student community in educational and other institutions in the State.

Land is as dear to a tribal folk as it is to a farmer of non-tribal areas in the country. Before independence, the latter was considered a victim of centuries-old customs; he was kept alive for economic exploitation which varied according to the accessibility, the fertility and other good conditions of the village from where the exploited hailed. Invariably the exploiter had his eyes on the

* "The more developed and highly organised the culture of a country, the less is the effect upon it of our own people.......We have had little effect on social structure, on the caste system, one language or religion, and it is noteworthy that the greatest effect has been in those parts of India where the indigenous culture has remained at a relatively low level........An examination of our times makes it clear that in this direction it is material culture which counts and counts alone........ To the uncivilised they are of small importance besides the purely material aspects of culture," writes Dr. Rivers when discussing the effects of Western culture on the people of India. (Psychology and Ethnology by W.H.R. Rivers, pages 300, 302 and 303).

farmer's land, and as a result the farmer suffered. This is not the case in the Himalayas. How many plains people, in recent times, have gone to Himalayan States and dispossessed locals of their land? Not many. Further, in mountainous terrain cultivation of land is not an easy affair, to be taken up by every one and anyone. Therefore it is ludicrous to imagine that the people of NEFA would be dispossessed of their land by land hungry plainsmen. The example of Mikir Hills* may be cited to support the argument that the tribals of NEFA would be dispossessed of their land by refugees from other States** and countries. This argument may be applicable to the plains bordering the central or the southern hills of Assam but not to NEFA. After Partition in 1947 how many refugees thought of even entering the Himalayan territories, let alone permanently settling down there? NEFA territory will be the last to be invaded by outsiders unless Government connives at or encourages immigration from one Himalayan State to another as the British did when they watched passively the migration of the Gorkhas into Margherita region. Today, the Gorkha population in the

* A few refugees from Eastern Bengal, after Partition of India, were allowed to temporarily settle down in the foothills of the Mikir Hills by the State Government of Assam. The refugees cleared the land of forests and developed it. The Mikirs, after a few years felt suspicious of the refugees' intentions and in 1969, forcibly ejected them from the tribal land. Questions concerning the incident were asked in the State legislature and the Indian Parliament and in both of these Government supported the ejectmtnt. However, the refugees were assured of alternative arrangement for their rehabilitation.

** Assam has also been experiencing the mass migration of Mymensinghias since 1906, but all the intruders have occupied fertile tracts in the plains. They did not intrude into the hilly areas.

Digboi-Margherita-Ledo sector dominates the original inhabitants of the State.

Land ownership is of three kinds. There is personal land, the clan land and the village land. The sentiment of personal property is very strong among the tribal groups like the Apa Tanis, the Monpas and a few others who practise permanent cultivation, and the area of land one possesses determines his status and prestige in the society. The Apa Tanis have rice fields which are passed on from father to son; then they have clan land for pastures and the burial ground. Forests on the periphery of the Apa Tani plateau are the village property.

Among those who practise shifting cultivation the laws governing land are different. Every village knows its 'jhum land' and the village council every year allots land to almost all individual families. Thus, there, private land is evolved from clan or village land. If the village land is properly surveyed and marked in maps in local areas, then in due course village council will allot it to the village families thus avoiding any opportunity for outsiders to buy land and dispossess the locals of their fields. The sale of land is already forbidden and it is up to the NEFA Administration to see that the 1945 Regulations are strictly observed. The difficulty is that the survey of many major tracts is yet to be completed. After that, how long it will take to complete village records is anyone's guess.

Forest is linked with land. As land is the main source of subsistence for a Nefaite, so is the forest. From the land he produces foodgrains, various vegetables and fruits; from the forest he fetches meat, fish, edible roots, timber bamboo grass fuel etc.

There are three categories of forests. The first includes Forest Reserves which cover a very small area. The second comprises forests which have not been brought under Reserves and where individual or collective proprietorship has so far not been established. The third embraces forests which definitely come within the village boundaries and belong to the locals. The second and the third categories are termed as 'Unclassed' State Forests and the State is authorised to realise revenues from them but because of strong tribal feelings the rules governing the royalty for extraction of forest produce are such more lenient in NEFA than anywhere else in the country. For instance, the tribal people living in or near Forest Reserves also have the right to collect timber and minor forest produce for their customary personal use (but not for sale, barter or gift); to graze cattle; to hunt and fish freely; to collect flowers; and to keep skins, hides, tasks and horns of animals hunted in the Reserve as trophies. "The management of the third category of forests will now vest in the existing tribal councils which are recognised under the various 'Jhum' Land Regulations. These powers will not be given immediately to tribal councils all over NEFA but, for the time being, only in the more advanced areas, where forest extraction has already been begun or will be begun soon, such as in the lower villages of Siang, the Roing area of the Dibong Valley, the Khampti low lands of Lohit and those parts of Tirap which are adjacent to the plains. The entire revenues from the forests under their control will be given to these councils, which will use them for the development of their villages[6]." This new arrangement will bestow much greater responsibility on the tribal councils and strengthen them.

A Philosophy For NEFA' by Dr. Verrier Elwyn (a NEFA Publication), was first written and published in

1957, but Mills in respect of the Naga Hills, an administered area since 1866, where outsiders with some effort could buy some land and exploit forests writes: "There has been little or no exploitation of forests, minerals or agricultural lands, but the future cannot be held to be secure as long as the ruling of the Government stands that jhum land, which the owners have bought or inherited as immovable property which can be held by an individual or a clan is all unclassed State Forest at the absolute disposal of Government, on which there is no liability to pay compensation in the event of being taken over[7]." The 'Jhum Land Regulations' of 1945 which were promulgated in 1947-49 and the present policy concerning forests have mitigated the concern expressed by Mills and now there should not be any apprehension that outsiders will enter NEFA in large numbers and dispossess the simple folk of his land and forests in the territory where geographical and climatic conditions are as adverse as they can be for human habitation.

For some reason known only to the NEFA Administration, political exploitation has not been given any place in their assessment as stated on page 232, though it is a most delicate item, in the face of the current Sino-Indian trouble. The political loyalty of the NEFA people does not extend beyond their clan territory. If Indian political parties of different ideologies are allowed to function among these politically unconscious people then the latter are bound to be confused and in their confusion they might be misguided. Limited political knowledge and the strictly local loyalties of the people combined with the confusion in political ideas will definitely create chaotic conditions in the territory which will harm the national interest. On the other hand, if the people are denied any political edu cation, the Communists will have a clean slate to write upon. Therefore, a balance has got to be struck between the political education and the intellectual inactivity of the people. This can be done by allowing the tribals to have more contacts with their countrymen and simultaneously by accelerating the growth of 'Kabang' to self-Government administering at least, one tribe on a non-party basis.

Since March 31, 1959, NEFA is said to have gained strategic importance. On January 12, 1960, when a correspondent asked Pt. Nehru for how long NEFA region would be kept shut to the rest of India, "Mr. Nehru said it must be realised that this was a strategic region and 'you must not think of discussing it'[8]." In fact NEFA after Independence became a strategic area and its defence right from the beginning of the new era should have been given priority over all other considerations. The Kuomintang Government's protests and Dalai Lama's demands[9] were a strong indication for this line of thought and action. Agreed that the absurd demands of the Kuomintang and Tibetan Government were suitably dealt with and they were accordingly informed of Government of India's views, still as long as the territorial claims had not been withdrawn how could one imagine that defence requirements of NEFA were relegated to an insignificant place? If NEFA is a strategic region today then it has been since the dawn of Independence. Therefore, the strategic importance of NEFA is belated excuse for keeping the territory shut off from the rest of the country. The excuse is not convincing, because Jummu and Kashmir is also a strategic area, and it is not closed even to foreign tourists. For security reasons, the Government or the Armed Forces may cordon off the areas held by troops, as is done in the Jammu and Kashmir theatre. It appears that the protests of the Koumintang Government and demands of Tibet made Government of India more cautious in dealing with the North-East Frontier people and terms like 'winning over', 'emotional integration' etc. were given undue emphasis in writings and utterances concerning the Agency.

From the above analysis it is evident that the question of lifting the Inner Line restriction is not easy of solution, but at the same time it cannot be held in abeyance indefinitely. The Government can start relaxing the entry restrictions from now so that by the next generation the people of NEFA are automatically integrated, if not assimilated, with the people of the rest of the country. This present isolation is neither serving the interests of the tribal people nor of the country. It must be removed. "As a matter of fact, nothing can protect such a minority or a group less than a barrier which separates it from the majority. It makes it a permanent isolated group and it prevents it from coming closer to the other groups in the country[10]." Dr. Guha has ably expressed his views on isolation. "A simple policy of segregation, while preserving the primitive man from exploitation, is a static remedy and at best a negative one and does not supply the machinery for enabling him to adjust himself to the changing conditions of his surrounding environment, and until this is done on the basis of his cultural potentialities and cultural accessories, no amount of spoon feeding or uplifting measures are likely to be effective,[11]" says he. Surely, circumstances will force the country to reorientate its NEFA policy, but then will it not be too late?

1. JASB 1951, Vol. XVII
2. The "Pioneer" November 27, 1959 p. 39
3. Pt. Nehru's speeches, November, 1948 p. 41
4. Ten Years' Progress in NEFA
5. Dr. Elwyn p. 222
6. „ p. 60
7. Mill's Report
8. The "Pioneer" January 12, 1960
9. Ibid
10. Pt. Nehru's speeches, November, 1948 p. 41
11. JASB 1951 Vol. XVII p. 38

CHAPTER XIV

Conclusion

The British were bound by self-interest and they could not think beyond it; their policies were conservative, short-sighted and lacked dynamism. India was their political laboratory, as such she neither gained economically nor industrially—the standard of living of her people was the lowest amongst all the colonies or possessions of the Imperial Powers and her industrial potentialities were so badly neglected that during the Second World War, the industrial void was condemned by a Great Britain sponsored commission and attempts were made to rectify the neglect. She suffered much, but unfortunately she has not yet learnt enough to overcome the difficulties left over as a legacy from the British. India should have shown some imagination and drive in tackling the problems inherent in frontier territories, especially in NEFA where the international boundaries of three countries*—India, China and Burma—meet and where the Sino-Indian boundary is yet to be recognised by the leading nations of the world and where the political loyalties of the people are confined to their clans.

In NEFA the process of assimilation of the hill people with those of Assam was in evidence from the earliest times of which records are available in the Buranjis, Hindu scriptures, and the Tantras. This process was stopped by the British. After Independence the country failed to appreciate the needs of the NEFA people and followed,

* Tibet is recognised by India as an integral part of China, therefore, it is not included in the discussion.

rather strengthened, the previous rulers' policies as applicable to Assam and the North-East Frontier territory. The very fact that the territory has not yet been given any Indian or Assamese or Tribal name indicates that except for the 'laissez-faire' there is no other policy in the field.

India did show imagination, and deviated from the British in framing her Foreign Policy, but how far she was correct in watching the 'rape of Tibet' passively and in believing China's professions of Panch-Sheel, only time will tell. China has occupied areas of India's territory at different places and is not vacating her occupation. This attitude has classed her as an 'aggressor' and her acts of intrusion as 'aggression' in the eyes of Indians.

In the History of Asia the 18th century will be marked as a crucial period. During the century China launched her expansionist policies; Great Britain made inroads into India and South East Asia, and Russia also had covetous eyes on States bordering China and India in the east and north respectively. The Tibetan Plateau, where the interest of these three powers overlapped, played an opportunist game, some times she suffered for her flirtations with China, Russia or Britain, and at others she succeeded in maintaining her integrity and independence. China being the oldest nation, played her cards well on the table of power politics and in the long run, came out as a winner. The British, probably, underrated China's potentialities and suspected Russia's intentions. They took every precaution against any Russian expansion towards India, and as corollary to this tried to keep Tibet free from Russian influence. In this latter design, they co-operated with China and for a long time their policy towards China was characterised by appeasement of the latter. Tibet suffered in this political game. Prolonged political association with the Chinese made the British realise their mistake. They resurveyed their Asian affairs and by the 1870s, they were fully conscious of China's intentions. But then it was too late. However, they tried to rectify their mistake. They succeeded in annexing Burma as British territory. In exchange they surrendered certain concessions in Tibet. But the game did not end here. The Chinese engineered the Peking Convention of 1906 in which the British recognised the suzerainty of China over Tibet. Russia, in 1907 also confirmed the suzerainty of China over Tibet. The British virtually handed over the Plateau to China. Later they tried to neutralise the effects of suzerainty but did not make much headway. Then they tried to delimit the Indo-Tibetan boundary and arranged the Simla Convention to which the three plenipotentiaries—British, Tibetan and the Chinese—were the signatories. China did not ratify the Convention. However, the McMahon Line became the Indo-Tibetan boundary. Both India and China started showing the Line as the international boundary between India and Tibet in their maps. The McMahon Line extended to Burma also. According to the latest Sino-Burma border agreement China has recognised the McMahon Line as the international boundary dividing the two countries—China and Burma. After August 15, 1947 India came on the scene and what the British had not already lost to China, India lost in a few months. The British considered Tibet as vital to India's interest while Indian diplomats and administrators sincerely believed that British policy with respect to Tibet was wrong. These politicians considered Tibet as an integral part of China, and they let China occupy the Plateau undisturbed. India watched the rape of Tibet passively. Afterwards she signed the 1954 Trade Treaty with China and withdrew all of her extra-territorial rights from Tibet. Until December, 1960, India and China were entangled in negotiations over the boundary question. In the absence of any common ground between the claims of the two Governments the negotiations seem to have been temporarily suspended. Failing peaceful settlement, India has got to prepare herself for every eventuality and in this age *'Industrialisation, Industrialisation,* and *Industrialisation'* is not the only answer to every problem, including that of the Chinese incursions, India must also become internally strong. The Kashmir problem has to be solved and in the larger interest India and Pakistan have got to come to some mutual agreement to frame a common defence policy in order to ward off the yellow menace from the North decisively and permanently. The crucial point in our border negotiations is that according to geography, history, and local traditions the existing boundaries, based on water-shed principles have to be recognised by China. For China has not yet fully expressed her views about her territorial claims. She is said to have been basing her claims on a '1717'* map drawn by a couple of Lamas on hearsay and which will be interpreted by the Chinese to include practically all the Himalayan States. It is a big and sinister demand. The Chinese have not come out with it yet (in open words) but in due course

* It was only at the 6th meeting held on 27 June 1960 that for the first time an authoritative map showing the whole alignment claimed by the People's Government of China had been made available." (Report of the Officials......, Comments under item one, page 5). According to this claim the Sino-Indian Boundary runs along the edge of the southern outer hills of the Himalayas in NEFA. The claim has still to ravel itself for a fuller comprehension and the author does not feel justified in withdrawing the prophecy.

they will, unless an agreement between India and China is soon reached on some valid principle, such as topographical features or the water-shed. In short, this is the history of the political game started by the British and the Chinese outside India. But, in the meantime, what was happening within India on the North-East Frontier?

The Ahoms were the paramount power of Assam and the tribals of NEFA owed allegiance to them. *Ipso facto* the Ahom Empire claimed most of the territory of present-day Assam and in the Brahmaputra Bend, much beyond the McMahon Line. Unfortunately the middle of the 18th century witnessed the weakening of the Ahom power. The more the Ahom influence loosened the more the tribals showed signs of unrest and in many cases encroached upon the Ahom territory. The terrain of NEFA is mountainous, interspersed by deep river valleys clad in evergreen tropical forests. These obstacles have nurtured small groups of people who are isolated from each other and because of this age-old isolation, they have developed suspicion and fear against each other. Many a time their jealousies took a violent shape and one group tried to wipe out the other. When the Ahom ruled Assam, they managed to administer the tribe, of course according to the conveniences available at the time. During the declining years of the Ahom Empire the tribal people of NEFA had virtually become independent of the Central authority. In 1826 the British occupied Assam and shouldered the responsibilities of the Ahoms. By then the tribals had tasted the fruit of freedom and they grudged the encroachments of the British into their territory. The British also were not keen to extend regular administration into an unknown wilderness. Their main consideration was trade. The NEFA territory was unproductive and future prospects for trade did not appear satisfactory. Therefore, the rulers did not consider the territory worth the candle and detached it from Assam. When realisation about the Chinese ambitions dawned on them they tried to develop NEFA as a 'Crown Colony'. The British never posted Indian administrators to these areas which they wanted to retain as their special reserves, and NEFA only occasionally received visits from the British POs. These POs, apart from giving political presents like opium, beads and pieces of cloth etc. to the tribal chiefs, did very little for the people. If the British had not occupied Assam then NEFA would not have been separated, and its history would have been the history of the State. The British changed this and allowed the tribals 'to live on their own'. The rulers were only concerned with the problem of Law and Order' within the territory and with defence on the Indo-Tibetan border. The Welfare of the people was never their concern. Then India attained Independence and inherited all that was left by the previous rulers.

In spite of Prime Minister Nehru's admission in the Lok Sabha that barriers are detrimental to the economic, social and cultural growth of a people, the Inner Line stays, segregating the people of NEFA from Assam and the same British policy of 'laissez-faire' is conducted in developing the territory. The basis of this policy is that the people of NEFA are considered like the aborigines of America, Australia and other Pacific islands who need protection and their identity preserved lest other people overwhelm them. It is not realised that the people of NEFA have been and are a part of Assam, as the Kumaonis and the Garhwalis are of U.P. Instanees of other aborigines of the world are quoted, and measures taken to protect such people against outsiders. Who are the outsiders? The Indians! Under this plea the people of NEFA are being developed as a separate entity. Their integration, and not their assimilation, is the goal of the NEFA Administration. But isolation will hardly transform itself into integration. The Inner Line is like a dagger thrust in the heart of Assam and it has stayed there for quite a long time. Even if it is withdrawn it would leave a wound which would take a very long time to heal. However, steps may be taken to strengthen the physical health of Assam so that she may be able to withstand the shock of the withdrawal of the sword and to heal the wound so caused in a shorter period than is generally expected.

At present the people of NEFA are accustomed to consider themselves as a separate race. They are likely to have forgotten their heritage from an old association with Assam. They consider themselves as the people of NEFA, a term styled after NWFP (North Western Frontier Province) in the North-West of the Sub-Continent. If the intention is to keep the people separate from Assam, then some definite name, after the Indian or the Assamese or the tribal tradition, should be given to the territory so that the people develop loyalty to some particular region with a significant name, and take pride in that. If the Government is planning to act according to the words of the Indian Constitution, then the NEFA Administration should be wound up and each Division be treated as a separate entity according to its special needs. Tirap has to be provided with food. The Inner Line has to be withdrawn to touch Roing, Tezu and Brahma Kund so as to allow these vast stretches of land to be appropriated by those who are willing to till them. The Abors in Siang are ready for taking a real part in the administration of their country; while Subansiri and Eastern Kameng will ever welcome better communications and Western Kameng welfare institutions. To integrate the people of NEFA among themselves, they should be given a chance to learn the Assamese language which always has been their Lingua Franca at least from the Ahom period. Side by side with their material development their spiritual needs should not be forgotten. This can be done by erasing the Inner Line, thus broadening the circle of their association to include not only Assam, but all of India. Many wrong notions appear to have found their way in the minds of administrators and now and then voices are heard that NEFA like the NAGA Land will be a separate State. Dr. B. S. Guha has expressed his opinion in this respect.

> "The proposal is not feasible either from the practical or the political points of view of the country, and the assumption at its back is not anthropologically sound. India is not ethnically a homogeneous country but with several racial and cultural spheres in different parts. It is true that the Assam tribes are not similar, say, to the inhabitants of Rajputana or the Punjab, but if they are compared with their neighbours, the people of Assam, it will be found that for centuries there has been constant cultural interchange and even some admixture of blood, with the result that to-day Assamese language is understood to some extent and forms the medium of communication between the tribes themselves, who, it must be remembered again, are not of one race, language or culture but of many, and on that ground alone they could

hardly be collected under one political system, distinct and separate from Assam."

(JASB VOL. XVI No. 2, 1950).

On November 11, 1960 "The times of India" published the news under the heading "Transfer of N.E.F.A.H.Q. Rs. 2 crore Plan" according to which "The North-East Frontier Agency Administration has finalised a Rs. 2-Crore plan for shifting its headquarters from Shillong to Yacholi, in Subansiri frontier division." If the report is true then it appears that the Government of India is finalising a plan to create a separate State of NEFA independent of Assam. Constitutional changes will be made accordingly. It means disintegration of Assam is a reality. One cannot but conclude that 'British sowed the seed of disintegration. The Congress party Government nurtured the plan. Who will reap the fruit'?

APPENDIX

Serial No.	Name	Date
1.	Sukapha	1228-1268 A.D.
2.	Sutenpha	1268-1281 ,,
3	Subinpha	1281-1293 ,,
4.	Sukhanpha	1293-1332 ,,
5	Sukhrangpha	1332-1364 ,,
6.	Sutupha	1364-1376 ,,
	Interregnum	1376-1380 ,,
7.	Tao Khamti	1380-1389 ,,
	Interregnum	1389-1397 ,,
8.	Sudangpha	1397-1407 ,,
9.	Sujanpha	1407-1422 ,,
10.	Suphangpha	1422-1439 ,,
11.	Suenpha	1439-1488 ,,
12.	Suhenpha	1488-1493 ,,
13.	Supinpha	1493-1497 ,,
14.	Suhungmung, Dihingia Raja—I. Swargnarayan	1497-1539 ,,
15.	Suklenmung, Gargyin Raja	1539-1552 ,,
16.	Sukhampha, Khora Raja	1552-1603 ,,
17.	Susenpha, Pratap Singh, Budhi Narayan or Burha Raja	1603-1641 ,,
18.	Surampha, Bhaga Raja, Jayditta Singh	1641-1644 ,,
19.	Sutinpha, Naria Raja	1644-1648 ,,
20.	Sutamla, Jaydhwaj Singh	1648-1663 ,,
21.	Supengmung, Chakrdhwaj	1663-1670 ,,
22.	Sunyatpha, Udayaditta	1670-1672 ,,
23.	Suklampha, Ramdhwaj	1672-1674 ,,
24.	Suhung Sunaguria Raja for 20 days	
25.	Gobar Raja for 20 days	1674-1675 ,,
26.	Sujinpha, Arjun, Dihingia Raja—II	1675-1677 ,,
27.	Sudenpha, Parvatia Raja	1677-1679 ,,

Serial No	Name	Date
28.	Sulekpha, Ratnadhwaj Singh, Lora Raja	1679-1681 A.D.
29.	Supanpha, Gadadhar Singh	1681-1696 „
30.	Sukhrungpha, Rudra Singh	1696-1714 „
31.	Sutanpha, Siv Singh	1714-1744 „
32.	Sunenpha, Parmatma Singh	1744-1751 „
33.	Surampha, Rajeshwar Singh	1751-1769 „
34.	Sunyeopha, Lakshmi Singh	1769-1780 „
35.	Suhitpangpha, Gauri Singh	1780-1795 „
36.	Sukhlingpha, Kamleshwar Singh	1795-1811 „
37.	Chandrakanta Singh, first time, Sudingpha	1811-1818 „
38.	Purendra Singh	1818-1819 „
39.	Sudingpha or Chandrakanta Singh, Second time	1819-1821 „

1821-1824 A.D. Burmese rules, with a puppet Ahom Monarch Jogeshwar Singh on the throne.

1825 A.D. British Conquest of Upper Burma. 1826 Feb. 24. Treaty of Yandebo, by which the King of Burma ceded Assam to British.

1833 A.D. April, Raja Purendra Singh installed as tributary ruler of Upper Assam.

1838 A.D. October, resumption of the territories of Raja Purendra Singh by the East India Company.

INDEX

U

V

W

ERRATA

p.	21	Line	6	from the bottom	for 'Tezpur' read 'Tezu'.
p.	24	„	1	„ „ „	„ '1324' „ '1224'.
p.	32	„	11	„ „ „	„ „ „ „
p.	46	„	5	„ „ top	„ 'oncredible' read 'incredible'.
p.	49	„	23	„ „ „	Delete the line MAP............
p.	57	„	17	„ „ „	for '1780' read '1870'.
p.	65	„	1	„ „ „	„ 'Part II-NEFA administration' read 'Part II-Tibet'.
p.	63	„	1	„ „ bottom	for 'NEFA' read 'NHTA'.
p.	67	„	12	„ „ top	„ '1842' „ '842'.
p.	71	„	15	„ „ „	„ '13th' „ '18th'.
p.	79	Item	7	read 1836 for 1936.	
		„	29	„ PASB 1869.	
p.	82	Line	5	from the bottom	for 'wiss' „ 'wise'.
p.	94	„	20	„ „ top	„ 'has' „ 'was'.
p.	137	„	29	„ „ „	„ 'Pite Pul 8' read 'Pite Pul'.
p.	138	„	31	„ „ „	„ 'evthali' read 'devthali'.
p.	159	„	21	„ „ „	„ '1853' read '1953'.
p.	162	„	22	„ „ „	„ 'miscarriage of injustice' read ' „ „ justice'
p.	239	„	6	„ „ „	for 'Sinkang' read 'Sikang'.
p.	275	„	22	„ „ „	„ '232' read '266'.
p.	287	„	1	„ „ bottom	„ 'plan' „ 'plant'.

4400 14688
30/1/2020 ED